S0-BKO-951

THE CHICANO HERITAGE

This is a volume in the Arno Press collection

THE CHICANO HERITAGE

See last pages of this volume for a complete list of titles.

SPANISH ARCADIA

Nellie Van de Grift Sanchez

ARNO PRESS
A New York Times Company
New York — 1976

Editorial Supervision: LESLIE PARR

Reprint Edition 1976 by Arno Press Inc.

Reprinted from a copy in the State
Historical Society of Wisconsin Library

THE CHICANO HERITAGE
ISBN for complete set: 0-405-09480-9
See last pages of this volume for titles.

Manufactured in the United States of America

Library of Congress Cataloging in Publication Data

Sanchez, Nellie Van de Grift, 1856-1935.
Spanish Arcadia.

(The Chicano heritage)
Reprint of the 1929 ed. published by Powell Pub. Co., Los Angeles, which was issued as v. 2 of California.
Bibliography: p.
1. California--History--To 1846. 2. California--Social life and customs. I. Title. II. Series. III. Series. IV. Series: California ; v. 2.
F864.S23 1976 979.4'02 76-1579
ISBN 0-405-09524-4

A SPANISH GENTLEMAN

A breath of days gone by, of leisurely living and mirthful pastimes, comes in the autograph (reproduced below) of Juan J. de la Guerra, born in the great Arcadian mansion "La Casa Grande," Santa Barbara, before the recognition of American sovereignty in California.

The grandfather, Don José Antonio Julian de la Guerra y Noriega, founder of the de la Guerra family in this country, came to Alta California in 1801. In 1810, he was made Habilitado General of both Californias, and became comandante of the presidio of Santa Barbara in 1815.

The wedding festivities of the aunt of Juan J. de la Guerra in January, 1836, are vividly described by Richard Henry Dana, Jr., in his TWO YEARS BEFORE THE MAST. *The father of Juan, Francisco de la Guerra, was one of the emissaries in connection with preliminaries of the treaty of Cahuenga, made with General John C. Frémont.*

Juan J. de la Guerra, who is one of the few remaining scions of an old family of Spain, always has been a loyal citizen of the United States. He served "Old Glory" in war in the '60's; in '67 and '68, was clerk of the California Assembly, and in '69, '70, and '71 was junior clerk of the Senate.

We trust that the remaining years of Don Juan will be as pleasant to him as the memories of his ancestral shrine are intriguing to Californians of today.

Juan J. dela Guerra

Spanish Arcadia

SPANISH ARCADIA

By Nellie Van de Grift Sanchez

Author of "*Spanish and Indian Place Names of California*"; "*California Under Spanish and Mexican Rule,*" *Etc.*

of the series

CALIFORNIA

Edited by
John Russell McCarthy

POWELL PUBLISHING COMPANY

San Francisco *LOS ANGELES* *Chicago*

Powell Publishing Company
Los Angeles
California

TO

YSABEL AND RAMONA SÁNCHEZ

CONTENTS

ILLUSTRATIONS

Specially Produced for this Work

By Franz Geritz

PREFACE

History as it is usually written is largely confined to events of major importance. This is inevitable, for those who set down events for the information of posterity are naturally most impressed by political and other public happenings. And yet it is only by the relation of the lighter phases of human existence, the intimate story of the common people—how they lived, what they ate, how they dressed, of their joys and sorrows, of their every-day doings, in short—that we gain a true picture of what lies behind us. It is upon personal memoirs, naturally, that we must depend for this picture, and here in California we are singularly rich in such sources, relating to both the Spanish-Mexican and early American periods.

The earliest Spanish documents are so taken up with the struggle for mere existence by the first comers—the tremendous battle by those bold navigators in their tiny ships in unknown waters, the desperate straining of the trail-makers over snow-covered mountains in the dead of winter, the supreme sacrifices of the missionaries for their faith, the hardships of life in the frontier settlements, and all the rest of the brave story—that not much time or space is left for the recital of private griefs or joys. Yet now and then the veil lifts, and we get a passing glimpse of the true nature of the men who suffered and died that we, their successors, might receive this priceless heritage at their hands. These first days are full of inspiration for poems; in fact, the whole period is one great epic; but for the real romance of California's story we must turn to the Mexican period, the days of the cattle barons, when the *ranchero* galloped over his broad domains on his beautiful Arabian horse, the freest and the happiest man on earth.

By this time the hard conditions of pioneer days had

been much ameliorated, and the people had leisure to live, to play, and to love. Above all, they had the time and the will to take pen in hand and write of their experiences for our benefit. Nearly every prominent Californian of that epoch set down his recollections in writing, many of them at the request of Hubert Howe Bancroft, to whom we are eternally indebted. Through these reminiscences it is possible to form a quite accurate picture of the daily lives of the Californians of that time; of their occupations, amusements, dwellings, dress, social customs, education, administration of justice, etc.—all illustrated by many personal stories, tragic, comic, or romantic, as the case may be. Through them we may recall some of the glamour of the day that is gone, when the Spanish *caballero* jingled his spurs along the *Camino Real*.

It is unfortunate that much of this material is in manuscript in the Spanish language, still untranslated, and therefore unavailable except to those who are qualified to read it. It has been my pleasant task to glean from these memoirs facts and incidents which throw light upon the manner of living and characters of those who came before us in the land we love, making them appear as real human beings, rather than as shadowy heroes with whom we have little in common. I take the liberty of offering the results of my research in this field to California writers of romance and poetry, modestly hoping that they will find there some of the "color" for which they are always in earnest quest.

As a last word, I wish to express my sincere gratitude to Dr. Herbert E. Bolton, Chairman of the Department of American History in the University of California, for his reading of the proofs of *Spanish Arcadia* and his generous approval of its contents; and to Dr. Alfred Louis Kroeber, for his reading and approval of the Indian data used in this book.

NELLIE VAN DE GRIFT SÁNCHEZ.

Oakland, 1928.

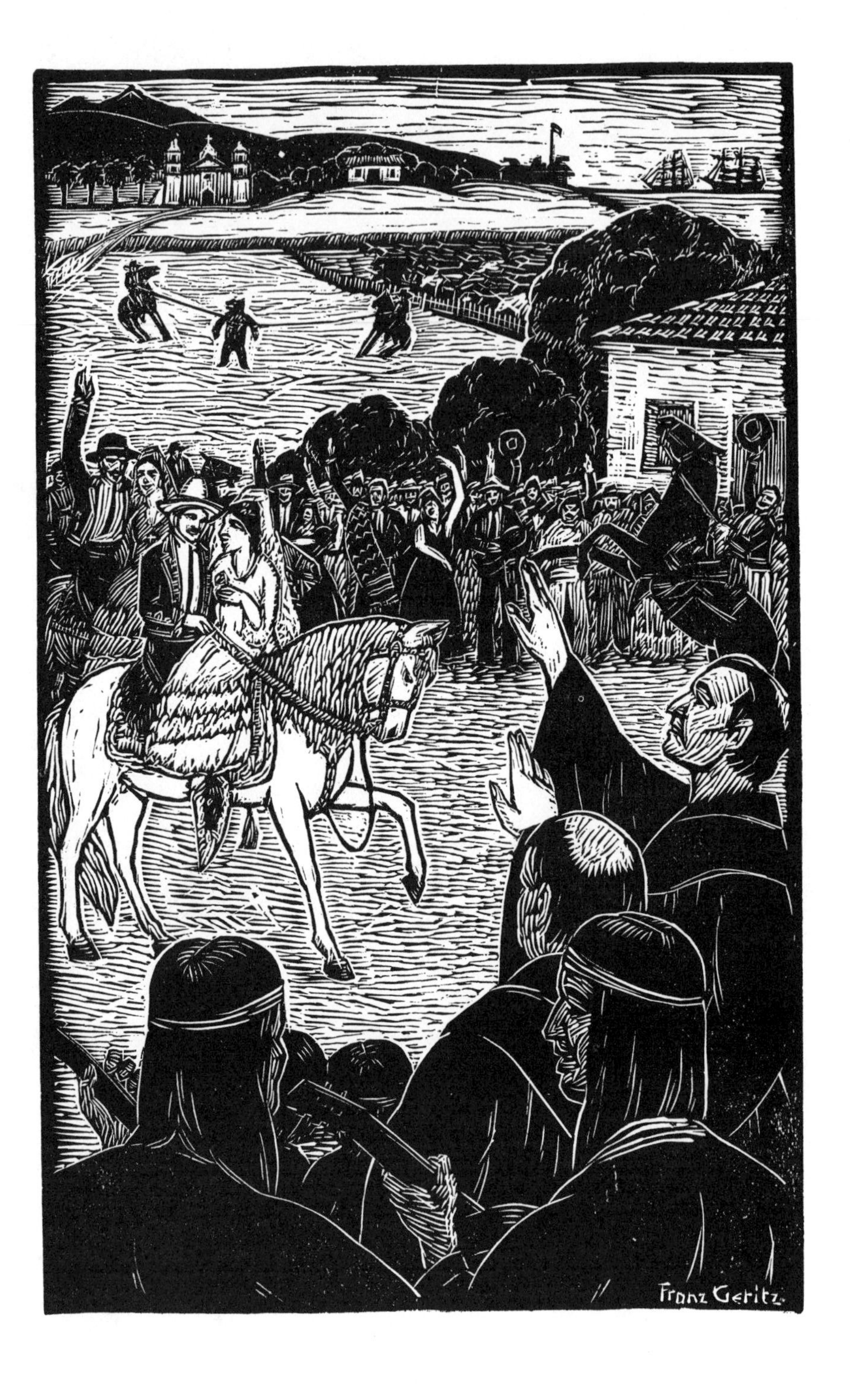
Franz Geritz.

SPANISH ARCADIA

CHAPTER I

Social Beginnings of California

SOCIAL LIFE in the earliest days of the Spanish colonization of Alta California can hardly be said to have existed at all. The very term carries with it the idea of leisure and opportunity to cultivate some of the graces of intercourse with one's fellows, circumstances which were almost entirely lacking in this farthest frontier post of Spain's possessions in America. In the very beginning the colony consisted of a mere handful of soldiers placed here to hold the country against possible invasion by the Russians from the north, with a few devoted friars, whose only object was to save the souls of the barbarous native inhabitants. It was a man's world at first, for lovely woman, without whose presence society cannot exist, did not immediately appear upon the scene. Living conditions were so primitive and uncomfortable that officers were not willing to expose their wives and children to such hardships. Most of these officers, or military *comandantes*, came on temporary commissions, and few indeed had any idea of remaining in what they regarded as a benighted wilderness. So they lived here as exiles, awaiting eagerly the day of their release when they might return to the bosoms of their families and comparative comfort in Mexico or old Spain. That brave and dutiful soldier, Gaspar de Portolá, leader of the first expedition to settle California, remained only long enough after his famous march from the peninsula to locate the points for settlement and see the settlements started, when he took his departure, never to return. The erratic Rivera, after a short and troublous term as comandante, also went back to Mexico, only to die at the hands of the Indians on the banks of the Colorado. Juan Bautista de Anza, perhaps the most outstanding figure in the whole Spanish period, led the first colonists for San Francisco from Sonora to the sea, delivered them to the comandante, explored and selected the site for the new colony; then, picturesque in plumed *sombrero* and flying *capa*, mounted his hardy frontier horse and rode out of the picture forever.

The first settlers to come accompanied by families were hardly of the sort to inaugurate and maintain anything that might properly be called society. It seems strange now to read that it was difficult to persuade respectable people to try their lot in distant California, and that it was necessary to recruit them from the class "submerged in poverty," for whom any change would be for the better. The missions were the only branch of the colonization scheme that took on an air of permanency at once, and even in them conditions were at first extremely primitive and comforts were few.

The social beginnings of some of the towns and cities of California which now bear the proudest names were exceedingly humble. San Francisco, one of the presidial towns which had their origin in the gathering of settlers and traders around military forts, was settled by people so poor that Captain Anza, in his recommendations to the authorities, declared that it would be necessary to

Franz Geritz '27

clothe them from head to foot, even to shoes and the ribbons to tie their queues. They were to be paid in advance, but only in the form of clothing and outfit, for they were such inveterate gamblers that if they were paid in money they would immediately wager it all away. A very elaborate equipment was taken, including—besides the absolutely necessary items of arms, horses, mules, cattle, and rations—shirts, underwear, jackets, breeches, hose, buckskin boots and buttoned shoes, capes, hats, and handkerchiefs for the men, ribbons for their hats and hair; and for the women, chemises, petticoats, jackets, shoes, stockings, hats, *rebozos* and ribbons; items for children's needs also concluded with ribbons. Spurs, bridle and bit, saddle and cushion, and a leathern jacket of seven thicknesses to ward off the arrows of the Indians, were added to each man's quota, while every family was provided with household utensils, from frying pans to blank books. This list shows that the king of Spain recognized the love of finery inherent in human nature, so he dangled the ribbons and other gewgaws before the eyes of these simple people, and heaven knows it was small enough inducement for the long, agonizing trek through the waterless sands of the Colorado desert and over the snow-covered heights of the sierra in the dead of winter.

Monterey, Santa Barbara, and San Diego also belonged to this class of presidial towns, and were for a long time under military rule, but each finally had its own civil government. Progress in these sleepy little *pueblos* under the easy-going Spanish and Mexican rule was so slow as to be scarcely visible, but they became in time the principal social centers of the colony. The officers and the missionaries were generally of pure white blood, and formed the aristocracy of the province. By the situation of these military towns on the principal ports they had the advantage of an occasional visit from foreign ships, and the consequent intermingling with educated men from other countries. One of the early writers ascribes a superiority in manners and speech which he observed in the citizens of Monterey to this cause. The appearance in port of a foreign vessel, no matter of what nationality, was the signal for a succession of *bailes* and *meriendas* which lasted as long as the visitors remained. Such was the monotony of existence in California and so unbounded the hospitality of the people that they found it difficult not to welcome even an enemy.

Besides the military towns there were three which were established from the beginning as civic communities—Los Angeles, San José, and Branciforte. The first of these to be founded was San José, for which purpose nine soldiers and their families were chosen from the *presidios* of Monterey and San Francisco and sent to the banks of the Guadalupe River, where, early in November of 1777, they founded California's first *bona fide* municipality. The growth of the town was very slow, and for many years it consisted of but a few scattered houses of settlers who obtained only a meager living from the products of their lands, supplemented by the supplies furnished by the government. The paternal rule of Spain seems to have been destructive to ambition—waiting for a supply ship was so much easier than sweating over a hoe and shovel.

But however derelict the inhabitants may have been in matters of industry, they were attentive to their religious duties, and travelled three miles every Sunday to attend mass. In order to make the journey from the town to the mission of Santa Clara more agreeable, Father Maguin de Catalá laid out an *alameda* between the two places, planting a fine avenue of willow trees which once comforted the wayfarer with their shade. The original trees have long since died or been replaced with others; the old alameda has vanished, and its place has been taken by a handsome wide boulevard between San José and Santa Clara where now the automobiles whirl by, replacing the plodding oxcarts of Spanish days. Thus arose, as though by magic, from a handful of mud-daubed huts on the banks of the Guadalupe, the charming, rose-embowered city of our day.

No higher in the social scale were the first settlers of Los Angeles, which was founded on September 4, 1781, with twelve colonists and their families, forty-six persons in all, on the site of the old Indian town of Yang-na. The Portolá party were the first white men to visit this place, which they passed on August 2, 1769. Father Crespi says in his entry of this date, "On seeing us the Indians came out on the road, and when we drew near they began to howl, like so many wolves." August 2nd being the feast day of Nuestra Señora la Reina de los Angeles, as the Virgin is often called by the Spaniards, this name was given to the place. For identification, the name of the river was added to it, so that the complete title of the great city which now stands on the spot where the Indian once raised his wolf-like howl is *Nuestra Señora la Reina de los Angeles de Porciúncula* (Our Lady the Queen of the Angels of Porciúncula).

The first social circles in this city of the lengthy name were anything but aristocratic, for the blood of the first settlers was mainly Indian and African, with but a trace of Spanish. They were the very off-scourings of Mexico, in fact, picked up at random from the very poor and even the criminal classes. This motley collection of pioneers went to work, nevertheless, and soon had temporary mud-roofed shelters built, which served as a protection while they were making the dam and irrigating ditch. By 1784 they had so far advanced that the first rude huts had been replaced by substantial adobe houses, the public buildings completed, and the foundations of the church laid, so that after all these unpromising settlers do not seem to have been utterly worthless. Five years after the first settlement a commissioner came down and conferred upon each inhabitant full rights to his property. Each received a separate deed, to which he affixed his cross, for not one could write his name. It is like a story from the Arabian Nights—this transformation of the little collection of squalid huts, inhabited by illiterate, half-criminal mulattoes and *mestizos*, into the magnificent present city of Los Angeles, a center of wealth and culture.

The third civic community, Branciforte, founded at the present site of Santa Cruz, was a failure almost from the beginning, and soon passed out of existence. The chief cause of the failure is to be found in the class of colonists sent to settle it, who were if anything lower in the scale than the first inhabitants of Los Angeles and San José. When the ship *Concepción* arrived at Monterey with the party, Governor Borica was aghast at their destitution and state of ill-health, while Comandante De la Guerra remarked of them, "To take a charitable view of the subject, their absence for a couple of centuries, at a distance of a million leagues, would prove most beneficial to the province and redound to the service of God and the king." The policy of the Mexican government in unloading its undesirables on the province, making of California a sort of penal colony, was beginning to arouse great resentment among the respectable citizens, and was, in fact, one of the principal causes of later ruptures with the home government. Californians were determined that their beautiful land should not become a second Botany Bay.

The brilliant hopes for the future of the third municipality, Branciforte, were doomed to disappointment, and fifty years later when the Americans arrived it was almost forgotten that such a place had ever existed. In justice to its first settlers, it must be admitted that there were other reasons for its failure besides their own unpromising character. Too much aid was given to them by the government, to the destruction of the self-reliance which must always be the first quality of the pioneer; and the near presence of the Indians, who could be forced or hired for a small percentage of the crops to do all the work, was another drawback. Father Salazar said of them: "The people are a set of idlers. For them the Indian is errand-boy, vaquero, and digger of ditches—in short, a general factotum." Moreover, there was no market for surplus products, hence there was no incentive for ambition.

A great effort was made by the authorities to regulate the morals of these pueblos, and some of their laws recall old Puritan days. Religious duties were to be faithfully fulfilled, the penalty for failure to attend mass on holidays being three hours in the stocks. No person might leave the church after mass had begun, and each day's labor was to be closed with prayer. Colonists were to refrain from drunkenness, gambling, and concubinage; they were not allowed to have company late at night nor to be out late. In all the pueblos it was necessary to obtain a permit from the *alcalde* for a dance in a private house, and Vallejo records that even for his wedding it was obligatory to get such a license.

The alcalde, who practically ruled the town, was a highly important and picturesque figure. His duties were multifarious, ranging from the promulgation and enforcement of laws, drawing up contracts, summoning citizens by the beat of the drum, setting an example in his own person of exemplary behavior, restraining vice and punishing crime, protecting the widow and orphan, etc., to the settlement out of court of family and neighborhood quarrels. Every Tom, Dick and Harry carried his little troubles to the Señor Alcalde, who had need of the wisdom of Solomon to decide some of the cases laid before him. And for all this he received no salary, but only honor, as his recompense. This, however, went a great way, for the Spaniard has a high respect for office, and the alcalde was a bigger man, almost, in his town than was the king in his court, and when he passed down the street carrying the tasseled cane, which was his staff of office, all bowed low before him.

The two civic pueblos which attained permanency, Los Angeles and San José, with the presidial towns, became the centers of social life as the years passed and more and more persons of old Spanish blood came to live in them. Besides these there were the mission towns, Sonoma, San Juan Bautista, San Juan Capistrano, and San Luís Obispo, aggregations of houses which gathered about the missions and played their part in developing the society which in time added so much to the charm of life in California.

We come now quite naturally to an event, which, though not of great importance in itself, may be regarded as the real beginning of social life in Alta California, the arrival of the first lady of quality, Doña Eulalia Fages, wife of one of the first Spanish governors, Don Pedro Fages. This is the tale of the domestic troubles, as related in the archives, of this mighty bear hunter, Indian fighter, and explorer, and one of the most original and attractive characters of his time.

Fages, who was a native of Catalonia in Spain, came to California with the Portolá expedition of 1769 as military comandante of the ship *San Carlos*, having under him twenty-five Catalan volunteers, who came to quell any resistance that might be offered by the natives to prevent their landing. After Portolá left California, Fages served as military comandante of the province until 1774, when he was superseded by Captain Rivera y Moncada at the request of Serra, who had some difficulty in getting along with Fages. It was not long, however, before the president of the missions found he had jumped from the frying pan into the fire, so he asked for the return of Fages, who then served as governor from 1782 to 1791.

Don Pedro is described as a peculiar man, industrious, energetic, hot-tempered, but good-hearted, ready to quarrel with everybody from his wife to the father president, but never bearing malice. Naturally a man of his brusque temper and manners was certain to have many disagreements with the friars, but most of them were in time made up, and in his report to the government in 1787 we find him referring to the missionaries in terms of the highest praise: "If we are to be just to all the Franciscans, as we ought to be, we must confess that the rapid, gratifying, and interesting progress, both spiritual and temporal, which we fortunately are able to see and enjoy in this vast country, is the glorious effect of the apostolic zeal, activity, and indefatigable ardor of their friars."

La Pérouse, the great French navigator, whose visit to California happened at a time when there was some discussion between the governor and Father Lasuén, found room to admire the good qualities of both. He says, "The missionaries, who are so pious, so worthy of respect, are already at open quarrel with the governor, who for his part seemed to me to be a loyal soldier." Mariano G. Vallejo writes of him in his *Historia de California:* "Governor Fages was an excellent hunter, a man hardened by his labors, moderately well educated, and with a sound heart—that is to say, he desired to do all the good that he could without for that reason failing to maintain with dignity the elevated position to which he had been raised."

During the very first years of the settlement of Alta California conditions were so hard and rough that the governor had not ventured to bring his wife, a lady of high family, born in the lap of luxury in the same province as himself in Spain, and quite unaccustomed to the hardships of a frontier camp. The loneliness of his life was partially mitigated by his hard and constant care in putting a raw, new country on a solid basis. At one time we see him spending three months in the San Luís Obispo Valley, laying in a supply of bear meat to relieve a scarcity in the mission at Monterey. After this he was known by the nickname of *El Oso* (the bear), but whether in allusion to his skill as a hunter or to his irascible temper history does not say.

In 1770 and again in 1772, he led exploring expeditions to San Francisco Bay. The country was found to be a perfect paradise of wild game, many bear tracks being seen, antelope in herds of fifty or more, and geese so numerous on the marshes of the bay shore that they could be knocked down with a stick.

In 1781, he was sent in command of a force of soldiers to the Colorado River to bury the bodies of the victims of the Yuma Indian massacre, which had occurred the year before, and ransom the women and children who had been carried off as captives. He found the bodies of the dead where they had fallen and, after giving them decent burial succeeded in rescuing all the women and children.

We are now ready for

The Story of the Henpecked Governor

One would think that with all the strenuous business related above Don Pedro would have had little time to miss his wife, but when in 1783 he heard that she had at last been persuaded by friends that California was not after all such a barbarous place of residence, and had undertaken to make the long journey thither, he was overjoyed, and in fact the whole province was thrown into a state of pleasurable excitement at the news. The happy husband and father hurried to Loreto in Baja California to meet her and their little son Pedrito, and in the middle of January the party arrived safely at San Diego.

From this point up to Monterey the journey became a triumphal procession, prophetic of stories of the coming of the first American women to the mining camps in the days of '49. Troops, settlers, officers, Indians, and even the padres, hastened to do honor to the high-born Spanish lady. The governor wrote to his wife's mother in Mexico: "The Señora Gobernadora is the Benjamin of all who know her; she is getting along famously, and Pedrito is like an angel."

Nevertheless, no sooner had Doña Eulalia arrived than she received a severe shock to her sensibilities in the sight of the multitudes of naked Indians who trooped to the governor's house to satisfy their curiosity by gazing upon the wonderful new visitor. Never reflecting that this was their natural condition, she was so seized with pity that she began at once to distribute both her own and her husband's clothing among them, no doubt to their great delight, until Don Pedro appeared and gently reminded her that if she gave everything away they would have to go naked themselves, as there was no place in California where a new outfit could be obtained.

It would be pleasant to record that these happy relations between husband and wife continued, but as time passed the Señora Gobernadora grew more and more discontented with the rough life of the country and longed constantly to return to her own home, where she might enjoy some of the comforts of civilization. The conditions which she had to endure must be taken into account before judging her too harshly for her frantic efforts to force her husband to abandon his post.

When the Englishman, George Vancouver, visited the coast in 1792 he was filled with amazement and compassion at the sight of the lack of the most ordinary comforts in the house of the comandante of the port of San Francisco. He describes the place as consisting of two rooms and a closet, divided by massive walls, which communicated with each other by very small doors. In winter it must have been a very uncomfortable abode, for the windows were destitute of glass, and any defense put up to keep out the wind shut out the light. The roof was covered with rushes, and the furniture was very scanty, including only the most indispensable articles. The floor was of the natural earth, not boarded or paved or even smoothed to a level surface. Vancouver was pained to find the chief official living under such comfortless conditions, without even necessary table utensils, but he generously admitted that the very poverty of these people made their fine courtesy and free-hearted hospitality all the more admirable. Everything that this most poverty-stricken establishment had was placed at the disposal of the visitors, including a ship load of meat and other provisions, and when the Englishmen sailed they tried to return the favors by leaving gifts of necessary implements, including table utensils, variously estimated as worth from $2,000 to $10,000.

As time passed and things became more settled, conditions changed very much for the better, and Californians began to live with some degree of comfort, even luxury, but in poor Doña Eulalia's time it was all still very primitive. Her discontent finally reached the point of a bitter quarrel with her husband, who wrote to his mother-in-law that his wife gave him no peace in her desire to leave the country, but he had no mind to leave a lucrative and honorable position to gratify her whim. The annals of Monterey at that period are filled with the domestic troubles of the governor, which seem to have been carried on with a maximum of publicity. Everybody, including the padres, became involved in the scandal, which culminated in a demand for divorce by Señora Fages on the ground of her husband's alleged infatuation for an Indian girl named Indizuela whom he had rescued from slavery on the Colorado River and brought up to be a servant in his household.

At last the distracted man enlisted the padres to bring her to reason, but this only added fuel to the flames, for the enraged lady flatly declared the devil might take her before she would again live with her husband. After examining witnesses, the ministers decided she had no ground for divorce, and Fages, being compelled to go south on business, placed her in their care at San Carlos Mission, though so much against her will that he had to break down the door into her apartment and remove her practically by force. No doubt the old bear hunting and Indian fighting days began to seem to him decidedly peaceful by contrast. The cloistered quiet of the mission must have been greatly disturbed by her stay, for the records relate that her outbursts of fury, some of which evidently took place in the sacred precincts of the church itself, finally brought threats of flogging and irons. It may be considered quite certain that there was no intention of putting these threats into execution.

At this juncture Captain Nicolás Soler, an old family friend, courageously stepped into the breach and endeavored to effect a reconciliation, but found it such hot work that in one of his letters he compares the explosive nature of the situation to a fire in a powder magazine. Being an old man, he ventures gravely to reprove the angry woman for her strong hankering after worldly pleasures, advising her in future to moderate her behavior toward the ministers and bear with patience the insult put upon her by their threats of stripes and irons. In a letter to Fages this brave intermediator admits that on account of the "indocility of her temper" his efforts had met with but little success, but at the same time he expresses the opinion that no governor ought to permit his Señora to be humiliated by public threats of flogging, even though she were guilty of the acts with which she was charged. The governor answers that although he is aware of the respect due the position and high birth of his wife, yet he cannot endure the outrageous calumnies with which she has publicly defamed him, and which he fears will cause, through their very nature, a crisis in his affairs.

So things ran on, until either through Soler the peacemaker, or because the lady realized the futility of her line of attack, a reconciliation was effected. In a letter to Father Palóu in which one can almost hear the harassed husband's sigh of relief, he writes: "My family are well. It is now about five or six months since Eulalia suddenly called me one morning, and with a thousand excuses and tears, humbly begged my pardon for all the past. She spontaneously confessed that it had all been a mere illusion and falsity, and that she herself had suborned Indizuela to entrap me. Afterwards she summoned Don Hermenegildo and Sergeant Vargas and other persons and told them the same, so that they might make it public in discharge of her conscience. Thanks to God that we are now living in union and harmony."

This *amende honorable*, however, did not prevent the Señora Gobernadora from continuing her efforts to have her husband recalled, and she adopted the bold plan of writing a letter to the *Real Audiencia* of Mexico to ask for his removal to some other part on the ground that the climate of this country disagreed with his health. Getting wind of this attempt, the embarrassed governor was compelled to write to a friend in Mexico post-haste and ask him to try to prevent the letter from being sent to Spain. Nevertheless, although it took her nine years to do it, the determined woman finally won her fight to have him recalled, whereupon she immediately sailed with her children for San Blas, although her husband could not follow for a year.

The Fages family and their domestic discords, so rare in that time and place, now disappear from the pages of California history, but it would certainly be unfair not to set down the good report given in private memoirs of the impulsive Doña Eulalia's reputation for charity and goodness to the poor. Vallejo says of her: "During the nine years that she lived in Monterey she never lost an occasion to do all the good that lay in her power. Whenever Don Pedro was compelled to go out on a campaign to restrain the disorders of the heathen barbarians and returned bringing wounded, she, like an angel come down from heaven to relieve misfortunes, personally waited upon the suffering men, and to the convalescents she sent food suitable for their condition."

So ends the story of "the henpecked governor," and it was worth the telling if only to prevent the name of a good man from being maligned by the false accusations against him.

The primitive social conditions which caused such bitter discontent to Doña Eulalia Fages continued for at least two decades longer. For the first sixteen years of the history of Alta California her isolation was almost complete. The people continued to lead their calm, uneventful lives, almost as indifferent to events in other parts of the world as though they were on another planet. They were even so ignorant of what was occurring on their own continent that they seem not to have known anything about the great conflict between England and her colonies on the Atlantic side until long after it was over. But the time was coming when they were to be awakened from their long sleep. With the coming of the French scientist-navigator, La Pérouse, in 1785, of the

Englishman, George Vancouver, in 1792, of the Russian Count von Rezánof in 1806, besides whalers and fur traders after 1804, the sea-wall of exclusion set up by Spain was gradually broken down. It is in connection with the coming of Rezánof that we have to tell the heart-touching story of the lover who never came back.

In the early part of the nineteenth century, when José Joaquín de Arrillaga was governor of California and José Darío Argüello comandante of the port of San Francisco, society was in much the same state as has been related in the preceding pages—that is to say, it was still primitive. Señor and Señora Argüello lived with their fifteen children and the rest of the inhabitants of the sleepy little military post in almost complete isolation from the outside world. Empires might rise and fall and they would know nothing of it. Placidly pursuing the monotonous round of their homely duties, it would have seemed like a fantastical dream to them if any one had suggested that something new and strange was about to project itself into their dull lives from across the broad ocean which washed the shore at their feet.

To get a proper understanding of this, California's most famous and saddest romance, it is necessary to give just a glance at the political reasons which led to the occupation and settlement of Alta California by Spain in 1769. The chief factor was alarm caused by the Russian settlements in Alaska, which the Spanish government feared might presage further movement to the south and finally encroachments upon the Spanish colonies in North America. In a general way it was known that the mysterious land called Alta California was a rich country, and the missionaries burned with desire to save the souls of its teeming population of barbarians, but the real reason for its occupation was to provide a barrier against foreign approach to the Mexican states, and Russia was the power chiefly dreaded.

The great trek of the Cossacks across Siberia in 1578, and the voyages of Bering and Chirikof to Alaska in 1741 were of much importance to California, for out of them grew the fur trade and the establishment of the supply post at Sitka, which frightened the Spaniards into taking active steps for the occupation of the coast north of the peninsula of Baja California. So the tremendous epic of the sufferings and sacrifice of the brave men of the Russian race who established this trade in the northwest—sailing as they did in wretched boats made of planks tied together with leather thongs, navigating without instruments, making their way by guess from island to island, perishing in large numbers from starvation, cold, scurvy, and the enmity of the fierce natives, losing as many as one-third of their vessels each year—had its part in the unfolding of the stirring drama of the opening of California to civilization.

Conditions in the Russian outpost in the frozen Arctic were vastly different from those met by the settlers in semi-tropic California. Nothing could be raised to aid in subsistence, there was no bountiful supply of wild game to tide over a time of scarcity, and if by any chance the supply ship failed to arrive with provisions, dire calamity stared the colonists in the face.

In 1805, Count Nikolai Petrovitch Rezánof, chamberlain of the Russian imperial court, was sent out by the Russian-American Fur Company to inspect the condition of the colonies in the North Pacific. Arriving at Sitka, he found the little settlement in the first stages of starvation. One of the supply ships had been wrecked and another had failed to make its usual trip. Only a pound of bread a day was being issued to each of the two hundred men on the island, and even at that rate the supply would be exhausted in a few weeks. The season for fish was over, and the provision of dried seal meat was almost gone. The men were now glad to eat eagles, crows, devil-fish—anything eatable, in fact. The dread specter of scurvy had made its appearance and was making fearful havoc among the sufferers. Incessant cold rains added to their misery; despair seized upon them. But just when things looked darkest a ship suddenly appeared out of the lonely waste of waters. It turned out to be the American vessel *Juno*, Captain Wolfe. Rezánof bought both ship and cargo, but the relief was of course only temporary. The eyes of the half-starved colonists finally began to turn longingly toward that sunny land to the south, of whose bursting granaries and great herds of cattle they had often heard glowing accounts from American traders. As it was the nearest point from which food could be obtained in time to save their lives, Rezánof decided to take the *Juno* and run down to the California coast. Accompanied by the surgeon and naturalist, Dr. Georg Heinrich von Langsdorff, and Lieutenant Davidoff, with a crew already sick with the scurvy, he sailed from Sitka on March 8, 1806.

Apart from the immediate purpose of securing supplies for the emergency, Rezánof, who was chamberlain to the Czar, had an ambitious plan for founding a permanent settlement at the mouth of the Columbia. In a letter to the directors of the company on February 15, 1806, he says: "From this settlement we could gradually advance toward the south to the port of San Francisco, which forms the boundary line of California. If we could but obtain the means for the beginning of this plan, I think I may say that at the Columbia we could assemble population from various localities, and in the course of ten years become strong enough to make use of any favorable turn in European politics to include the coast of California in the Russian possessions. The Spaniards are very weak in this country, and if in 1798, when war was declared by the Spanish court, our company had possessed adequate means, it would have been easy to seize a part of California north from the thirty-fourth degree (latitude of the mission of Santa Barbara) and to appropriate this part forever, since the geographical position of Mexico would have prevented her from sending any assistance overland. The Spaniards, on account of their shiftlessness, have hardly made any use of their lands, and have advanced toward the north only to secure the boundary."

Nature herself repulsed this plan, for on the arrival at the Columbia the little ship with its nearly incapacitated crew was driven from its mouth by the powerful outgoing current. With all the food aboard practically used up, there was nothing left to do but proceed to San Francisco. Many were the misgivings of Rezánof as he hovered outside the Gate, for he was thoroughly aware of the strictness of the regulations of the Spaniards against foreign vessels. The situation was such, with a starving crew, as to allow of no hesitation, for a refusal of permission to enter meant to perish at sea, so he resolved, "at the risk of two or three cannon balls, to run straight for the fort at the entrance."

As the *Juno* drew opposite a loud hail of "What ship?" came through a trumpet from shore. "Russian!" was shouted back. "Drop anchor!" thundered the Spaniard. "Si, señor! Si, señor!" replied the Russian, but the ship kept on going until she was inside the harbor and well out of range of the guns, when the anchor was dropped. There she was safe, for the Spaniards had not even a rowboat with which to reach her.

It still remained, however, to cajole the authorities of the port into giving the supplies so urgently needed both for the ship and the starving settlement at Sitka. This the astute Rezánof wished to accomplish, if possible, without exposing the weakness of Russia's hold in Alaska, lest the old-time ambition of Spain for conquest might be aroused.

After waiting some time for boats to come out, and finding that none came, for the very good reason as they afterward learned that there were none, the commander of the *Juno* sent Langsdorff and Lieutenant Davidoff ashore, where they were met by Luís Argüello, in temporary charge at San Francisco in the absence of his father, Don José Darío Argüello, then comandante of the port. One gets the impression that the whole Argüello family were above the ordinary both in looks and in intelligence. This same Don Luís afterwards became governor of California, and won a reputation second only to the famous Gabriel Moraga in exploration of the interior. Langsdorff gives an attractive description of his appearance in his Mexican *serape*. "We were received by a Franciscan monk and several military officers. The comandante was a good-looking young man. He wore over his uniform a sort of mantle of striped woolen cloth, which looked like the coverlid of a bed, his head coming through the opening in the middle, so that it hung down over the breast, back and shoulders. He wore richly embroidered boots and extravagantly large spurs. Most of them wore long cloaks."

It is stated that the conversation was carried on in Latin by Langsdorff and Father Francisco Uría, since none of them knew both Spanish and Russian. Fortunately for the visitors, the Mexican government had had word some time before of a projected Russian voyage of discovery, and had sent orders to the California officials to treat the foreign navigators with every courtesy if they should arrive there. Argüello at first believed the *Juno* might be one of these ships, and so gave its officers a friendly reception, entertaining them at his father's home, where they were received politely by Señora Argüello.

Langsdorff describes the habitation of the comandante as a small mean place, having a sort of parlor with white-washed walls, scantily furnished, with about half the floor covered with matting to serve as a reception room. In strange contrast with these poor surroundings dinner came in served on a handsome set of silver plate, possibly an heirloom in the Argüello family which they had managed to bring with them. The Russian remarks on the loving family relations exhibited in the whole behavior of "these worthy, kind-hearted people," and the "simple, artless attachment" shown by the Argüellos for each other, adding that in such a place there were scarcely any pleasures except in family union and domestic cordiality.

While the officers of the ship were thus being made welcome, the emaciated, pale-faced men of the crew were not neglected. The comandante sent out for their use four fat oxen, two sheep, onions, garlic, cabbage, etc. With this good living Langsdorff says they were all changed in three weeks from miserable, lean, melancholy figures to healthy people, with a good color. There was one unexpected result from this pleasant change which was not so agreeable to the commander of the Russians. The contrast between this sunny, bountiful land and dreary Sitka, with its empty larder, brought discontent among the crew, two of whom managed to desert from the ship and remain in California.

Governor Arrillaga, hearing of the arrival of the Russians, took horse and hastened up from Monterey to meet them. Then ensued a long diplomatic discussion between Rezánof and the governor in the endeavor of the former to secure the coveted supplies. He had already won over the friars and the military to his side by tempting them with gifts of articles brought on the ship—linen and woolen cloth, tools for trades, axes, saws, iron cooking vessels, bottles, glasses, plates, leather, shoes, hats, cotton goods, shawls for the ladies, etc. When one remembers the utter lack of such manufactured goods in California at that time and the extreme discomfort of life for want of them, one feels that the temptation must have been almost irresistible.

Arrillaga, described by Langsdorff as a "polite, respectable man," though he received the Russians with the cordiality due to guests, was troubled in his mind at the idea of furnishing the supplies without permission from his government. He remarked, "After living sixty years without reproach I cannot take such a trick on my conscience." Rezánof, on the other hand, could not forget the colonists at Sitka, now on the verge of starvation, and resolved to procure the provisions at whatever cost.

The Lover Who Never Came Back

It is at this point that the element of romance enters into the cautious sparring between the two diplomats. Among the numerous progeny of the Argüellos there was one—a daughter named Concepción—who attracted the particular attention of the strangers by her vivid, colorful beauty, and her vivacity and intelligence. She was but sixteen years of age at this time, but, like the fruits and flowers of her land, had early blossomed into maturity. Langsdorff thus describes this California girl of long ago: "She was lively and animated, had sparkling, love-inspiring eyes, beautiful teeth, pleasing and expressive features, a fine form, and a thousand other charms, yet her manners were perfectly simple and artless."

Everything was done to make the stay of the foreigners agreeable. Horses stood ready every day if they wished to ride. Every afternoon they were entertained at the Argüello home with music and dancing. The ladies taught the Russian officers the dances of the country, and they in turn instructed the Californians in the English country dances, which "made a great hit."

An opportunity was given the officers of the Russian Czar to inspect a good part of the country by a trip to Santa Clara Mission. The sight of the rich soil and abundant crops put dreams in the head of the ambitious chamberlain—dreams of a colony in this genial land which would insure a regular supply of corn and flour for the Russian possessions in the continent of North America and contiguous islands in the north. Mingled with these thoughts of the true patriot that he was, were others of a tenderer sort. Why not for once make inclination and duty go hand in hand and work to the same end? Let us permit his friend and companion von Langsdorff to relate what happened next: "Our constant friendly intercourse with the family of Argüello, the music, the singing, the sports, and the dancing, awakened in the mind of the chamberlain von Rezánof some new and very important speculations, which gave rise to his forming a plan of a very different nature from the first, for establishing a commercial intercourse between the Russian and Spanish settlements. The bright eyes of Doña Concepción had made a deep impression upon his heart; and he conceived that a nuptial union with the daughter of the comandante at San Francisco would be a vast step gained towards promoting the political objects he so much desired. He had therefore nearly come to a resolution to sacrifice himself by this marriage to the welfare, as he hoped, of the two countries of Spain and Russia."

The hint about a "sacrifice" points to the suggestion that it was not love alone that influenced the decision of the chamberlain, yet the description of the young Spanish girl, who Langsdorff said was reputed to be the greatest beauty in California, makes it easy to believe that he did not find the sacrifice a painful one. And how stood the affair on the señorita's side? Though there was some disparity in age, for she was just flowering into womanhood and he was past his first youth and was a widower, yet he possessed unusual personal attractions. With a tall, erect figure, fair-haired and blue-eyed, with a singularly handsome face, all set off by the Russian uniform of dark green and gold lace and the glittering order of Saint Ann on his breast, in appearance he was distinguished. Add to this the elegant manners of the European noble of his time and fine intellectual attainments, with the prestige of courts and high station, and surely it is not difficult to understand that his task of winning the heart of the unsophisticated country girl was an easy one. To her he must indeed have seemed the very prince of romance. But evidently he did not depend solely upon his personal attractions for success, but day by day, in the intervals of the dancing and singing and horseback riding, painted in his talk lively pictures of the splendors of life in the capital of Russia and the luxury of the imperial court. As compared with the monotony and plainness of life in California it must have seemed like a glimpse into fairyland to the imaginative young girl. In this way he soon brought her to the point when to become the wife of the Russian chamberlain became the dearest object of her life.

But still no progress had been made with the governor in the matter of the sale to the Russians of breadstuffs. Writing with great frankness to his minister, the chamberlain says:

"Seeing that my situation was not improving, expecting every day that some misunderstanding would arise, and having but little confidence in my own ship's people, I resolved to change my politeness for a more serious tone. Finally, I imperceptibly created in Doña Concepción an impatience to hear something serious from me, which caused me to ask her hand, to which she consented. My proposal created consternation in her parents, who had been reared in fanaticism. The difference in religion and the prospective separation from their daughter made it a terrible blow for them. They ran to the missionaries, who did not know what to do; they hustled poor Concepción to church, confessed her and urged her to refuse me, but her resolution finally overcame them all. The holy fathers appealed to the decision of the throne of Rome, but if I could not accomplish my nuptials I had at least the preliminary act performed, the marriage contract drawn up, and forced them to betroth us."

"From that time," says Tikhmeneff, the Russian chronicler, "Rezánof, in the capacity of a near relative of the comandante, had better success in the accomplishment of his object. In the Argüello family no more secrets existed for him, even in matters which did not belong to family affairs. All the officials belonging to the port gradually changed their disposition and relaxed their vigilance. The governor, besieged from all sides with requests to grant the demands of Rezánof with regard to supplying the colony with provisions, was not only forced to give him the necessary quantity of breadstuffs but to place his men at Rezánof's disposal for the purpose of loading the ship. The brothers of Doña Concepción early succeeded in getting ready the greater part of the breadstuffs, while the remaining portion was gradually furnished by the missionaries. The loading of the ship went on with great dispatch and Rezánof, without paying the least attention before the Spaniards to the rumors of war which became more and more distinct, continually entertained them with dinners and festivals, and by that means strove to wean them from even the idea of possible hostilities between the two powers in the near future."

"From this time," says Rezánof himself, "I managed

this port as my interests required." The *Juno* was soon loaded with all it would hold, 4,600 pounds, of wheat, flour, barley, peas, beans, tallow, and a small quantity of dried meat. Tikhmeneff admits that it was through the powerful influence of Concepción, who seems to have been a young woman of unwonted independence of spirit for her day, that the colony at Sitka was saved from death by starvation.

On May 8, 1806, Rezánof sailed away, while the whole Argüello family stood upon the heights at the presidio and waved farewell with hats and handkerchiefs. Little thought they that they had seen the last of their interesting foreign friend! The understanding when he left was that immediately upon his arrival at St. Petersburg he would go to Madrid as ambassador extraordinary from the Imperial Russian Court and there clear up every kind of misunderstanding between the two powers. Thence he would proceed to Vera Cruz or some other Spanish harbor in Mexico and finally come on to San Francisco to claim his bride and settle all matters relative to the commerce he so much wished to promote.

The little colony by the Golden Gate dropped back into its former dull round of monotonous duties; but for Doña Concepción, promised bride of the fascinating Russian, the dullness was relieved by day dreams of a brilliant future. But when week after week, then month after month, and finally year after year passed without a sign from her departed lover the rainbow colors of her dreams began to fade. Every summer the fog rolled in from the wide ocean while she scanned it vainly for the sail that never came; but, if doubt ever entered her heart, she kept it concealed from all. If others expressed the belief that he had been false, she always replied, "If Rezánof does not come back it is because he is dead; to him I have given my love, and to no other will I ever give it."

True to her troth, she remained unwedded until the day of her death. It was all in vain that the many suitors of her own race and others strummed their guitars beneath her window, for she would have naught to do with them. When at last hope died, she took on the habit of a *beata*, and devoted the rest of her life to charity, in teaching the young to read, in caring for the sick, and aiding the poor Indians. It was not until 1842, thirty-six years after Rezánof waved his farewell from the deck of the *Juno*, that news was brought to her by Sir George Simpson, the English navigator, of the lonely death of her lover on the cold steppes of Siberia as a result of a fall from his horse. He had never reached St. Petersburg. At last she knew he had not been false, but that cruel fate had interposed to prevent him from carrying out the plans that were to end in his return and marriage. It may seem strange that so long a time should have elapsed before she received the news, but it must be remembered not only that California had little and slow communication with the rest of the world, but that no one in Russia had enough knowledge of or interest in the waiting girl far across the world to inform her of his death.

It is said that many were the young men among the friends of Concepción who endeavored to persuade her to give up her vows of a religious life, but all failed, and she lived to a comparatively old age true to the lost lover of her youth. On December 23, 1857, at the age of sixty-six years, this heroine of California's most touching love story died in the convent at Benicia, when, as is written in the records of the institution, "A tired soul was dismissed out of the storms of life into the divine tranquillity of death." She lies buried in the convent cemetery under a brown stone cross bearing the simple inscription: "Sister María Domínica, O. S. D." (Order of Saint Dominic).

Chapter II

CHAPTER II

Days of the Cattle Barons

AFTER THE first meager years of frontier life in the colony of Alta California, with growing prosperity conditions began to improve, and a distinctive society gradually developed. This social life reached its fullest flowering under the flag of the Mexican Republic, the most romantic period in the whole history of the province, in what may fitly be called the "days of the cattle barons."

Although the paternal government of Spain supplied its colonists with every necessity, even to hair ribbons for the queues of the men and petticoats for the women, and continued to send supply ships for their maintenance long after the first establishment, yet it desired greatly that they should become self-supporting as soon as possible. The missionaries accompanying the Portolá expedition brought with them all kinds of seeds of grains and vegetables, and farm implements, besides 200 head of brood cattle contributed by the missions of Baja California. It was known that they were going to a fertile land, and they went prepared to take every advantage of it. As soon as they were sufficiently settled, artisans in all the principal trades were sent out to teach the Indians the practice of these industries.

Of the three branches in the colonizing plan—military, civil, and religious—the last named was by far the best managed and most successful. The reasons are self-evident: Spain sent out her very best as missionaries, generally university graduates of the highest character and endowed with special talents for administration. Moreover, their hearts were in their work, which always makes a vast difference. Many of them were men of an inventive turn, and they became jacks of all trades, able to give elementary instruction in farming, building, weaving, blacksmithing, etc., and always willing to lend a hand for the encouragement of the child-like neophytes. Even Fray Junípero might often have been seen bending his frail shoulders beneath a heavy timber for some church building. Every mission became an industrial school, a busy hive of native workers under the tutelage of the men of God. It was found that the Indians readily acquired a working knowledge of most of the manual trades, notwithstanding their almost complete lack of native arts except basket-making.

Efforts were made by the government to introduce a variety of occupations into the country, but the only one that ever reached any magnitude was stock-raising. There were many reasons why this should be so. Lack of a market for surplus products limited even agriculture to raising only what was required for the maintenance of the small community of whites and the Christianized Indians. Why raise more when it could not be used or sold? The same conditions existed in the trades and professions, for which there was little call in this new land. When a new party of colonists was sent to California in 1834 under the leadership of José María Hijar, although as a class they were vastly superior to those who had gone before, the great error was made of sending persons skilled in professions for which there was no opening. There were artists and printers for a land where there were no newspapers or books; teachers of music and dancing for a people who knew, seemingly, how to play their instruments and dance their folk dances by instinct; goldsmiths where there was as yet no gold to use and no one with money to buy the jewelry when made; blacksmiths in a country where even the horses went unshod and the wheels of the only vehicles were made of the solid rounds of tree trunks; carpenters where adobe and tiles were the principal building materials; painters in a region where paint was seldom used; shoemakers and tailors for a people who shod themselves with rawhides and wore blankets instead of coats; school teachers in a community where there was little interest in education. Naturally the new settlers got into trouble, and finally became objects of charity until they could be sent back to Mexico. Some of the best of them remained, however, and scattered through the province, to become respectable members of the community and leave to their descendants such honored names as Coronel, Abrego, Noé, Serrano, Covarrubias, Prudón, and many others. It was a well-meant but ill-managed enterprise.

The one great industry for which all conditions were eminently suitable was the raising of cattle, both great and small, as the Spaniards distinguished beef cattle and sheep. First was almost unlimited pasture land, generally well watered, to be obtained at a minimum of expense or effort. The cost of securing possession of an allotment of land was about twelve dollars, and in early times a settler could borrow from the nearest mission a start of cattle for nothing at all except the promise to return the same number of cattle to the mission as soon as the increase warranted it—say, in five years. So that it required no great outlay of capital in those days for a man to lay the foundation of a large and lucrative business. It was a poor man indeed, or an exceedingly shiftless one, who had no land or cattle of his own. Other advantages were the mild climate, which obviated the need of providing shelter for the animals, and the saving of expense in the matter of fencing, for the cattle were allowed to roam at large. Indian herders could be had at very slight expense, for the natives quickly became experts with the *reata* and on the horse, and for their labor expected little more than food and saddle and bridle. The open air freedom of the life, involving so much less actual drudgery than farming or the trades, appealed to the natural temperament of the Californian, for, although he had no great love for work, yet neither was he slothful, and to be up at the dawn and away on a bounding steed to look after the stock—this he considered an ideal life, healthful while not slavishly laborious. And who shall say that he was not right? Then, too, the possession of land and cattle put a mark of standing and respectability upon a man, which, as a proud Spaniard he valued highly. And there was little difference in grading; he who had four thousand cattle was as high in the social scale as he who owned forty thousand or more. In either case he belonged to the landed gentry. Almost every native Californian had his *rancho* and herds of cattle and sheep, while a grandee like General Mariano Guadalupe Vallejo had land without limit, with from 12,000 to 15,000 head of neat cattle, 7,000 or 8,000 head of horses, and from 2,000 to 3,000 sheep.

Most important of all the reasons for the adoption of this industry by so many Californians was that a revenue could be obtained from it. It was the one thing for which they could get a market. In the earliest years there was no more sale for the cattle than for other products of the province, but finally reports of the great California herds reached South America, and in 1813 the Lima trade was established by the arrival of the *Flora* and the *Eagle*, which brought up cargoes of cloth and a variety of manufactured goods to exchange for hides, tallow, grain, wine, and other products of the missions. In 1822, the English firm of John Begg and Company, engaged in business at Lima, established a branch of their house at Monterey, this being the first mercantile house opened on the coast. The company was represented in California by Hugh McCulloch and William Hartnell, who arrived in June, 1822, on the ship *John Begg*. A three-year contract was signed by the authorities by which the John Begg Company was bound to send at least one vessel a year, to touch at each harbor, to take all hides offered and at least 312 tons of tallow, and to pay either in money or in such goods as should be desired.

As a side line the firm also contracted with the Peruvian government to supply it with salted beef, and a number of salters and coopers were brought from Ireland and Scotland to prepare the meat under the superintendence of David Spence. For some reason the meat branch of the business proved unprofitable after a few cargoes had been shipped and it was therefore abandoned. The lack of a market for the meat made it practically worthless; hence only about two hundred pounds of the best parts of each bullock was saved and dried, while the balance was left for the buzzards and wild beasts. The number of carcasses finally became so large that these volunteer scavengers could not dispose of them all, and the stench became so great as to threaten a pestilence. On November 15, 1833, the *ayuntamiento* of Los Angeles passed an ordinance compelling all persons slaughtering cattle for hides and tallow to cremate the remains.

The tallow was tried out in large pots brought by the whalers for use in rendering the whale blubber, and was then run while hot into bags made by sewing up hides, an opening being left near the neck through which the tallow was poured. These hides filled with fat were called *botas*, and when ship-masters signed bills of lading they acknowledged having received so many botas of fat. The hides were cured by first soaking them for some days in sea water to soften them, then stretching them on the ground fastened down with small stakes. They were then carefully scraped with a knife, and placed on racks to dry. Next the inside was powdered with salt, they were folded lengthwise with the hair outward, pressed to flatten them, and packed in the ship with the aid of jack-screws. It was not uncommon to see a brig of 160 tons loaded with 14,000 hides, and a three-masted American schooner of 360 tons with 30,000. It may be imagined that for odoriferous qualities these ships were comparable to the whalers.

Besides the trade with the ships, some of the hides and tallow were disposed of to local rancheros, who found as many uses for the products from these half-wild cattle as the Indians of the plains once found for the buffalo. Strips of the skins were used for reatas, and in building *corrals*, for the tops and floors of oxcarts, and for many other purposes. Many of the farmers tanned their own leather and made their own shoes, using cowhide for the soles and deerskin for the uppers. The hides were also used for covering saddle-trees, for beds in lieu of mattresses, for cuirasses to be used in Indian fighting, knapsacks, horse blankets, stirrup covers, and, in fact, in ways too numerous to mention. Large quantities of the tallow were used by the rancheros in making candles and soap, which were sold to the Russians for export to Alaska.

Naturally it was not long before the Yankee traders began to take a hand in this new business in hides and tallow. It was chiefly owing to the representations of William A. Gale, a former fur trader on the northwest coast, that the Boston firm of Bryant and Sturgis and others were induced to fit out a vessel and engage in this trade with the Pacific, exchanging the manufactured goods of

New England for the hides and tallow of California. By the voyage of the *Sachem* in 1822, the direct trade between the two coasts was opened. From this time on the "Boston ships" carried on a regular commerce with California, leaving their cargoes of goods in all the harbors from San Diego to San Francisco and taking on hides and tallow in exchange.

When the horses and cattle brought up from Mexico increased to such an extent that the owners could no longer care for them, they were allowed to run free over the broad plains of the Sacramento and the San Joaquín. All California became one vast pasturage, where the cattle roamed at will. So it was that the small herd brought up by the Portolá expedition in 1769, augmented by additions at later periods, including what were left alive of those brought by Anza in his famous crossing of the sierra in the dead of the winter of 1775-76, became the nucleus of the only great industry practiced in Alta California during the Spanish-Mexican period. This traffic brought wealth to some of the Californians, and in fact it was then that the foundations were laid for the great fortunes which in some instances have endured to our own times. The period of the greatest prosperity of the ranchos was from 1828 to 1846, when the trade with the English and American ships flourished most. This was the pastoral age, when the people enjoyed a degree of comfort, and even luxury, not before known. They could now have glass in their windows, silks and laces to wear, knives and forks for table use, good furniture for their houses, even books to read, as we shall see later. Gone were the days when the discomforts of the comandante's house in San Francisco aroused Vancouver to such pity! And all owing to those dumb friends of man, the patient cattle!

In the transactions with the trading vessels money was

seldom passed, hides and tallow being usually the only legal tender exchanged for the manufactured articles brought by the ships. It was the time when a man's word was as good as his bond. Merchants trusted the *rancheros* largely for the goods they sold them, and the indebtedness was paid when the hides and tallow were prepared. José M. Estudillo relates a story illustrative of this custom and the honorable reputation of the rancheros in business matters: "Don José Aguirre, owner of one of these ships, once had a new supercargo, a young man who was a stranger to California and its customs. While the ship lay at San Pedro, Aguirre being absent on shore, Agustín Machado, a well-to-do ranchero and a man of sterling character, although he could neither read nor write, went on board to make purchases, his carts being at the landing. After he had made his selection from the goods, which were spread out on deck for exhibition, and was about to have them placed in a launch to be taken ashore, the supercargo asked him for payment, or some guaranty or note. Machado stared at him in great astonishment, hardly comprehending what the man meant, for such a demand had never been made from him before, nor indeed from any other ranchero. Presently the idea struck him that he was distrusted. Plucking one hair from his beard, he gravely handed it to the supercargo, saying, 'Here, deliver this to Señor Aguirre, and tell him it is a hair from the beard of Agustín Machado. It will cover your responsibility; it is sufficient guaranty.' The abashed young man took the hair and placed it inside his pocketbook. Machado carried away the goods. Aguirre was much chagrined on hearing that the supercargo had demanded a document from Machado, a man whose word was as good as the best bond, even for the entire ship's cargo."

No expense was incurred for exhibiting the goods brought by these ships, for the agents or supercargoes had stores fitted up on board, with shelves, show cases, drawers, and scales, selling from one pound of tea, shot, etc., to a box or bag, and again from a yard of silk or calico to a bale. One may imagine the delight of the señoras and señoritas of the town when a trading vessel hove in sight, for their wants were by no means neglected in the cargoes, and an exciting shopping trip was in store for them on board.

The vessels engaged in this traffic were of many nationalities—American, British, French, German, Swedish, Russian, and South American. Most of the hides went to England and the United States, and the tallow to Peru. A great variety of goods was delivered to the Californians in exchange—silk, linen, woolen, cotton; fine dress patterns, cashmere shawls and silk stockings; rebozos and serapes from South America; gold and silver lace; all kinds of hardware and window glass; farm implements from the United States; furniture of all kinds, some of it very elegant, of mahogany, nails, iron pots and kettles. But why continue the list? Enough has been quoted to show that the early abstemious days were a thing of the past. Payment for these articles was made almost entirely in hides, at two dollars each, and tallow at one dollar and a half for twenty-five pounds.

Before this trade had made the cattle worth something as a medium of exchange for articles brought by the ships, they were valued so low that nobody took the trouble to steal them, even though they wandered unconfined. "Formerly," says Salvador Vallejo, "our cattle roamed by thousands, yet not one was stolen, for the unwritten law of the land granted to the weary traveller the privilege of killing cattle whenever he wanted beef, so long as he placed the hide where the owner could easily find it. Since the transfer of California to the United States many native Californians have been hanged for stealing cattle, and I firmly believe that some of the victims did not know that under the new government it was a crime to kill a steer for which they had not a bill of sale."

It is asserted that the cattle increased at a greater rate in California than anywhere else, no doubt owing to favorable climate, the unequalled pasture, and the state of nature in which they lived. They were of the large-bodied, long-horned variety, and, being allowed to run free, soon returned to a wild state. They were so fierce that it was unsafe to go among them on foot, and a wise man did not approach them unless he was safe on the back of his swift horse. John Bidwell, who thought wild bulls more dangerous than grizzly bears, tells of dodging into gulches and behind trees to avoid them. The Russian, von Langsdorff, who was a visitor to California in 1806, describes a night of peril spent by himself and some companions in the woods while on their way to Santa Clara Mission, when they were obliged to defend themselves with their guns against wild bulls and bears, scarcely knowing which they feared most. Many cattle were lost by falling over cliffs, and many more fell victims to bears and lions, although they learned in time to give a good account of themselves against these lords of the forest. It was a common thing for a bull to come in with torn and bleeding sides, while the blood on its horns proved that the combat had not been altogether one-sided. J. Ross Browne tells of witnessing from the safe vantage of a tree such a battle royal in which both combatants were left dead on the ground.

Estates chiefly devoted to the raising of stock were called *ranchos*, while those used for planting crops were known as *haciendas*. Each mission had its rancho and its hacienda, and in the days of their prosperity these properties brought them a substantial income. San Juan Capistrano held fifteen leagues along the seaboard, extending

Franz Geritz

back to the mountains, interspersed with shady groves and fertile valleys, and covered with herds of stock and fields of waving grain. The mission of Santa Inés, although it had less land than some of the others, had vast herds of cattle and horses. At Purísima cattle increased at one time to such an extent that permission was granted by the presiding priests for free slaughter in order to reduce their number, and thousands were killed for the hides and tallow alone. Mission San José owned 62,000 head of cattle in 1825, besides horses, sheep, and mules. San Gabriel was one of the richest in stock and grain. In 1802 San Buenaventura possessed finer herds of cattle and richer fields of grain than any of its contemporaries, and its gardens and orchards were visions of wealth and beauty. Richest of all was San Luís Rey de Francia, which at one time had some thirty thousand sheep feeding on its pastures, to say nothing of its great herds of cattle. Private owners held stock in proportion to their lands; some of them had immense herds.

For the care of all this half-wild stock a great number of mounted herders, called *vaqueros* (cow-men) in California, were necessary. These herdsmen were generally Indians, who tended stock under the direction of a *mayordomo*. These Indians, who had never seen a horse or cow until the arrival of the Spaniards but a few years before, showed a special aptitude for this kind of work and soon became extraordinarily expert at it. They were said to be a very wild set of men. As for the Spanish Californians, they became through this occupation of stock raising the most skillful cavaliers in the world, not even excepting the Cossacks of Tartary or the *gauchos* of South America.

The free running of the cattle over broad unfenced ranges inevitably resulted in the intermingling of animals belonging to different owners, and some method had to be adopted by which each man could recognize and claim his own. Out of this necessity came the well-known California institution, the *rodéo* (round-up), for the branding of the cattle. Each ranchero had his own branding iron, which was required to be listed in the *libro de registro*, and no one could adopt or change a brand without the permission of the governor. As far back as 1770 every owner of horses, cattle, asses, mules, and sheep was compelled by law to brand his stock. Each man had two private brands, one called *el fierro para herrar los ganados* (the iron for branding the cattle), and the other *el fierro para ventear* (the brand for selling). Sometimes the cattle were marked by cutting their ears in a certain way, and even these marks had to be kept in the *libro de registro*. Even these strict regulations did not always prevent fraud, for at a later date California became infested with Mexican convicts, who forged the sellers' brand for cattle and caused great confusion. A few were arrested, but the local authorities did not understand the magnitude of the crime and simply exiled the prisoners to other pueblos, where they went on with the traffic.

The rodéos were held annually, when additions to the herds were counted and branded, old marks inspected, and stragglers from adjoining ranges restored to their claimants. The rodéo was held not only for branding and dividing stock, but to make the animals accustomed to a certain place, and to prevent them from going hopelessly wild. When the time approached for the stock taking, the alcalde called the people together by the sound of the drum, then announced that on a certain date the round-up would be held at a certain named place. The news was carried to all the ranchos for leagues around, for everybody came, bringing wives and children, to the rodéos, which were made occasions for so much feasting and merrymaking that one hardly knows whether to list them among occupations or amusements. The cattle were first driven into corrals, where the new calves were lassoed and held while the red-hot branding iron was applied to their flanks, amid much piteous bawling from the terrified creatures. The affair was conducted under the oversight of a regularly appointed *juez de campo* (field judge), who settled all disputes and saw that the regulations were strictly carried out. The bellowing of the frightened cattle, the prancing of the excited horses, which seemed to take the keenest delight in their part in the work, the furious struggles of wild bulls to escape from the lasso, and the daring feats of horsemanship of the young fellows who seized this opportunity to win the admiration of the fair spectators, made these affairs very thrilling. Bullocks were killed to feed the company, and in the evening guitars were tuned up and there was singing and dancing.

These round-ups and this system of cattle branding were adopted by American farmers who came in later and were continued up to a recent date. The custom is commemorated in the name of the town of Rodéo, not far from San Francisco. The soldiers at the presidios held their own annual rodéos, to count and brand the stock on the *ranchos del rey*, that is, the king's farms, which were maintained for the support of the military. These affairs always ended in a grand ball, which was attended by the comandante and all the élite of the place.

Less thrilling and more gory than the rodéos were the *matanzas*, or slaughterings, thus described by Bancroft: "When a ranchero wished to slaughter his cattle, he sent six men on horseback to ride at full speed through the fields with knives. Passing near an animal, one gave it a blow with the knife in the nerve at the nape of the neck, and it fell dead. These *nuqueadores* (neckers) were followed as by a flock of hungry vultures by dozens of *peleadores* (skinners), who took off the hides. Next came the *tasajeros* (butchers), who cut up the meat into strips for drying. The funeral procession was closed by a swarm of Indian women who gathered the tallow and lard in bags made of the hides by sewing up one end. A field after the slaughter looked like Waterloo after the charge of the old guard."

The *matanzas* naturally left much offal in their wake, and a multitude of dogs were kept to dispose of it. In every town there were a thousand dogs without a master; Constantinople was outdone. They became so numerous in Monterey that marines were ordered out to thin their ranks with muskets. Every farmhouse had from sixty to eighty dogs, and every Indian driver's cart was followed by thirty or forty. It was said that a ranchero riding to town was sometimes attended by a train of dogs half a mile long.

Every mission and rancho in old times had its *calaveras*, its place of skulls, or slaughter corral, where cattle and sheep were killed by the Indian butchers. The grizzly bears, which were very abundant in the country and very bold, used to come by night to the ravines near the slaughter corral where the refuse was thrown by the butchers. The young *caballeros* often rode out on moonlight nights for a little exciting sport in lassoing these bears, which they would then drag through the village street, past the houses of their friends, particularly those of the señoritas whom they wished to impress with their prowess. Two men could hold any bear with the strong rawhide reatas; but sometimes saucy bruin turned the tables by coolly taking a short cut through the village on his way to or from the calaveras, and then, as may be imagined, there was a wild scattering of persons who happened to be out. Several times a serenade party, singing and playing by the light of the moon, was suddenly broken up by two or three grizzlies ambling down the hill into the street, and the gay caballeros, caught armed only with their guitars, and having little faith in the old adage about music and the savage breast, had to spring over the adobe walls and run for their horses, which always stood saddled, with reata coiled ready for use at the saddle-bow. A Californian without his second self, that is, his horse and his faithful reata, was at a loss, but with them he could face any bear that ever growled a defiance.

Speaking of bears, they were so numerous and destructive that the governor of California at one time appointed an expert bear hunter to spend his whole time in destroying them, which he did by trapping them in pits, by shooting them, or lassoing. Settlers north of San Francisco Bay were in constant danger, from bears as well as from Indians. Even the women were in the habit of carrying guns and pistols when they went out to make calls. Señora Vallejo had a small rifle which she carried for this purpose, and she says that in the earlier years she had occasion to fire it at bears which attempted to intrude into the courtyard of her house.

The chief uses of the cattle were to provide food for the people, including the Indians at the missions, and in the exchange of the hides and tallow with the trading vessels for all sorts of commodities not produced in the country; but there were many other novel and interesting ways in which they were used. Some mutton was eaten, but beef was the staple meat, and the amount of it consumed was very large. The Californians ate it morning, noon, and night, and the amount given to the Christian Indians was considerable. At most of the missions as many as thirty or forty head were killed every week, enough meat being given to each Indian to last him and his family for eight days. To feed the 5,000 natives at Mission San José required the killing of a hundred head of cattle every Saturday. Some hogs were raised, but pork was never a favorite article of diet with the Californians, who valued it chiefly for the fat in soap making; and as for the Indians, they absolutely refused to touch it, just as they refused the cows' milk.

It was noticed with surprise by travelers that milk and other dairy products were rather scantily used by the Californians, but had they witnessed the milking of one of these half-wild cows they would perhaps have understood at least one of the reasons for the scarcity. The milking required the combined efforts of at least three persons; one held the animal by the head, another kept tight hold of the reata with which its hind legs were tied, while a third milked with one hand, holding the receptacle in the other. Milk pails were unknown, and the rancho's assortment of crockery was generally so small that if several cows were milked at one time all the tumblers, tea-cups, and bowls had to be pressed into service. Meanwhile the ranchero, his wife and family, such of the servants as were not busy at other occupations, and guests, of whom there were nearly always several, looked on with absorbed interest at this exciting performance. Some of the more temperamental of the animals objected strenuously to being milked by Indians.

Another use for the cattle was as work oxen. These patient creatures performed most of the labor not done by the Indians; they drew the ploughs, or primitive implements that passed as such; hauled the lumbering *carretas* which were for years the only vehicles in the country, and even ran races hitched to these carts for the amusement of the people, for they could gallop like horses. The heaviness of Sunday morning was lightened very much by a race to church with the oxen-drawn carts containing the families. The on-lookers and participants staked money or stock on the results, and even the oxen seemed to enjoy the sport, for they galloped at their best speed without being urged by the goad.

Another unusual custom was that of using the horns of slaughtered cattle to top off fences around wheat fields. On account of the lack of saws for cutting up timber, wood was not generally used for fencing, low adobe walls often serving the purpose. These walls were sometimes heightened and strengthened by a row of skulls of the cattle, with the long curving horns still attached. These came from the *matanzas*, where there were thousands of them lying in piles. So used they made a strong and almost impassable barrier against man or beast, and, set close and deep at various angles about the gateways and corral walls, they even helped to protect the enclosure from horse thieves.

As chief participants in bull and bear fights, these animals also contributed to the public entertainment.

A novel way was sometimes practiced to catch wild cattle. A trained domesticated animal was taken out with the hunter; the wild one was lassoed and tied, after which his horns were fastened to those of the tame one, which dragged him home to be slaughtered. This was done to avoid carrying the meat a long distance, especially in hot weather.

Dead or alive, the cattle were the outstanding factor in the life of the people during the pastoral age in California. Among the minor effects of the stock-raising business was the addition of a number of words which have now become an accepted part of the English language as spoken in California. Among these words are *rodéo* (round-up); *corral* (pen for live-stock); *rancho* (tract of land used almost wholly for pasturage); *reata* (a rope made of rawhide, used for lassoing animals); *vaquero* (cow-herder). In Mexican times a rancho covered not less than four square miles, and often as much as thirty, but since the American annexation the term, Anglicized into ranch, is applied to small farms and even to single houses. The old large, liberal days are gone forever. *Ranch* and *corral* are often used as verbs; a man speaks of ranching as he does of farming, and to corral anything is to catch and confine it.

The sheep industry, although there were extensive flocks throughout the province, never reached the great proportions of cattle raising. Two breeds of sheep were raised—those called *carneros* for mutton, and the *ovejas* for wool. They were generally small animals, and their wool, while strong and durable, was rather coarse and wiry. However, it served a useful purpose for making mattresses, for which it was more resilient and less likely to pack than finer wool, and for making a good though coarse cloth called *serga*, which was woven at the missions by the Indians. In 1842 there were many sheep, both in the mission flocks and in those of private owners. Vallejo had from 2,000 to 3,000, Sutter had 1,000, and the Livermore rancho had 6,000. Mission San José had 7,000; total in the missions was 31,600. At this time cattle stood at about $4.00 per head, hides at $2.00, tallow at $6.00 per 100 pounds. Broken oxen brought the comparatively high price of $25.00. Both private Californians and the padres had a dislike for raising sheep, which they felt were beneath the attention of rancheros and vaqueros. Then, too, these gentle animals were not so well able to hold their own against wild beasts as were the cattle, and large numbers were killed by wolves, coyotes, and bears.

Severe droughts were often experienced which caused heavy loss in both cattle and sheep. In 1820-21 the livestock of the missions, now increased to 400,000, had much difficulty in finding grass enough to keep them in condition. In the great drought of twenty-two months between the rains of 1828 and 1830, during which the wells and springs of Monterey gave out, and water for the use of families had to be brought from the Carmelo River, three miles distant, it was estimated that fully 40,000 head of horses and neat cattle perished throughout the province. When the year was dry and pasture short the padres ordered a *desviejar*, that is, the killing of old stock. On such occasions white men and Indians, armed with lances, entered the corrals on their horses and there quickly disposed of the poorer animals. The hides were taken off and the flesh left for beasts and birds, or for the Indians.

Two circumstances brought about the fall of this one great industry of the Californians from its high estate. One was the immigration of foreigners into the province, which put a value on both cattle and land. It was no longer possible to obtain any amount of pasture for a nominal sum, nor free cattle with which to stock it. The secularization of the missions, when the missionaries were removed from control and a secular branch of the clergy put in, also played a large part in the decay of the cattle business. The accusation has been made against certain of the friars of wanton destruction of the property, especially of wholesale slaughter of the mission cattle, when they saw the day approaching when they would have to yield up the fruits of their years of hard labor; but it is thought by many that the padres were not guilty of connivance in the slaughter of the cattle, but were simply unable to prevent it in the unsettled conditions following secularization. The Indians, having been told that they were free to follow their own inclinations, no longer had any respect for the authority of the friars, nor were they willing to work to procure their food, finding it easier to kill the cattle. Those neophytes who went back to the wild life of their ancestors soon learned that by stealing horses and cattle from the missions they could sell them to traders from Santa Fé and other points beyond the mountains. The wild Indians also preyed upon the mission herds, exchanging stolen animals for the bright-colored goods of the traders, for which they had a strong predilection. In fact, there were many agencies other than the resentment of the missionaries working for the destruction of the mission cattle.

Alfred Robinson writes that the friars were cheated in their dealings with unscrupulous dealers, who contracted to slaughter the animals and deliver half the hides and tallow to the padres. He says, "Thousands of cattle were slain for their hides only, while their carcasses remained to decompose upon the plains. The rascally contractors, who were enriching themselves so easily, secretly appropriated two hides for their portion to one on account of the missions." Bandini tells us that two thousand cattle were killed in a single day at one mission, only the hides being taken and the meat and fat left in the fields. Mrs. Ord (María de las Angustias de la Guerra) remembers that thirty thousand were killed at San Gabriel, causing fears of a pestilence from the rotting carcasses. It is said that some of the valleys were entirely covered with the decaying bodies, presenting a horrible spectacle, and that for years the country in the neighborhood was white with the skeletons. In some places the skulls and large bones were so plentiful that long fences were built of them. It is a gruesome picture, only to be matched by the slaughter by the American plainsmen of the buffalo for their tongues and hides alone. Conditions finally became so menacing to health that in June, 1834, the *diputación* (legislature) was obliged to take action forbidding the unnecessary slaughter of the mission cattle.

Increase of wealth, improvement of living conditions, and the consequent development of a distinctive society, were not the only debts owing by the Californians to the cattle. Both Spain and Mexico, always in dread lest some other power should wrest from them this precious bit of earthly paradise on the Pacific, attempted to postpone the evil day by putting up a wall of exclusion against the entrance of foreign commerce, either by land or by sea; but the hide and tallow trade brought ships in such numbers that the feeble efforts to keep them out broke down altogether, and the Golden Gate was finally swung wide to the world. As many as 134 of these ships arrived between 1841 and 1845.

Even more important to California than this breaking down of the wall of trade isolation was the fact that many of the officers of these vessels, some of whom were men of superior character and education, fell permanently under the spell of the new land. They ate of her fruits; they basked in her sunshine; they breathed her "soft Lydian airs"; they looked upon her fair daughters; they enjoyed the generous hospitality of her people; they tasted of the ease and peace of the life; and, like the lotus eaters of old, they forgot home and family and determined to remain forever in this Arcadia beside the western sea. From this "peaceful invasion" came the matrimonial alliances between the Anglo-Saxon immigrants and the Spanish Californians, from which originated the old families which constitute our true aristocracy, occupying the same position as the descendants of the Puritans on the other shore. From this most unromantic trade in hides and tallow came one literary classic—Richard Henry Dana's *Two Years Before the Mast*—and from it flowered many a charming romance between the *hijas del pais* (daughters of the country) and the officers of the Boston ships. One of the most delightful of these romances will be related in a succeeding chapter.

Chapter III

CHAPTER III

The Tilling of the Soil

THE CREDIT for introduction of agriculture into California belongs almost entirely to the missions. In the selection of sites care was taken to be not far from a landing for ships, and yet not so near as to expose the Indian neophytes to contamination by the soldiers and sailors. Three circumstances were absolutely required—an abundance of good water, so situated as to be available for irrigation, enough arable land, and a good extent of pasturage. The wise judgment of the missionaries is nowhere more evident than in their choice of these sites, for the chain of twenty-one missions eventually established occupied the most fertile land in the country.

The friars were the first farmers, who taught the natives how to till the soil and win their living from it, in spite of the fact that in all the untold centuries of their occupation of this rich land, the Indians had never planted a single thing, except perhaps the seeds of wild tobacco, which they sometimes scattered about their huts and allowed to grow untended. The reason for this lay not altogether in lack of intelligence or industry on their part, but rather in their natural surroundings, where bountiful Nature gave them a free living from her rich supply of game, fish, nuts, fruits, roots, and above all the acorns, which were their staple, as maize was in all other parts of America. It cannot be truly said that they enjoyed this bounty wholly without effort, for the women at least labored hard in gathering and preparing these natural products. Father Boscana, historian of the mission of San Juan Capistrano, says it was painful to see the Indian women groping about in the fields, with their babies strapped to their backs, while they swept the seeds from the plants with long-handled baskets into others used as receptacles; and if meals were not ready on time they were abused by their lords and masters in quite civilized fashion. Stephen Powers says, "The Indian women were eternally working, and the first sound to be heard on approaching a village was the everlasting pounding of the pestles in the mortars." The acorns and some of the other seeds and roots required elaborate preparation before they were fit for food. Some of them, such as the soaproot, were poisonous in their natural state and had to be roasted in underground pits forty-eight hours before they could be eaten. When the Spaniards tried to eat acorns they were made ill, because they did not know how to leach out the tannic acid as the Indians did.

Notwithstanding that the whole business was new to them, these aboriginals became the chief, in fact almost the only laborers in the flourishing fields of grain, the fruit orchards, and the vegetable gardens which soon surrounded every mission, as well as in those of the presidios and private owners. This kind of work did not suit the temperament of the Spanish Californians so well as the free life of the cattle ranger, and even the soldiers at the presidios, who were allotted land for cultivation as well as for grazing, did not see why sons of Mars should stoop to this slavish labor when Indians could be got to do it for their food or a small share of the crops, or even less.

It is said by Markoff, speaking of affairs in 1835, that the Indian laborers were well satisfied with a fathom of black, red, and white glass beads for a season's work. Beads were in great demand among them, and commanded high prices. In addition to the payment of beads the workers had to be furnished with parched unground corn for food. There were some among them who had become accustomed to living in houses and had acquired a considerable knowledge of domestic work. To these the Californians either paid a salary or clothed them and fed them at their own tables.

In any case it was cheap labor, but there were still many among the whites who could not afford even that, and they rose long before the dawn and worked indefatigably in the cultivation of their fields and other labors. One has only to read the manuscript account of José del Carmen Lugo, *Vida de un ranchero* (Life of a Rancher), to realize that there were many hard-working Californians. Much has been said about their ease-loving tendency, which is generally ascribed to their Spanish ancestry, but travellers in old Spain have always noted that the inhabitants are rather exceptionally industrious and thrifty, as well as abstemious in their habits. It is not necessary to look farther than our own southern states to find a parallel to the conditions that lay at the root of the dislike for the tedium of manual labor among the Spanish Californians. The near presence of a large number of an inferior race whose labor is to be had for little or nothing always has a deteriorating influence on the industrial habits of the superior people. In both instances the same effect was produced by the removal of this free labor at a later date; after a more or less painful struggle to adapt themselves to the changed conditions, our Southerners and the Californians have alike learned the dignity of labor, and their descendants have become active and enterprising citizens of the Republic.

The Californians suffered from the added disadvantage of having too much done for them by a paternal government; the regular ship coming from San Blas with supplies was a bad thing for the ambition of the colonists. The lack of a market for surplus products also had much to do with restricting agriculture to little more than was required for home use. A limited amount of wheat was sold to the trading vessels and to the Russians, who never made a success of their farming operations at Fort Ross, perhaps because they had to turn their Aleut fur hunters and fishermen into unwilling and unskillful farmers.

Although the practice of agriculture never reached the same extensive proportions as cattle raising in California, it was of great importance, as representing the very beginning of that vast industry which has since made this strip of land on the western shore of North America the garden of the world. The missionaries were great experimenters, and they showed us the way. They were the first to prove that semi-tropical fruits could be grown here—oranges, lemons, figs, dates, olives, pomegranates, citrons, limes, wine grapes, etc. The date palms, two or three of which were planted at every mission, were placed there partly as symbols of the Holy Land, and partly to supply leaves and branches for Palm Sunday. It was proved, too, that the climate and soil were suitable for the successful growing of cotton, flax, hemp, and other textile plants. Maize, which up to that time had been entirely unknown to the California Indians, was introduced by the missionaries, and soon every mission had its corn patch.

Progress was slow at first, for the priestly farmers had to learn by their failures, the first crops had to be saved for seed, and the Indian laborers had to be trained in the

Franz Geritz '27

art; but in an astonishingly short space of time, considering all the conditions, the missions were raising more than enough food stuffs for their own use, and, besides assisting the presidios, were able to ship a surplus of meal, wine, oil, hemp, hides and tallow to San Blas, there to be exchanged for clothing and other necessaries. Payment was always made in goods, for in this country, where nothing could be bought, money was of no use.

In a country where rainfall was not always to be depended upon, artificial watering became a necessary accompaniment of agriculture, and there was no form of industry in which the inventive genius of the missionaries was more evident than in the construction of irrigation works at the various missions. They were the real pioneers in the great water conservation system which now covers a large part of the state with a network of canals. Perhaps the most notable example of their work was at San Diego, where the remains are still to be seen. About three miles above the mission the river was dammed by a solid stone wall, thirteen feet in thickness, and coated with a cement that became as hard as rock. From this dam an aqueduct lined with hand-made cement slabs carried a stream one foot deep and two feet wide to the mission lands. This conduit was built through a precipitous gorge impassable to horses, and in places it crossed gulches from fifteen to twenty feet wide and deep. In these places it was supported on cobble stones set in cement, but the conduit was so strong that it supported itself after the foundations were removed. Considerable portions of the dam and conduit still remaining in a good state of preservation and standing in place, having withstood the winter floods of almost a century and a half, are mute testimony to the quality of the work. This irrigation project was the first constructed by the missionaries, and was built by the labor of Indians but newly rescued from barbarism, under the direction of men who were not qualified engineers. So that the friars were not only the first farmers, the first horticulturists, the first stockmen, the first teachers, the first manufacturers, the first builders in California, but also the first engineers and irrigationists. The list of our obligations to these able and indefatigable men is almost without end.

At Santa Barbara extensive irrigation works were constructed. In front of the church, built of solid masonry, was a series of tasteful fountains, a pool and a reservoir seventy feet long. Water was brought from an adjoining hill through an open stone aqueduct, near which were the grist mill and bath house, the latter a stone structure six by ten feet, over the door of which was a stone lion's head from which a large jet of water issued. The water was made to serve various uses in its passage, finally being spread over the soil in irrigating ditches.

The waters of the beautiful San Antonio River were conducted to the mission of the same name and carried for twenty miles in paved trenches to be dispensed over rich tracts of land.

There were elaborate regulations for the contribution of Indian labor by the rancheros for the construction of these works, for keeping them in repair and preventing wastage, for keeping the ditches clean, etc. Any person who washed clothes in the main ditch, who threw filth into it, or allowed swamp land to be formed, was liable to very severe punishment.

Mission San Gabriel Arcángel was the mother of agriculture in California. This mission occupied one of the most charming spots in the province. Its gardens were crowded with oranges, grapes, figs, pomegranates, peaches, apples, limes, pears, and citrons, and the air was sweet with the perfume of their flowers. Wheat was raised there at a very early date and sold to the Russians, and it was there that the orange and the vine were first planted. The padres made mistakes at first, and it took several years to find out how to grow good grain.

At Mission San José a tract about a mile square was planted to wheat. Fences were almost unknown, timber not being used because there were no sawmills. Sometimes the planted fields were surrounded by a hedge of willows, but this one at San José was guarded by a ditch, dug by the Indians with their hands and sharp sticks, so deep and so wide that horses and cattle never crossed it. The old field is now occupied by several fine farms, and the course of the ditch can still be traced. In other places stone or adobe walls or hedges of prickly pear cactus were used in lieu of fences. As has already been described in the chapter on cattle raising, sometimes these walls were heightened and strengthened by a row of cattle skulls with the horns still attached. The *milpas*, or garden patches, sometimes had no other fence than a troop of half-naked Indians, who warned off trespassing animals with loud, harsh cries. At night this living fence camped near the fields, "making night hideous with their excruciating melodies," and whiling away the long hours in gambling, when the ranchero permitted it.

Methods of sowing and reaping were almost biblical in their simplicity. The ground was ploughed once or twice, merely scratched with a primitive wooden plow made of the crooked limb of a tree shod with an iron point, then harrowed by dragging over it large branches of trees. When there was no iron to be had, hard oak limbs were used. Oxen, guided by Indian laborers, did all the work of husbandry. Barley and wheat were sown by hand, broadcast, and corn and beans were planted four or five grains to the hill. So rich was the virgin soil which had lain fallow since the beginning of time that even with these simple methods the yield was enormous. John Bidwell speaks of wheat fields in the vicinity of San Francisco Bay which produced from 70 to 110 fold. Harrison G. Rogers, a member of the Jedediah Smith expedition of 1826, remarks that "this mission of San Gabriel, if properly managed would be equal to a mine of silver or gold. There annual income, situated as it is and managed so badly by the Indians, is worth in hides, tallow, soap, wine, brandy, wheat, and corn from $55,000 to $60,000."

Wheat growers saved themselves the trouble of replanting by cutting so high that enough seed was left to sow itself. Sometimes a third crop was raised in this way. When the grain was ripe it was cut with hand sickles and thrown into *coras* (baskets), which were carried on the backs of men, women, and children, and when full emptied into carts. Pío Pico says the grain was threshed by men with *garrotes* (sticks) and winnowed by women who tossed it in wooden bowls called *bateas*. The grain was stored in bulk, in immense granaries called *trojes*. A still slower and more laborious way was for Indians to rub the heads of grain between their hands, blow the chaff away, and then grind it between two stones. The usual method of threshing, however, was as follows: First a circular piece of ground was fenced in and its surface watered and pounded until it was very hard; the wheat was then thrown into the enclosure and seventy-five or a hundred mares driven in and round and round until the grain was all trampled out. This was a noisy business, accompanied by much loud shouting by the Indian drivers. Next came the winnowing by tossing it against the wind in shovels. The whole process was such as had been in use in Spain for centuries. The grain was then packed in bags made of sail cloth, and some of it stored and some sold to the Russians. It is said that wheat threshed in this way always came out in whole grains.

The close of the wheat harvest was celebrated by a special religious ceremony. The last four sheaves taken from the last field at San José were tied to poles in the form of a cross, and then were brought by the reapers in a harvest procession to the church. The bells were rung, and the father, dressed in his robes, carrying a cross and accompanied by boys with tapers and censers, chanting the *Te Deum* as they went, set forth to meet the bearers of the sheaves. Seed time and harvest were epochs in the quiet life of the missions.

Those who had no granaries put the grain in leather bags, holding from three to six *fanegas* (bushels). Horsehides were generally used, hides from the cattle being reserved for sale. The maize was kept in the ear and shelled by hand when needed. The grains were freed of their outer shell by soaking in water mixed with lime for some hours, then thoroughly washing in fresh water. Treated in this way the corn made a hominy very superior to that obtained by modern machinery. Prices in 1788 were approximately, per *fanega*, wheat, $2.00; barley, $1.00; maize, $1.50; beans, $2.50; flour, $1.25 per 100 pounds. Frijoles, peas, lentils and chick-peas were kept in bags or in dry places. Much trouble was experienced with grubs, which attacked the grain when stored, but these pests were not so numerous as now. Rats and mice also did damage, but worst of all were squirrels, moles, crows, and a bird called *sanate*. Bird catchers were employed against them, who set traps and killed them with small arrows.

At first the only means of grinding was by hand, with Indian stone pestles and mortars, a most tedious process which kept large numbers of women busy all day long. Every hacienda had a number of women who did nothing else, and little rest did they get from this monotonous task. Monsieur de Langle, a French visitor who came in early times, pitying the poor creatures, made the missionaries a present of his handmill, of which he says, "A greater service could not have been rendered them as by that means four women could perform the work of a hundred." The fathers, however, were of the opinion that labor-saving machinery would be detrimental to the morals of the Indians, as it would leave them too much time for the works of Satan. Speaking on this subject, Markoff says, "The Californians have neither wind-mills nor water-mills with large stones. Some of them, but only a few, have hand-mills, while for the most part they obtain flour by crushing the grain between two large stones. You can imagine how much flour one man can make in this manner in a day. This is the reason why in California, where wheat may be said to grow wild, flour is dear."

Grinding by the *arrastra* marked one step in advance of the Indian *metate*. The arrastra, also used in crushing quartz, consisted of two mill-stones, the lower one of which remained stationary, while the upper was attached to a cross beam and dragged around in a circle by a mule or horse which was hitched to the beam. The grain, which was first carefully washed by the women, was ground between the two stones, and the flour then passed through hand sieves, as they had no bolting cloth. These sieves make a very important item in the lists of supplies sent from Mexico to the colony in Alta California. The stones used in these mills were of granite, and were sometimes obtained from the beds of streams, in the form of flat boulders. Mill Creek in Tehama County, originally *El Rio de los Molinos* (the river of the mill-stones) evidently received its name from this circumstance.

At a later date water-mills were built at Santa Cruz, San Luís Obispo, San José, and San Gabriel. In 1833 there was an adobe grist-mill run by water at Mission San Juan

Capistrano, which was destroyed by a flood and afterwards replaced by a wooden structure.

The food furnished a farm hand at the missions included neither liquor, which the padres regarded as an instrument of the devil for Indians, nor coffee nor tea. Rations were given him weekly, consisting of as much as he could consume of beef, lard, maize, beans, and lentils, and the Indians were great consumers. Von Langsdorff expressed astonishment that any one could eat so much extremely nourishing food three times a day. Other things, such as pumpkins, onions, and chiles, the laborer raised on land which he was allowed to make use of. At the proper season the neophytes were permitted to go out to the forest and gather nuts, seeds, and fruits, to which they were accustomed, and of which they were very fond. This store, with the regular food of the mission crops, especially after cattle became plentiful, made a great abundance. In the very earliest times this was not always the case, and sometimes the padres were glad to fall back upon the seeds and other contributions brought in by the Indians.

In regard to agriculture in general it may be said that, while the implements were of a very rude sort, results were surprisingly good. The principal cereals cultivated gave abundant harvests, amply sufficient for the use of the missions and their large body of dependent Indians, and a sufficient surplus to aid the whites and the soldiers at the presidios, and to exchange for clothing and other necessaries at San Blas. The missionaries did not go at this work blindly, but made every effort to learn the proper methods, as far as could be done in their isolated situation. "From my own conversation," says Señor Coronel, "and from what I learned from frequent talks with Padre Zalvidea of San Juan Capistrano, the system of agriculture, manufactures, and instruction in operation at the missions was based on a work entitled *Casa de Campo y Pastoril*, a treatise which contained full information regarding the proper management of the property and the laborers." It would be interesting to unearth a copy of this work.

In a few years abundant crops of all kinds were being raised at the missions on land which had previously raised only acorns and wild fruits. Mission San José, which for years supplied the Russian settlements with grain, raised 8,600 bushels of wheat from eighty bushels of seed in one year, and in the year following 5,200 bushels as a volunteer crop from the scatterings of the first harvest. The accounts of Vancouver and others of the early visitors mention a great variety of the products of temperate and semitropical countries grown by the padres in the mission gardens. Alfred Robinson, writing of San Gabriel, says, "There are several extensive gardens attached to this mission, where may be found oranges, citrons, limes, apples, pears, peaches, pomegranates, figs, and grapes in abundance."

Among the private rancheros grain culture was a small industry before 1825-30, only enough being raised for home use. Poor people who had no stock of their own were generally employed as vaqueros to handle the stock, work in matanzas, and to some small extent in cultivating the soil. The *gente de razon* (people of reason, that is, the whites) did the principal work, handling stock, marking, branding, and killing. The roughest labor was done by the partially Christianized Indians. They worked at the various processes of agriculture, such as clearing the land, ploughing, planting, building irrigating ditches, harvesting the crops, threshing the wheat and barley, husking corn, picking beans, lentils, peas, and garbanzos, and gathering grapes. Coronel says that the white Californians occupied themselves exclusively in caring for the cattle and horses, and this only during the season of the rodéos, that they might protect their own interests, and when the slaughter of cattle took place, in order to collect the hides and tallow, which were the only medium of exchange to make purchases and pay their debts. They were not devoted to agriculture, for they could obtain what grain they wanted at the missions. Some, however, cultivated land for their own use, and later, as the missions decayed, all were compelled to pay some attention to cultivating the soil. About 1846 a change of view, as regarded agriculture, came on gradually, when Americans came in and began to cultivate the land. It cannot be said that agriculture was extensively practiced until after this date, when many foreigners settled in the Santa Clara Valley and around the bay.

Among the products of the soil for whose beginnings we are indebted to Spanish days is the homely but invaluable potato. When the French navigator, La Pérouse, visited California in 1786, he was received literally with open arms, his hosts lavishing true Spanish hospitality upon him and the other members of the expedition. During the ten days' stay of the French vessels in Monterey Bay the Spaniards busied themselves in loading the visiting ships with prodigal supplies of cattle, vegetables, milk, poultry, hay, and grain, for none of which would they accept one *peso* in payment. Overwhelmed by this generosity, the visitors endeavored to reciprocate with presents of blue cloth, blankets, beads, tools, and, above all, with seed potatoes from Chile, which they rightly believed to be "not the least of their gifts, and that the root would succeed perfectly in the light and fertile soil around Monterey." This was the origin of one of the largest and most profitable industries of modern California, although it seems that potatoes were not extensively raised until they were brought in from Oregon.

Olives were planted in all the mission orchards, and they produced enough to supply the home wants in the pickled fruit and oil, leaving a surplus for export to San Blas. In this industry also the missionaries pointed the way, which has since been followed with such success by modern California olive growers.

Cotton was planted in 1846 and found to grow well. The cotton grown in California was pronounced better than that of Acapulco, and attracted the attention of the Tepic manufacturers. At San Luís Obispo cotton clothing of good quality was made, as well as rebozos, quilts, and other things of the same material. José de Jesus Pico informs us that during Father Luís A. Martinez's management of Mission San Luís Obispo, down to 1830, its Indians were better clothed than the soldiers and other *gente de razon*. "At the mission," he says, "good blue cloth was made for cloaks and pantaloons, because there were plantations of cotton which yielded considerably." Some of the mission archives refer to rooms full of cotton in storage. Again this represents the beginning of what is now a large California industry, producing the best cotton in the world. Enough flax and hemp were raised to meet all home necessities for rope and textures and leave some for trading purposes.

Some of the Californians tried to raise tobacco on their farms. It grew luxuriantly but was inferior in quality to that of the eastern coast of the continent. When the Spaniards first arrived here they found the natives smoking the leaves of the wild tobacco, which was said to have a particularly vile odor. The Indians had no intoxicating drink, properly speaking, but they prepared a sort of narcotic by mixing powdered burnt shells with wild tobacco juice, crushed wild cherries, and water, which they called *pispibata*. This decoction was so potent that they dared only to touch the forefinger to the tongue after dipping it in the mass, and even this when repeated three or four times threw them into a complete stupor, from which there was sometimes no awakening. This drug was said to produce the dreamy, but false, delights of hasheesh.

Sugar was made by the Indians, in very small quantity but of a fine flavor. There were several saccharine producing plants native to the country from which their sweet content was extracted by various methods. In the Tulares a certain reed grew which, if gathered when ripe and crushed on metates, yielded crystals something like rock candy. Little sweet *tamales* were made of these crystals by rolling them in leaves of the reed. Señor Hijar speaks of coffee-colored bulbs called *torogüi*, which, after being roasted underground on a bed of hot stones, were used to sweeten *atole* (porridge). Then there was a wild reed growing near the missions from the dried leaves of which a sugary substance exuded. All these native sources of sugar were, of course, so slight as to be negligible, and during practically all the time of Spanish occupation of Alta California the inhabitants were compelled to rely on the supply ships from San Blas for this commodity. But this was not because the thought of producing it at home had not come into their minds. Bancroft relates an amusing story illustrative of this point:

"In the year 1838, there came to Monterey one Octavio Custot, surnamed *El Azucarero* (the sugar-maker), so called because he did *not* know how to make sugar. He was a sharp fellow, this Octavio; and, thinking that among the simple-minded people of our lotus land it were easy to live by one's wits, he deserted from his ship. It was at Sonoma that he acquired the title of *El Azucarero*, and it was in this wise. Closeted one day with the autocrat of the frontier, he revealed the startling intelligence that he could make sugar; he could fabricate the genuine saccharine substance from beets.

"Vallejo was a man of progress. All his life he had spent in this far-away wilderness, and there were now coming to these shores so many strangers with so many strange tales, ideas new to him, and things never before heard of, that he was ready to believe almost anything. Indeed, there was no reason why sugar should not be made from beets, and perhaps tea from oak leaves, and coffee from manzanita berries.

"'Doubtless all is as you say,' remarked Vallejo, 'but where are the beets?'

"'Grow them,' replied Custot.

"'I have no seed,' said Vallejo.

"'Send for some,' answered Custot.

"Indeed, the cunning Octavio had all along reckoned on this—on the absence of facilities, and the restful days in store for him while awaiting them; for this, to a deserting sailor, was a fat country, with balmy air and beautiful women.

"To his mayordomo at Petaluma Vallejo finally sent the fellow, with orders to place at his disposal four yoke of oxen, eight Indians, and a dwelling and provisions. 'Civilization is indeed a boon,' thought Octavio, as he lay under a madroño smoking his pipe, while the slow-stepping oxen furrowed forty acres.

"Seed was found at Mazatlan, and when it came it was pronounced of good quality—very good quality. 'But,' said Octavio, 'nothing can be done now; it is too late to plant this season.' So there was nothing to be done but to extend to Azucarero his free and easy living at Petaluma through the summer.

"At length the rains came, the seed was put into the ground, the beets grew, sun and virgin soil combining to make the biggest and reddest roots on record. The master came frequently from Sonoma to see the beets grow, and in his mind to compute the quantity of sugar each contained, and how much that would be an acre, and what was forty times that, and it was about time to think of getting barrels ready.

"Finally came to Sonoma July, 1830, and with it a fine box of sugar from Custot to the Señora who pronounced it fine, very fine; equal to her loaf-sugar brought from Peru. 'Here is an industry worth having,' mused the master, 'oxen, Indian labor, unlimited lands; why, I will have in beets millions of acres, and presently ships carrying hence the great staple to every quarter of the earth.'

"But what is this the Señora says, as she returns with the servant from putting in the storehouse with the other the new production? Her sugar is gone! A dozen loaves of her best Peruvian stolen! Ah! all is clear; she always knew that Octavio to be a thief. Vallejo hurried to Petaluma, demanded to see the process, but was told it would not bear too much light. 'True; nor yourself,' replied Vallejo as he ordered Chief Solano to take the impostor to Yerba Buena. Solano obeyed, landing El Azucarero waist-deep in water."

But this is a great deal of discussion about an industry which never materialized, for the Spanish Californians never produced a pound of sugar.

Wine making was a different matter, for it was soon found that the climate was eminently suitable for the variety of fruit adapted to this purpose, and soon every mission had its flourishing vineyard. At San Gabriel wine and brandy were produced in abundance, and Santa Barbara became famous for its choice wines. In a beautiful plain north of San Gabriel was the mission of San Fernando, founded in 1797, where was made annually two thousand gallons each of wine and fine brandy. This manufacture was considered a perfectly legitimate industry for the missions to engage in, and most of the padres became expert wine and brandy makers. The fact that in the days before the advent of foreigners the abuse of alcoholic liquors was rare, accounted for the lack of discredit attached to the business. Señor Arnaz, one of those who writes of early days, says drunkenness was not common; few intoxicated men were seen, although liquor was common and cheap. Most people took wine at dinner at Los Angeles, where it was made; elsewhere water was used. Drinking was more prevalent in the north, though not excessive there. Richard Henry Dana also comments on the fact that he never saw an intoxicated Californian while he was on the coast. So it was thought perfectly respectable for Father Durán to make good wine and brandy at his mission of San José. His *aguardiente* was as clear as crystal, or when treated with burnt sugar became of a clear yellow. "It was doubly distilled," says Bancroft, "and as strong as the reverend father's faith."

Most of the missions manufactured aguardiente from grapes, apples, and pears. The brandy of San Fernando acquired a great reputation in California. A bottle of Catalan brandy cost twelve *reales*, or an oxhide. One Gamboa used to fill an empty brandy keg with water, expose it to the sun half a day, then put in burnt sugar and ground chile. This mixture he would sell to the savages as brandy, and when they complained that there was no happiness in it, he would say that he had kept it so long that it had lost its strength.

The wine of pastoral days was made in the primitive European manner, the juice trod out by the feet of Indians (reassuringly said to be "well washed"), then kept in tubs or vats until it fermented. Heat was applied to aid evaporation. For white wine the first juice only was taken and stored. Liquor distilled from wheat, maize, and barley was considered prejudicial to health, and in 1840 the *diputación* (legislature) passed a resolution prohibiting its manufacture from those materials. Any one wishing to make wine or brandy was required to take out a license, and strict regulations governed the whole process. Violation of any of the rules laid the offender liable to a fine of $50 (a large sum in those days) or two months in the *calabozo*. Many complaints were made concerning the ill effects on the morals of the people of the introduction of "bad liquor" from abroad, and several of the governors made earnest efforts to prohibit it. Both wine and brandy were produced in sufficient quantity for exportation. The brandy of the country sold in the late years of Mexican domination at $50.00 a barrel.

At San Antonio Mission the remains of the great circular *bodegas*, or wine vats, may still be seen a short distance away from the church. Here was stored the wine made from the grapes that once grew in luxuriant profusion over the arched corridors of the church. The pear trees planted by the missionaries are today alive and each year heavily loaded with fruit, and the scarlet of the pomegranate flowers still flames against the ruined walls. At San Juan Bautista there is a clump of the original pear trees, planted in the earliest days of the mission, still healthy and bearing good fruit. Every spring, in their annual re-birth, they put out their sweet-smelling flowers and green leaves, and every autumn their branches are heavy with juicy pears, silent reminders of the busy hands which have long since mouldered into dust, the hands which brought agriculture to California.

In 1806 the Russian von Langsdorff describes a dinner enjoyed at Santa Clara Mission as consisting of vegetable soup, roast fowl, leg of mutton, different vegetables, salad, pastry, preserved fruits, dairy products, wine, tea, chocolate—all home grown products except the tea and chocolate—showing how greatly agriculture and horticulture had prospered since the first days. A decided change from the days when Pedro Fages went bear hunting in San Luís

Obispo Valley to save the little colony at Monterey from starvation!

Stories of the extraordinary productiveness of the land and the variety of its fruits were undoubtedly carried back to the eastern states of the Union by returning traders and trappers, and certainly helped to stimulate the influx of immigration later. The Spanish ranchos actually saved the American pioneers from the stage of starvation which usually initiates such movements, for the first comers gathered about the principal Spanish settlements and lived on their products. The sight of the enormous yield of grain, and of the oranges, lemons, figs, olives, grapes, etc., growing in the mission gardens, led to the planting of the great wheat fields and orchards of semi-tropical fruits which have since made California famous. It may be said that in this sense the vast fields of grain which ripen every year under the hot sun of the San Joaquín Valley; the tons of golden fruit gathered from the orchards of Riverside and other parts of Southern California; the potatoes now produced in huge amounts in the valley of the Salinas, to say nothing of the innumerable other products of every part of the state, are a direct heritage from the Spanish missionary-farmers. Primitive as were their methods and their tools, they pointed the way, they showed us what a mine of wealth lay hidden in the soil, far beyond all the gold of the mountains.

Chapter IV

CHAPTER IV

Building and Other Occupations

AMONG ALL the occupations followed by the Spanish settlers of Alta California, none left a more lasting impress, reaching down even into our own day, than building. This is not because of the extent or grandeur of their operations in this respect, but rather because they succeeded in evolving a distinctive architecture, which, as the years pass, shows more and more its peculiar adaptation to the country and climate. Once more we must lay our tribute of gratitude at the feet of the missionaries, for it is largely to them that we owe this heritage which sets California apart from all the other states in the Union. And let us not forget the poor Indians, for if the friars were the brains which planned the work, they were the hands which put it into execution.

The very first buildings erected, by both the friars and the private citizens, were mere brush shelters. Then came something a little better, primitive huts made of poles driven into the ground for walls, and roofed over with tules or grass smeared with mud or asphalt, sufficient at least to keep out the rain, but with no pretense at comfort or beauty. Even the first churches were constructed in this way, to be supplanted by better ones as conditions permitted. At some of the missions as many as three churches were built before those whose still imposing ruins meet our eyes, and at Santa Barbara the stone building wrecked in the earthquake of June 29, 1925, was the fourth erected on that site. The first buildings of San Carlos Borroméo at Monterey were of the very rudest construction, mere huts of sticks, plastered with mud or clay, with tule or mud roofs, the whole surrounded with a stockade at the four corners of which cannon were set up. As time passed the cannon were allowed to rust, for there was never any occasion to use them upon the inoffensive natives of this region. In these comfortless abodes the padres lived for some time without furniture, probably without doors, windows, or fireplaces, without light except by day, for candles were too precious for anything but the altar. The chapels, constructed in the same humble fashion, were partly furnished with bells and altar utensils and ornaments. The permanent buildings which are familiar to us in their ruined state were of slow growth, accomplished by years of toil after Indian labor was better trained. Few of the pioneer missionaries ever saw the finished structures; the stone walls of San Carlos were never hallowed by the bodily presence of the illustrious Serra. He and his companions had been dead nearly ten years before the first stone of those now remaining, except Dolores, was laid. How wild were the surroundings even at the time of the erection of the permanent buildings is attested by an interesting relic at San Juan Bautista. The floor tiles, made of clay found in the neighborhood, were left outside to dry, and in the night prowling animals walked across them and left the impress of their feet in the soft clay. The marks hardened as the earth dried, the tiles were fortunately put in just as they were, and so to this day the footprints of foxes and wildcats remain in the floor of the central nave of the church, mute remind-

ers of the day when this once imposing building stood as an outpost in the midst of the wilderness.

In building the missions the padres, by what seems an almost heaven-born inspiration, evolved from a combination of ideas brought from Spain in which both Moorish and Roman influences may be traced, with variations in design for convenience and suitability to environment, an original type, what is now known as "California mission architecture." In this connection Blackmar says:

"The traveller views with astonishment these interesting structures that have endured the storms of a century of seasons, monuments to the wisdom and perseverance of the founders who sought, not to transplant, but to build a new civilization out of crude materials. They have produced a distinctive California architecture, with open court, long colonnades, round arches, corridors, tile roofs, a style unique and picturesque as well as commodious and convenient for the purposes for which it was designed."

Experiences with earthquakes, by which church buildings were damaged again and again, no doubt had something to do with the thick and substantial walls, in some cases reenforced with heavy buttresses, which give the buildings their massive and impressive appearance; while the red tile roofs were the result of many sharp lessons from fire. In order to guard against this danger one of the fathers at Mission San Luís Obispo, whose buildings were burned down three times from having the thatched roof set on fire by burning arrows shot by hostile Indians, invented a method of making fire-proof tiles of burnt clay, which were first put in use at this mission and afterwards adopted at all the others. This is the origin of the red tile roofs which blend so harmoniously with the mellow tones of the California landscape. Out of need came beauty.

The evolution of this distinctive architecture is largely

owing to the isolated situation of California and the poverty of the resources at the command of the missionaries. The use of stone and adobe was resorted to because of the want of sawmills to work up the timber with which the country was so richly supplied. It was not until 1844 that some Frenchmen built a sawmill near Santa Cruz; there was one erected at San Gabriel in 1846; and the following year Monterey had one. This very dearth of means to make use of the timber gave us the buildings of solid and permanent appearance characteristic of the mission period. Simplicity was in a sense forced upon them by lack of tools and skilled artisans, and out of it came dignity and an absence of the over decoration that mars many of the churches of Mexico. Let us quote an excellent authority, Rexford Newcomb:

"The influence of the country, the geography, the topography, the climate, has played a larger part in the development than has its ancestry. The style is, above everything else, California; her sloping hills; her beaches; her mountains; her sunshine. It being hard to get artisans and artists to come to California, the priests and Indians, with humble materials and unskilled hands, were compelled to build simply, and, meeting squarely and frankly their problem as they saw it, they were able to create a style, which, for the country in which it was developed, has not been excelled."

Without going into technicalities, it may be said that the California mission style, although Spanish-Moorish in its general feeling, has enough new features, either in form or in application, to establish it as separate and distinct from any other in the world. One of these unique features is the campanile or bell tower of Pala, which is the only known instance of a campanile detached from the main body of the church.

It is to the missionaries that we owe this new type of

architecture, so admirably adapted to the Mediterranean blue of our sea and sky, to the warm brown of the rolling hills in autumn, and to the ever-visible mountain peaks. Its influence upon present-day building in California is everywhere evident, in both public and private structures. The massive walls with piers and buttresses, the arched corridors, the terraced bell towers, the inner patio with fountain or garden, the broad, undecorated wall surfaces, the wide projecting eaves, and the low sloping tile roofs, characteristic of the Franciscan edifices of early days, have served and increasingly continue to serve as the *motif* for many modern buildings. Schools, hotels, private houses, even railroad stations, everywhere adopt such of its features as are suitable for their uses. In this way this form of architecture, evolved by the genius of the missionaries from Old World recollections and New World needs, remains with us as a permanent heritage, not merely in the ruins of the dead missions, but as a living presence in the work of our modern builders.

When the Spaniards first arrived in Alta California they knew little or nothing about the character of the natives, whether they were to be feared or not. Hence the first building to be erected was always the presidio, whose fortifications and walls were of adobe, the latter sometimes eighteen feet high in places, while in other less exposed parts twelve or fourteen. The walls were generally six feet thick, and had iron or brass cannon at each corner. In time, as the docile character of the natives was recognized, these cannon were allowed to rust and become useless. The Indians referred to them as "thunder makers," no doubt believing that their sole function was to make a noise, and indeed that was about all they were good for.

In the very earliest times all the people were poor and all lived in the same primitive way, with few comforts and no luxuries. The reader will remember how amazed Vancouver was at sight of the comfortless living conditions of the comandante and his family at San Francisco. The massive style of the missions was imitated to a certain extent in private dwellings. Adobe was the material generally employed for the walls, which were sometimes two or three feet thick, making a deep embrasure for the rather small window openings. The poorer houses were thatched with straw or tules smeared with mud or asphalt, while the better ones had roofs of overlapping tiles. As a rule the rooms were few but quite large, and the houses were comfortable, roomy, warm in winter and cool in summer, as is coming to be recognized in our day.

At first there was no glass in the windows, and sometimes the doors were made of rawhide stretched over sticks, while the more ambitious had painted wooden doors. None of these doors had locks, for there was little fear of thieves where there was nothing to be stolen. The rafters were made of straight young trees with the bark stripped off. Often no nails were used, but these rafters were tied to the cross-beams with thongs made of oxhide. The remains of these thongs could still be seen at Mission San Carlos before its restoration.

Those with fastidious tastes had their dwellings plastered and white-washed, inside and out,which gave them a fresh, clean look, but this was not always done. Some of them had benches two or three feet high, also built of adobe and also white-washed, running around the outside walls. These benches, usually shaded by the overhanging roof, made pleasant lounging places on a hot day. One of them is still to be seen at the old customhouse at Monterey, where one might sit and dream while looking out over the deep blue waters of the bay.

Few of the houses had chimneys or fireplaces except in an outhouse used for cooking. This was not because of any superstition against fire in the house, as Bancroft says, but partly as an inheritance from old Spain, and partly because it was thought weakening to the health to sit by a fire. Also, it kept the heat and odors and noise of the kitchen away from the main part of the house. In fact, there are many things to be said in commendation of this plan as far as the cooking is concerned. Many of the town houses had large adobe ovens built in the yard, where the neighborhood came to bake their bread. The only method of heating in cold weather was often that brought from Spain, the open brasier sitting in the middle of the room, and even this was used but seldom. The people depended upon extra clothing and active exercise to keep warm.

The houses of the poorer people had only earth floors; even Comandante Argüello had no better, but at a later date those who could afford it had them boarded. The lack of sawmills in the country was the cause of the small use of wood about these structures, except for doors, window-frames, and roof timbers. The houses of sun-dried clay brick called adobe took the place in California of the log cabins in our pioneer middle west. The word *adobe* is one of the building terms that have come down to us from that period.

After 1834, when a large number of colonists came in, some of them from the better class in the city of Mexico, material changes took place in California. A more luxurious mode of living was adopted, and some of the wealthier residents constructed commodious and even handsome houses after the Spanish fashion, built around an inner court filled with luxuriant plants watered by a fountain in the center. All around the court ran a corridor, upon which opened the large, dimly lighted rooms, with low ceilings, furnished sparsely, after the manner of the abstemious Spaniard. Here in peaceful California grated windows were quite common, a relic from a day and place where a man's house had in reality to be "his castle." The houses were usually of one story, never more than two. They had a look of solidity and permanency rather unusual in a new, frontier land.

Tile roofing was generally used on the better houses, but after foreign immigrants began to drop in, bringing with them their different usages and above all their trades and tools, some of the richer Californians adopted the shingled roof. A little story, illustrative of the large, easy ways of the times and the people, is told by Bancroft about General Vallejo, and how he had his roof shingled. About that time George Yount, for whom the town of Yountsville was afterwards named, dropped in to see the autocrat of Sonoma, and offer his services.

"What can you do?" demanded Vallejo.

"Many things," said Yount.

"I do not want you to do many things; what one thing can you do that no one else does here?"

"I have seen no shingles in California; your new house yonder is about ready for them; I can make shingles."

"What are shingles?"

Yount explained the complete process of barking the felled tree, cross-cutting in blocks eighteen inches long, splitting and shaving, and all with the simplest tools.

"Very well," replied Vallejo, who had followed him attentively though half incredulously; "you shall make me some shingles and roof my house."

The work was done, and the owner was highly pleased; he had a shingled house, the first in all the two Californias, and he was very proud of it. This indeed looked like civilization.

Again the mechanic stood before the master.

"What shall I give you?" asked Vallejo.

"I would like some land in Napa Valley, if you would

lend me a few heifers so that I might start a herd," said Yount.

"How much land?"

"Half a league."

"You can't have half a league; we don't give half leagues here, with five hundred miles on our north and a thousand on our east unoccupied. You must take four leagues."

"I will take a league," said Yount, who was thinking of the care and cost attending the ownership of so large a tract.

"You can have two leagues, and nothing less," replied Vallejo; and so the matter ended.

In 1836 there was great excitement in the town of Yerba Buena over the building of the first frame house, the first real structure, by an American from Ohio, Jacob P. Leese, who married General Vallejo's sister. This house was completed in time for a grand celebration on July 4, which was attended by all the prominent residents, Californians as well as Americans, for leagues around. The festivities were managed by the Americans attached to the three or four American vessels in port and those living on shore. To enable families around the bay to attend, boats and schooners were sent from town to different points a day or two before, returning in the same way. All the beauty and wealth and fashion of Northern California graced the occasion. Feasting, dancing, picnics at Rincon Point, were kept up for three days, and only ceased on account of the exhaustion of the ladies. Salutes were fired at intervals from vessels in the bay, and during the whole time the Mexican and American flags flew amicably side by side over Leese's house.

Alfred Robinson, writing at the time of his first entrance into the bay of Monterey in 1829, gives a description of the house of the comandante, Don Mariano Estrada, which may be regarded as typical of the finer dwellings:

"The residence stood in the central part of the town, in the usual route from the beach to the presidio. Its external appearance, notwithstanding it was made of adobe, . . . was not displeasing, for the outer walls had been plastered and whitewashed, giving it a cheerful and inviting aspect. Like all dwellings built in the warm countries of America, it was but one story in height, covered with tiles, and occupied, in its entire premises, an entire square. Our Don was standing in the door, and as we approached, he, with true Castilian courtesy, sallied forth to meet us, embraced G., shook me cordially by the hand, then bowed us ceremoniously into the 'sala.'"

Shipbuilding was practiced but slightly by the Californians, but Sir George Simpson was mistaken in his statement that in 1842 there was not, on the waters of San Francisco Bay, nor anywhere upon the coast from that point to San Diego, any boat, barge, canoe, or other floating craft except the native *balsas* made of bulrushes; for some few vessels were built both before and after the coming of the first Americans. Joaquín Gómez built at Monterey a famous schooner which he called *Peor es Nada* (worse is nothing), and during Alvarado's rule some small vessels were built at Santa Cruz for the coast trade between Monterey and San Luís Obispo. The captain of the port of Santa Barbara was somewhat chagrined when on the eighteenth of April, 1839, the ship *Monsoon* arrived from Boston and he had no boat in which to visit her officially; whereupon he petitioned the government and a boat was provided for him. Among the early American arrivals there were several ship carpenters, and licenses were given to them for building schooners for otter hunting and coast trading. The very first craft made by white men in California was the *cayuco*, or dugout, made from the trunk of a tree on the Carmelo River and used by Captain Ayala in 1775 in exploring San Francisco Bay after his first passage through the Golden Gate. The construction of this rude boat may fairly be said to be the forerunner of the vast ship-building industry which now turns out the great leviathans in the yards of the Pacific Coast.

Fur hunting was another occupation engaged in to a limited extent by the Californians, but nearly always as trappers in the employ of foreigners, seldom as principals. At one time Alvarado and Castro went into the business, but as Alvarado himself remarks, "We made money, but we were two gay young men, and whenever we were in funds we gave a grand ball, to which the whole world was invited; so the money did not last long." Bancroft says, "The Californians could have done well in furs had they had more enterprise. Sea-otter skins were purchased at twenty dollars a piece, while the animals swam about in San Francisco Bay." Fur and hair seal and sea otter were numerous all along the coast, and plenty of bear, beaver, fox, and deer, for the skins of which there was a certain sale, were to be found in the interior. But the Californians allowed the Russians and Americans to seize the lion's share of the trade, and so greedy were these foreigners that in a few years the whole coast was practically stripped of these valuable animals. It was said that 80,000 otter skins were taken in one year from the Farallon station alone. Some of the American trading ships formed a partnership with the Russian commander at Sitka, Baránof, furnishing his trappers and hunters with food supplies, without which they would have starved. They were furnished in return with companies of expert Aleut hunters and their *bidarkas* (skin canoes), in which they caught the sea otter in every bay, inlet, and river mouth along the coast as far south as Santa Barbara.

During the time when the fur business was at its height the Californians were in an unfortunate situation. The jealous policy of Spain interdicted all trade with foreign vessels, and at the same time the government supply ships were prevented from coming by the activities of the privateers working in the interest of the seceding colonies in the south, at that time engaged in revolution against Spain. Lean years began for the Californians, who at first remained loyal to the mother country. Having practically no manufactures of their own, they had depended almost entirely upon the regular supply ships from San Blas, and so were now reduced to a state of utmost destitution. There was nothing left for them but to engage in illicit trade with the foreigners and in that way procure the necessities for which they were suffering. The time came when even the officials winked at the smuggling and the friars took part in it openly.

When Sola, the last of the Spanish governors, arrived in 1815, he came with a mind strongly prejudiced against the Russian intruders, but the sight of the raggedness and poverty of the people forced him to appreciate the utter necessity for foreign trade. Want prevailed at the presidios, where the soldiers had not received their pay for several years. The governor himself said "to see the good troops of California going through their evolutions entirely naked and their families in a like situation pierced him to the heart." So extreme was the destitution that in 1817 Sola parted with needed clothing of his own to cover the nakedness of the troops compelled "to pursue the Gentiles in their wild retreats." At Monterey many of the soldiers and other inhabitants were unable to attend church services for want of decent clothing, and the padres had neither wearing apparel, nor supplies for the churches, nor agricultural tools. Otto von Kotzebue, the Russian sailor-scientist, who made two visits to the coast during this period, writes of the destitute condition of the people.

"The military at San Francisco seemed to be dissatisfied with both the governor and the missions, having received nothing for these seven years, and being almost entirely without clothing; at the same time the inhabitants are entirely deprived of European clothes, since no trading vessel is allowed to enter any port of California; and it is truly lamentable to see this beautiful country thus neglected."

The distressed condition of the Californians at this time was a powerful ally of the traders, who soon discovered that the easiest way to obtain, not only the hides and tallow of the beef cattle, but also the skins of the fur-bearing animals, was by tempting the half-naked inhabitants with the manufactured goods in their cargoes, which they were careful to select in accordance with the wants of both the Indians and the Spaniards. Coarse cottons and agricultural implements were brought for the workers, while silks, laces, and linens came to please the fancy of the leisure class. It was a fair exchange between the mills of New England and the natural products of California, but the Mexican authorities, as well as the Spanish, looked upon it at first with great disfavor, for the viceroys and governors rightly dreaded the enterprise of the American fur traders more than that of all others combined. Stringent regulations were passed to prevent intercourse between these traders and the people, but necessity knows no law, and a flourishing contraband trade sprang up. The people and the missionaries hailed the arrival of one of these ships with joy, and the officials interposed but a spasmodic interference, for their own wants were nearly as dire as those of the others. This state of affairs was the opportunity of the foreign traders. Of money there was little or none, but furs were to be had for the trouble of hunting them and could be exchanged for the coveted articles in the ships' cargoes.

The padres were the chief customers of the vessels, and they spent freely from the ample stores of otter skins which they accumulated by stimulating the hunting by Californians and instructing the Indians in the art of trapping. Frequently they fitted out the boats and furnished and paid the hunters themselves, or bought the skins from men not in their employ. The goods they secured from the vessels were not for their personal use and enjoyment, but most of them were sold to the rancheros at a profit, the funds thus acquired being devoted to the benefit of the missions over which they presided, and to purchase clothing and other necessities for the Indians. Thus they acted as "middle men" between the traders and the hunters, acquiring an excellent reputation as first-class merchants and shrewd purchasers, but strictly honest and reliable, so that "it was a pleasure to deal with them."

So the smuggling went merrily on, more or less winked at by the officials. By it the Californians were enabled to live with some sort of decency and comfort during this time of stress, while many a fine mansion on the shores of New England was built and furnished from the proceeds of these voyages in the far Pacific. The chief sufferers were the poor animals, which were soon hunted to the point of extermination, and then the business came to an end.

There were a few other occupations in which the Californians engaged to a limited extent, and it seems strange to say that gold mining was one of the least of them. In the peace and ease of life in pastoral California, the descendants of the gold-mad *conquistadores* who ravaged Mexico and Peru in their frantic search for the precious metal had apparently lost interest in the chase. Several reasons are advanced to explain the failure to prosecute the search for gold in California. Alvarado says the Spanish Californians were never sufficient in numbers to overcome the determined resistance of the Indians in the Sierra, which was more formidable than Americans have imagined. The truth is that by the time the Americans got here the path had been smoothed for them by the Spaniards, who had many a hard fought battle with the natives before the country was safe for prospectors.

Another and a more valid reason given for the neglect of this industry, which afterwards became of such overwhelming importance, lies in the stern opposition made against it by the missionaries. They held, and with how much justice later events show, that a general knowledge of the presence of gold would result in the destruction of their wards, the Indians, to whom they had become genuinely attached. They knew enough of the frightful atrocities perpetrated in the southern Spanish colonies to dread a repetition of them in their beloved California. And never was fear based on truer foundations, for when the fatal news finally went out to the world death and destruction descended with fearful rapidity upon the first owners of the soil.

But, as a matter of fact, gold was discovered long before the "days of '49," and was even exported from the country in appreciable quantity. Just why this first discovery should receive so little attention in the annals of the state, and why the credit, if such it be, is always ascribed, quite erroneously, to the American, James W. Marshall, is one of the mysteries in our history. Early accounts record its discovery by at least two persons in 1841 or 1842. John Bidwell says it was found by Baptiste Ruelle, presumably a Frenchman, in the vicinity of Los Angeles in 1841. Better substantiated is the relation of its discovery by Francisco López—for years mayordomo of Mission San Fernando—in the San Feliciano Cañon, forty miles northwest of Los Angeles and eight miles westerly from the present site of Newhall. Abel Stearns says this discovery occurred in 1842, James M. Guinn gives it as March 9, 1841, but in any case it is certain that it was at least six years before Marshall's reputed find. How completely accidental it was, how entirely the luck of a "tenderfoot," is shown in Abel Stearns' brief account:

"López with a companion while in search of some stray horses, about midday stopped under some trees and tied their horses to feed. While resting in the shade, López with his sheath knife dug up some wild onions and in the dirt discovered a piece of gold. Searching further he found more. On his return to town he showed these pieces to his friends, who at once declared there must be a placer of gold there."

At a later date Stearns says in a letter:

"I find by referring to my old account books that Nov. 22, 1842, I sent to Alfred Robinson, Esq., 20 oz. California weight of placer gold to be forwarded by him to the U. S. mint at Philadelphia for assay. The placer mines from which this gold was taken were first discovered by Francisco López, a native of California, in the month of March, 1842."

These placers were worked more or less continuously, mostly by miners from Sonora, down to 1846. On March 2, 1844, Don Manuel Castañares, deputy for California to the Mexican Congress, reported to his government that placers in the vicinity of Los Angeles had produced, previous to December, 1843, 2,000 ounces of gold dust, the most of which had been sent to the mint of the United States. William Heath Davis, pioneer of 1831, estimated that from $80,000 to $100,000 was taken out in a period of two years, but it is now thought that this estimate was excessive.

Davis says that gold was known to exist in the Sacramento Valley long before the discovery at Sutter's Mill. It was often brought in to the missions by the Indians, but the priests cautioned them to keep it secret, for they regarded it as the root of all evil, and dreaded the effect of the immigration that would surely result from its discovery. Two of the priests showed nuggets to Davis.

There is evidence that gold was discovered even earlier than 1841. José de Jesus Pico, speaking of gold found near the mission San Luís Obispo, early in the century, says:

"To several of us Father Luís Martínez, in 1829, gave gold; to myself, Raimundo, and Gabriel de la Torre, and Francisco Soto, he made a present of about twenty ounces of gold, not coined, but in little balls of one ounce each; because he had much affection for us who had been his pupils and acolytes here in the mission. The father had many flasks of quicksilver, together with tools and materials for working gold and silver. This gold must have been found near the mission."

General Vallejo says gold was known since 1824, and that the failure of the Californians to search for it was ascribable to the tenacious resistance of the Indians in the Sierra.

Just why no greater excitement was caused by this first actual discovery of gold in California, either among Americans then resident there or among the people of the Spanish race, is hard to conjecture. It may have been because they already had a gold mine in their land and cattle, with less exertion than in digging the metal from the ground. Whatever may have been the cause, it is certain that in this industry, as in so many others, the Spanish Californians were the pioneers, and in the great gold rush of '49 many of their mining laws, methods, and terms were adopted by the Americans. *Placer* itself is a Spanish-American word of uncertain origin. The *arrastra*, which was no more than a large stone dragged by a mule around and around over a pile of broken ore, was found by many Americans to be a simple, cheap, and easily managed mill for pulverizing and amalgamating auriferous quartz, often better suited to the work than stamp mills. The *patio* process of amalgamation, in which pulverized ore was spread out in a paved patio, quicksilver spread on it, and then horses driven back and forth over it, was often used by the Americans.

The raising of wool sheep, although it never reached large proportions, served a useful purpose and on more than one occasion tided the people over periods of great necessity in the matter of clothing. At the missions a coarse but durable cloth called *jerga* (serge), perhaps somewhat similar to the linsey-woolsey of pioneer days in our middle states, was woven in hand looms by the Indians. During the time when the supply ships were stopped from coming by the Buenos Aires insurgents against Spain, and clothing got very scarce in California, ladies of quality were as glad to get the humble *jerga* as though it had been the finest silk. They were glad, too, to get the stockings knit by the Indians of this coarse wool, for otherwise they were reduced to wearing those that nature gave them. *Serapes* and blankets were also made of this wool, all of a coarse, heavy quality, for in the early days the government permitted no display of luxury. According to José María Amador, Mission San José had five looms making 150 woolen blankets weekly, and one which made nine serapes during the same time. In 1788 wool sold at from $1.25 to $2.00 per twenty-five pounds. The looms were all made by the Indians, of course under the direction of the padres, and Vancouver says of them, "Though they were rudely wrought they were well contrived. I saw some of the cloth, which was by no means despicable, and, had it received the advantage of fulling, would have made a very decent sort of clothing." In 1845 San Antonio Mission had two looms, Santa Inés two, Santa Barbara four large looms and one small one, and so on through the missions. Nor did they fail to introduce some ornamentation, for in Petaluma, San José, Santa Clara, and the more southern missions there were weaving factories where striped serapes with black and white borders were made.

In June, 1831, Governor Victoria wrote to the minister of relations complaining of the little interest taken in manufactures in California, where he said such work was done only at the missions, by the neophytes, who made ordinary cloth from the wool of their sheep. There was a lamentable lack of interest in these matters, so he says, due in part to lack of men and in part to the abundance of the actual necessities of life, removing the incentive to labor.

After the secularization of the missions the sheep industry went down rapidly. The Indians were no longer willing to work, and by 1842, at the time of Sir George Simpson's visit, there were hardly any left of the once large flocks of sheep. The Spanish Californians did not take kindly to this work, and so the sheep were destroyed to make way for the horned cattle, which paid better with less trouble. Simpson says the Californians were too lazy to weave or spin, or even to clip or wash the raw material, but he did not take into account that there was little inducement to make articles for which there was little sale beyond the small local demand, and which could be procured of better quality in exchange for the hides and tallow. As Bancroft says, "The Hudson's Bay magnate, like many another, throwing a glance at the country as he passes by or through it, though he might see much, could not see all." The lack of a market was always a discouragement to the enterprise of the Californians.

Among the lesser industries which nevertheless brought in some income by exchange with the trading vessels was soap making, no doubt instituted to use up the excess of fats resulting from the butchering of so many cattle. The best of the tallow was melted down, run into leather bags, and sold to the ships, while the poorer parts were used for soap. Pork fat was especially in demand for this purpose, partly because few, either of the whites or the Indians, liked it as food. It is said that they all, even the natives, not noted for their cleanliness, took kindly to the soap. At San Gabriel there was a soap boiling establishment, and Salvador Vallejo had a large soap factory at his Napa rancho which brought him in several thousand dollars a year. At a later date the Americans, Larkin and Fitch, made a good profit on soap.

Leather was manufactured to some extent, but in no proportion to the demands or needs of the country. At most of the missions some leather was tanned, the Santa Barbara inventory of 1845 showing a tannery house, five good vats, and other articles in proportion. Hall says the natives "made shoes from leather tanned by themselves. They used to take a large oxhide, gather up the corners, hang it on a tree or beam raised on posts, then fill the hide with water and oak bark and place therein the skins to be tanned. In this manner they prepared sole leather. The uppers for shoes were made from smoked deer skin, colored. Not a bad-looking shoe was the final result of their labor in skins." The uppers of these shoes were often elaborately decorated, at least those worn by the men. The Russian von Langsdorff speaks of the richly embroidered boots of Don Luís Argüello, son of the comandante of the port of San Francisco. Saddles, also often handsomely trimmed, bits, *botas*, and shoes were manufactured at San Gabriel. The Mojave, Cochane, and Yuma Indians used to bring at a certain time every year to Los Angeles antelope skins and *tirutas*, black and white blankets which they wove by hand with great perfection from the wool of wild sheep, once tame, which roamed the plains of Sonora. These *tirutas* were much sought after by the rancheros, who used them as saddle cloths. In exchange for them the Indians took mares and horses, and cast-off clothing. One gets the impression that all Indians were natural adepts at weaving, when one considers, in addition to the blankets, their skill at weaving baskets. The baskets made by the California Indians were among the best in the world.

There was a small trade with the interior in salt from the lagoons, *salinas*, situated between the ocean sand dunes of Monterey Bay and the river then known as the Monterey, now called the Salinas. This stream and the town of Salinas, now the county seat of Monterey, both acquired their names from these salt lagoons. Salt was obtained here for Mission San Carlos and the troops at the presidio at Monterey, the excess being sent to San Blas on the king's ship as early as 1770. Salt being a royal monopoly, no sooner did men begin to make and transport it than a guard was placed over it by order of the government. The commander of the guard brought Indians from Soledad and Carmelo, and gathering all the salt from the three lagoons into one pile, covered it with sticks and branches, to which they set fire, so as to melt the surface and form a crust over the mass which would protect it from the dampness of the neighboring ocean. When all was ready for the shipment, it was brought to the warehouse at Monterey and placed in charge of the *habilitado* (paymaster), and sent away in tanned leather bags brought by the ship for the purpose. In reading the documents one is always impressed by the high value put upon salt.

Several minor arts were practiced, such as the making of *dulces* (sweets), and *limonada* (lemonade), sent by Padre Sánchez to Spain. Nothing was made of stone, silver, gold, iron, copper, or lead; nor of hair, silk, feathers, or bones. Excellent mattresses were made of the coarse wool of the sheep, tiles were made of clay, and the hair of cattle and horses was sold to the traders, as also the horns of cattle.

From the earliest years the government provided master carpenters, masons, blacksmiths, weavers, soap-makers and other artisans for the instruction of the Indians. At first these men were placed at the heads of departments, but when the Indians were sufficiently instructed the teachers withdrew. The natives were quick to learn the mechanic arts and willing to work as long as they remained under the tutelage of the missionaries, but they were like children and did better when they worked in companies. It is said that sometimes a hundred men could be seen ploughing one field on Vallejo's rancho. This was one reason why the community system, so often decried by thoughtless critics of the missions, was adhered to by the friars.

From the above it will be seen that the list of occupations practiced by the Californians was not a long one, nor were they very vigorously prosecuted, but enough was done to show us the capabilities of the country in which we live. And mayhap there is something in the soft air of California to predispose men to love play better than work.

Chapter V

CHAPTER V

The Part Played by the Indians

"INDIANS ARE the most misunderstood people in the world; the whole history of their treatment is a list of mistakes and injustices; even their name is a mistake; more Indians die of broken hearts than any other white man's disease." So says Cary W. Hartman, who spent half his life among the Indians of North America. The aboriginals of California are no exception to this story of misunderstanding and mistreatment. In the first place, they were by no means the lowest of the human race, as they are often depicted, but had many interesting and useful qualities. No picture of the social life of Spanish California would be complete without them, for they had a large part in it. They were, as Don Juan Bandini says, "the working arms which made it possible to carry out agricultural and other projects to provide necessities." In the words of Dr. John Marsh, American pioneer of 1836, "Throughout all California the Indians are the principal laborers; without them the business of the country could hardly be carried on." Individually their efficiency was not high, but collectively they were the main factor in building up the fortunes of the white lords of the soil of which they themselves had been despoiled. And by assuming all, or practically all, the manual labor of getting this frontier community in running order, as farmers, herdsmen, carpenters, blacksmiths, masons, weavers, etc., they allowed the whites the opportunity to develop a society which charmed all early visitors to the province. Without them, in fact, the romantic, leisurely days of pastoral California could not have been.

The Spaniards understood the Indians better than did the Americans, perhaps because they made the first contact with them. They did not regard the natives as cowards, incapable of defending their own rights, for they had many a sharp brush with various tribes in which they were able to hold their own only by dint of superior arms. Vallejo says the natives of Alta California were "formidable because of their numbers, their indifference to death, and their great bravery, to which they added the astuteness of the fox." There is a story about the Tulare Indians illustrative of this wiliness of the savage. It is related that on an occasion of a hard fight with the Spaniards, the Indians, seeing themselves worsted, retired into the tules on the river bank, where they remained hidden. The Spaniards, not wishing to expose themselves to unnecessary risks, surrounded the place and waited for hunger to drive the enemy out, but the Indians concocted a clever scheme by which they made good their escape. With unexpected skill, they constructed manikins of tules and tossed them, unseen, into the current of the river. When these imitation men floated into the view of the Spaniards they took them for Indians trying to swim down stream, and so followed after them along the bank, shooting as they ran. Meanwhile the Indians quietly decamped in the other direction.

Writing of a battle between the whites under Alférez José Sánchez and the Suisun tribe, Vallejo says, "They only yielded after a fierce conflict in which we came out victors owing to the superiority of our arms and the swiftness of our horses. As to their bravery, I believe that the warriors of Chief Malaca were equal to us, for those Indians were valiant in the extreme, and their daring and impulsive boldness I cannot describe."

In 1829 the famous Chief Estanislao led a revolt of the Indians in the San Joaquín Valley which required the total military force of the Spaniards to subdue, and even then victory was won only by setting fire to the woods in which the natives had entrenched themselves after the manner of civilized warfare.

Vallejo has a story of Chief Pacomío, leader of a serious revolt at Mission Purísima in 1824, which throws an interesting light on the logic of Indian reasoning:

"He was a youth of gallant presence, slender figure, great intelligence, unwearying perseverance, excellent judgment, and proved courage. He had been given a superior education by the padres, but afterwards organized a revolution to kill all the whites. At the head of 2,000 natives he attacked Purísima and took the garrison prisoners. When reproached by Father Victoria for treachery to those who had always been his friends and had given him his education, he replied that he felt obliged to sacrifice his personal hopes for the general good, concluding by saying, 'It is better that a hundred barrels of blood should flow than a hundred thousand. If I kill all the whites in California in this war, not more than four thousand persons will perish, but if the whites triumph and kill all the Indians, many hundreds of thousands of human beings made in the image of God will lose their lives.' " Pacomío finally yielded to superior strength, and for the rest of his life was a "good Indian," in other words, a completely humbled one.

In illustration of their courage in the face of death in a

peculiarly terrifying form, and the ruthless cruelty of the Americans toward them, Stephen Powers tells

The Story of Bloody Rock

"In a fight with some Americans on the middle fork of the Eel River, a band of thirty or forty Indians were driven to the top of an isolated exposed rock jutting out on the face of the mountain. An American acquainted with the language advanced to the foot of the overhanging rock and offered the trapped Indians a choice of three alternatives—to continue to fight and be picked off one by one, to continue the truce and perish from hunger, or to lock hands and leap down from the rock. After a short consultation the savages replied that they would lock hands and leap down. Advancing in line to the brow of the cliff, they joined hands and began their death song, the hoarse unearthly rattle floating down to the ears of the waiting listeners. As they ceased and the weird tones of the dirge were heard no more there fell upon the little band of whites a breathless silence, for even the stout hearts of those hardy pioneers were appalled at the thing which was about to be done. The Indians hesitated only a moment, then, with one sharp cry of strong and grim human suffering, of the last bitter agony, which rang out strangely and sadly wild over the echoing mountains, they leaped down to their death."

Neither were the California Indians, if we are to believe some excellent early authorities, always the squat, ill-favored people so often described in modern writings. Among them were individuals endowed with good looks above the ordinary, and it was said that among the mountaineers there were many tall, well-made men, splendid specimens of humanity. Walter Colton, the first American alcalde at Monterey after the Conquest, gives a description of a chief who was brought in for horse-stealing that does not conform to the usual idea of the California Indian:

"The chief was over seven feet high, with an enormous blanket wrapped around him and thrown over the shoulder, like a Spanish cloak, which set forth his towering form to the best advantage. His long black hair streamed in darkness down to his waist. His features strikingly resembled those of General Jackson. His forehead was high, his eye full of fire, and his mouth betrayed great decision. His step was firm; his age must have been about fifty. He entered the court with a civil but undaunted air. After being taken aboard the American frigate in port he was attired in the uniform of one of the tallest and stoutest of the officers, with navy buttons, epaulettes, sword, cap with gold band, boots, and spurs, in which he looked every inch a chief. As the Indians left the vessel, the band struck up 'Hail, Columbia,' and they departed vowing eternal allegiance to the Americans. The sailors were delighted with these savages and half envied them their wild life."

Speaking of the Suisunes, Dr. Platón Vallejo, son of the general, says:

"Inhabiting the north and east shores of the Bay of San Francisco and far into the interior, was a great Indian tribe, known as the Suisunes, who gave the name to a bay and modern town, the sole reminder of their existence. Physically, instead of the weak, squat figures described in histories, my father and his friends always contended that the Suisunes were the finest developed people they ever saw—men and women cast in a noble mould, of which Chief Solano, with his six feet, seven inches, was a type. I used to sit on his mighty shoulders, when a boy, and the earth below seemed remote. I have heard my father say that he had seen several hundred of the active class together at a time, any one of whom might have served as a model for a sculptor. Talk about your eugenics! Here was a people who bred true, had no deformed nor unhealthy offspring, no word for disease, and a blood entirely without contamination. My father looked on the Suisunes as the most interesting savages in the world, and held them in high regard. He found them trustful and trustworthy, honest, truthful, and singularly faithful in their marital relations. Through the help of Solano he maintained a sort of militia force among these Indians, who gave a sense of security to all the settlers of the north." It is pitiful to read that this tribe was practically wiped out by the smallpox, brought by whites.

Stephen Powers, speaking of the beauty of some of the females of the northern tribes, says: "Some of the young women of the Karoks, with their smooth, brown skins, oval faces, full brilliant eyes, have a piquant beauty which in many instances, has won them white husbands."

To their good humor and gayety of spirit all the early diaries testify. Engineer Costansó, one of the officers of the Portolá expedition, tells us of the dancing by the women of the Santa Barbara Channel:

"They honored us with a dance; it was the first place where we saw the women dance. Two of these excelled the others; they had bunches of flowers in their hands, and accompanied the dance with various graceful gestures and movements, without getting out of time in their songs. We called the place *La Ranchería del Baile de las Indias* (the village of the dance of the Indian women)."

Bandini says they were very fond of fiestas, and would spend days and nights, almost without interruption, in singing and dancing and making speeches commemorating deeds of their ancestors. These fiestas were continued until all the food that had been gathered for the occasion was exhausted, and that would mark the end. To the en-

Franz Geritz 27

durance of the Indians themselves there seemed to be no limit, and their dancing was not without grace.

Vallejo writes of a celebration at Sonoma of a peace which had been concluded between the Sotoyomes and the Suisunes, in which they danced three days and nights; these dances were followed by bull and bear fights which lasted two more days. It was said that the Indians did not especially enjoy these fights, for they had the good sense to prefer diversions in which they themselves took an active part. Let us hear Vallejo's description of this celebration:

"Notwithstanding that thirty-eight years have passed by since then, I recall with pleasure the graceful movements made in dancing by the pretty daughters of the Suisun warriors and the wives of the robust chiefs of the Sotoyome nation. Their dances were much more enchanting than those invented by modern civilization, and their manner of dress was so simple as to leave exposed to the view of the curious the larger part of the dancer's body, and they presented a *tout ensemble* to cause a thrill, and give one an idea of the terrestrial paradise."

One sees here no reminder of the taciturn Indian of tradition. On the contrary, the first Californians seem to have been a light-hearted, merry people when the whites first entered their country, and they entertained the Spanish explorers with dancing and singing all the way from San Diego to San Francisco. All the visitors had to complain of was that they could get no sleep, so incessant was the entertainment. Father Font, diarist and chaplain of the Anza expedition of 1775, who saw nothing in any form of amusement but an invention of the devil, referred to their music as "songs of hell."

Recent studies of their mythology has brought out the fact that it is far more extensive and interesting than had usually been thought. Of religion they seemed to have none worthy of the name, and yet there are indications of a belief in immortality of the soul. Father Boscana says that when the coming of the new moon was celebrated an old man danced in a circle, crying out, "As the moon dieth and cometh to life again, so we also, having to die, will live again."

Among the myths which show some poetic feeling are the ideas that hearts never died, and that those of dead chiefs became stars in the sky; that meteors were children of the moon; that the sun had twelve houses, in each of which he lived a month; that an eclipse of the moon was caused by the attempt of some monster to devour it, which they tried to frighten away by beating on the ground with sticks. Among the Yosemite Valley myths which have been preserved is the one called:

The Rock of the Measuring Worm

"Very long ago two little ones were living in a place which the Indians call Ahwahnee, the Deep Grassy Valley, and the white men call Yosemite, Grizzly Bear Valley. One afternoon the little ones went swimming.

"They splashed and swam and played about in the water until they were tired out. Then they climbed onto a great boulder rising beside the water, to rest. It was sunny there, and warm. The two little ones fell asleep.

"They slept for a very long time—for many snows. As they slept the boulder grew, and grew, and grew; until finally its top was right against the sky, and the little ones' faces were scraped by the moon. And still they did not wake up!

"Down in Ahwahnee, the Deep Grassy Valley, every one was worried because the little ones did not awaken and because there was no way to get them down off the great rock. Finally all the animals came together in council to see what could be done. They decided that each animal should try in turn to jump up the face of the tremendous rock and seize the little ones and carry them down.

"Mouse jumped first—but he could jump only the length of an Indian's hand. Rat could jump a little higher. Raccoon went still higher, but even so it was only a very short jump that he could make. Grizzly Bear gave a jump and reached far up the wall of rock. But he came nowhere near the top, and he fell to the ground with a great thud. Mountain Lion gathered himself together and made a mighty leap that carried him high, high up the face of the towering rock. But he did not reach the top either. He tumbled to the ground and rolled over and over in the dust.

"At last all the animals had tried and failed except one. Now he came forward and asked for his turn. The other animals all looked at him and laughed. They said he could never succeed where they had failed. He could not jump at all. He was only little Tultókana, the Measuring Worm.

"But Measuring Worm went over to the rock and began to crawl up its face. Slowly up and up he climbed—past the place to which Mouse had jumped, past the point which Rat had reached, higher than Raccoon had touched, past the place that Bear had grazed, and up to and past the high point of Mountain Lion's great leap.

"And still Measuring Worm kept on crawling and crawling. He crawled far out of sight of the animals in the Deep Grassy Valley. He crawled for a whole snow, without stopping. At last he came to the top of the great rock. There the two little ones lay sleeping. Measuring Worm wakened them. He started to crawl back down the face of the great rock. He took the little ones with him. He crawled downward for a whole snow.

"At last he reached the foot of the rock and set the two little ones safely down on the valley floor. Then the other animals all praised him, and they all welcomed the two little ones.

"So the great rock has ever since been called by the Indians Tutokanúla, the rock of the Measuring Worm. It is the rock which the white men call El Capitan." [1]

Reproductions of the primitive music of the Indians of California recently made by Dr. Derrick N. Lehmer of the State University show what he calls a "lilting, lyric" quality in the musical notes, and a poetic feeling in the ideas which had hitherto not been suspected.

This aptitude for music was observable in the Indians from the beginning. Music was a powerful aid for the missionaries, who taught the cleverest of the neophytes to sing in the choir, and also to play upon various musical instruments. One of the fathers invented a method of making the notes in different colors, red, blue, etc., for it was found that it was easier for the Indians to recognize the notes if they were so distinguished. Some sheets of this colored musical score are still to be seen at San Juan Bautista. Father Durán of San José was especially successful in teaching this art, finally gathering together a band of thirty or forty musicians who played in excellent time, generally lively waltzes and polkas. San Gabriel had an orchestra of Indians who played flutes, guitars, violins, drums, triangles and cymbals. Alvarado says the Indians learned music readily, and played at dances for the whites, as well as at church services. Vallejo mentions that an Indian band furnished the music for his wedding. All of which goes to show that the mental capacity of the California aboriginals was not so low as many historians would have us believe.

But it is one individual among them with whom we are here chiefly concerned—that magnificent savage, Sum-yet-ho (mighty arm), called Solano by the Spaniards—six feet, seven inches tall and broad in proportion. Val-

[1] *Quoted from Galen Clark, former guardian of Yosemite Valley.*

lejo was much attached to this Suisun chief, who became his faithful ally in preserving order among the northern tribes. It was through his request that Solano County was named for the noted Indian, surely an honor that was fully deserved, for, as Vallejo goes on to say, "To the bravery, and in particular to the diplomacy of that great chieftain of the Suisun Indians civilization is indebted for the conquest of the territory which today composes the counties of Solano, Napa, Sonoma, Mendocino, and Lake." He could muster a force of one thousand plumed and painted warriors, which he used in supporting the rule of his great white brother and ally, General Vallejo. The latter trusted him completely. Speaking on this subject, Dr. Platón Vallejo says:

"The Comandante always held Solano, not alone as an ally, but as a personal friend and equal. He consulted him on all things. The chief was a most welcome guest at the hacienda when the Comandante settled in Sonoma. He might be savage still in some things, with the primitive ideals of war. When enemies opposed him he killed them if he could. But he also had the primitive virtues of truth, honor, and everlasting good faith, and the trust placed in him was never betrayed. My father often told me that he never came in contact with a finer natural mind. He was a keen, clear-headed thinker, readily grasped new ideas, learned to speak Spanish with ease and precision, and was so ready to debate that few cared to engage with him in a contest of wits."

Yet once the simple savage came near to causing trouble in a most undreamed-of way. To get the proper setting for this story, which shows that even romantic love was not a stranger to the hearts of these untutored savages, it will now be necessary to fly in spirit across the broad Pacific to far-away Russia. Here we will permit Don Platón Vallejo to take up the thread of the tale of

The Indian Chief and the Russian Princess

"In the year 1805 the Russian navigator, Kotzebue, son of a famous poet, visited the bay of San Francisco and saw something of the country surrounding its shores. The report he made to his master, the Czar, seems not alone dramatic but prophetic. It was because of the report of Kotzebue that the Russians took possession of Fort Ross and Bodega, despite the earnest protest of Spain. The language of the mariner was roseate enough to urge on a grasping nation in taking any chance . . . Far away, in an antipodean region, something took place that seemed to have no bearing possible on the affairs of distant California. That was the marriage at St. Petersburg of the beautiful Princess Helene, niece of the Czar, to a Russian noble by the name of Rotcheff. He was the overlord of Siberia and of all the possessions of Russia on both sides of the Pacific Ocean. And where do you suppose the young bride proposed to spend her honeymoon? In the gayeties of Paris, Vienna, London, or under the soft Italian skies? No, she chose to cross the Asian continent and the Pacific Ocean to view the land which Kotzebue described. Two warships conveyed the party from the Siberian shore to Alaska, late in the fall. Thence they sailed in leisurely fashion down the coast of America, spending some time in Puget Sound, and at length arrived in the late winter, or rather, early spring, at the large Russian settlements that we call Fort Ross."

It was not simply Kotzebue's roseate descriptions of the country that brought about the Russian settlement at Fort Ross, however, but the pressing need for a base of supplies for the almost starving fur hunters in the colony at Sitka. It was believed that in California's favorable climate sufficient foodstuffs could be raised and sent up on ships to support the trappers and traders in the north. So they diplomatically and courteously insinuated themselves into the country, much against the wishes of the Californians, who had not a sufficient armed force with which to oppose them, nor could they arouse the central government to the danger.

One thing to be said for the Russian government was that it made its representatives comfortable. The officers of the king of Spain looked at the furnishings and outfittings at Fort Ross with a rueful envy when they contrasted them with their own almost squalid quarters. We have already seen that Vancouver and other visiting notables were stricken with pity at sight of the primitive, painfully bare homes of the comandantes of the ports in California. At Fort Ross, on the contrary, there was a good house of six or eight rooms inside the stockade for the use of the officers, which was comfortably, nay, luxuriously for the place, furnished with carpets and pianos, even with glass windows, a thing then unheard-of in California. Du Mofras, a Frenchman who visited the coast in 1841, says:

"Fort Ross, with its beautiful gardens, is in a superb position; there is nothing in existence more picturesque, or more grandiose than the forests of gigantic pines which surround it. It is necessary to have led the terrible life of a trapper, that life of the 'long carbine,' to have been pursued by the yells of savages, to enjoy the pleasures of a well-chosen library, of the wines of France, of a piano and a selection from Mozart." So that even a high-born lady like the Princess Helena had no occasion to complain of her temporary home in the wilds of western America.

As was the case in most frontier posts, there was almost a complete absence of the gentler sex at Fort Ross; in fact, there were no women at all of the white race except one or two wives of officers in the later years of the colony. A notable exception was the lady we have just read about, the beautiful young Princess Helena de Gagarine, bride of Count Alexander Rotcheff and relative of the Czar, who came to Ross on her honeymoon trip early in 1841. Not long after their arrival the Count went to San Francisco to talk over the situation with Comandante Vallejo, taking his bride with him. While they were guests at that place a very curious thing happened, which we will allow General Vallejo to relate in his own words:

"When Señor Rotcheff, governor of Bodega and Ross, came to see me, he was accompanied by his wife, the Princess Elena, a very beautiful lady of twenty Aprils, who united to her other gifts an irresistible affability. The beauty of the governor's wife made such a deep impression on the heart of Chief Solano that he conceived the project of stealing her. With this object he came to visit me very late at night and asked my consent to putting his plan into effect. The story horrified me, for if it should unfortunately be carried out my good name would suffer, for no one would be able to get it out of his head that my agent had acted on my account; and besides seeing the country involved in a war provoked by the same cause which actuated the famous siege of Troy, I, who had never hesitated at expense or trouble to please my visitors, whoever they might be, would be stigmatized as the most disloyal being that the world ever produced. It was necessary for me to assume all the authority that I knew how to assume on occasions that required it to make Solano understand that his life would hang in the balance if he should be so ill-advised as to attempt to break the rules of hospitality. My words produced a good effect, and that same night, repenting of his conduct, he went to Napa Valley, where I sent him to prevent him from compromising, under the impulse of his insane love, the harmony which it was so urgent for me to reestablish with my powerful neighbors, who had had their residence fixed for thirty years in a land which did not belong to them. But, fearing that Solano might ambush them on the road, I went to escort my visitors to Bodega."

As for the lady, like the coquette that she probably was, she expressed herself as enchanted with the adventure, and especially with having been rescued from the splendid savage by such cavaliers. But what about the "splendid savage"? Who knows how deeply this experience sank into the heart of the Indian, of a race who never forget?

Chapter VI

CHAPTER VI

The Coming of the Blue-Eyed Man

ONE OF THE most interesting phases in the whole story of California, rivaling in romance the days of '49, is the period when the vast commerce which now radiates from the busy ports of the state had its beginning, bringing with it an influx of outsiders. Before 1822 the few foreigners landing here had been mere passing visitors, who, after a short time of friendly intercourse with the inhabitants, raised their anchors and sailed away, not to return. With the entrance of foreign shipping engaged in a regular trade with the country, a different class, and in larger numbers, began to arrive, many of them to stay. Most of those who elected to cast in their lot with the Californians became citizens of the province and property owners, and many intermarried with the leading families and became themselves progenitors of descendants whose names are still prominent in the social life of the state.

Although the government of Mexico was still actuated by its old inherited suspicion against strangers, conditions in Alta California at this time tended to change the attitude of the people in that respect, and a friendly governor, Luís Argüello, did much to modify this spirit. Moreover, long before overt trade was allowed, the Americans had established friendly relations with the people by furnishing them with smuggled goods, even the priests and the officers at the presidios being almost forced by the strict regulations of the government to procure necessities in this illegal way. A more liberal act passed by the Mexican Congress in 1824 by which foreigners settling in Mexican territory and obeying the laws were promised security in person and property, opened the way to the settlement of many in California.

Although among them were English, Scotch, Irish, Russians, etc., most of these first foreign settlers were Americans, who came in such numbers as to constitute what may be truly called a "peaceful invasion," which, had it not been for later ill-judged interferences, would almost certainly have accomplished the conquest of California by the United States without firing a shot.

While these sailor men were opening wide the sea gates to the golden land on the west, men of another and different sort were breaking down the barrier of burning deserts and snowy mountains on the east—the fur trappers and traders. Generally speaking, these land invaders were inferior in character to those who came by sea. They were a wild set of men, and although some few settled down and became worthy members of the community, others caused constant trouble to the authorities by their indifference to the law and their reckless disregard for human life. It was their custom to spend all that they had earned in the season in wild roystering in the coast towns, and then make their way back as best they could to their posts and begin all over again. The leaders were as a rule estimable men, often deeply religious, but their followers were too often a rough and turbulent lot of adventurers, the relation of whose doings, could it be completely bared, would no doubt make a dark page in the story of California and account for much of the distrust that the people felt for outsiders. To the best class belonged the famous pathfinder, Jedediah Smith, first among the American trappers to reach California overland. In the diary of Harrison Rogers, one of the Smith party and himself a very pious man, we find much to throw light upon social conditions at that time. Some of the entries show that the hunters, fresh from the trail in their rough clothes, were surprised to find a more cultured society than they had expected and somewhat embarrassed by their own inability to make a decent appearance. Writing at San Gabriel Mission, he says:

"They all appear to be gentlemen of the first class both in manners and habits. . . There was a wedding in this place today, and Mr. S. and myself invited; the bell was rang a little before sunrise; then the music commenced serenading, the soldiers firing, etc.; about seven o'clock tea and bread was served, and about eleven dinner and music. The ceremony and dinner was held at the priests; they had an elegant dinner, consisting of a number of dishes, boiled and roast meats and fowl, wine and brandy, grapes brought as a dessert after dinner. . . Mr. S. and I endeavored to apologize, being very dirty and not in a position to shift our clothing, but no excuse would be taken, we must be present. They treat us as gentlemen in every sense of the word, although our apparel is so indifferent, plenty of everything to eat and drink. . . I could see a great deal of satisfaction here if I could talk their language, but as it is I feel great diffidence in being among them, not knowing the topic of their conversation; still every attention is paid to me by all present, especially the old priest [Father Sánchez]. I must say he is a very fine man and very much of a gentleman. . . My situation is a delicate one, as I have to be among the grandees of the country every day. I make a very grotesque appearance when seated at table amongst the dandys with their ruffles, silks, and broad cloths."

These pioneers of pioneers, especially those who came by sea, were, generally speaking, superior in character and ability to the majority of the Forty-niners. To repeat the words of one who knew them at first hand: "Nature herself set them apart from other men, constituting them the vanguard of the long, transcontinental march of immigration's endless army." Years of travel in many lands and on many seas and association with men of all nations had broadened their minds and liberalized their attitude towards others not of their own race. With few exceptions they left an enviable record of character and honorable conduct toward the Californians. Alvarado says of them, "Many settled among us and contributed with their intelligence and industry to the progress of my beloved country. Would that the foreigners that came to settle in Alta California after 1841 had been of the same quality as those who preceded them!"

In various ways they left an indelible impress upon the country of their adoption. Some originated industries that have since risen to gigantic proportions; for example, the cultivation of the orange and the grape in a commercial scale may be traced back to the orchards of Louis Vignes and William Wolfskill, immigrants of 1831; and to Nathan Spear is due the credit of inaugurating salmon fishing and packing on this coast as a business. Many have left their names to geographical points—Livermore, Lassen, Yountsville, and others—as a reminder of their presence and influence here in that early day.

Among these earliest arrivals were men of the highest education and culture; for example, William Hartnell, who spoke half a dozen languages, and John Marsh, who was a graduate of Harvard University. Even those who had little book learning possessed excellent natural abilities; Thomas O. Larkin, although he had not enjoyed the advantages of a finished education, had acquired a large fund of useful information, and, besides, had in him the making of a great diplomat. In short, these first pioneers would have been marked out as a superior body of men in any community. In nothing does their superiority stand out more clearly than in their fair-mindedness and honesty toward the Californians. The latter, on the other hand, were quick to recognize the abilities of these new citizens, and were glad to make use of their talents in public office. Nearly all the foreigners of that period served, at one time or another, as alcaldes, justices of the peace, etc.

Of all the forces which operated to bind these first comers to the Californians by ties of friendship none was more powerful than the attractions of the *hijas del país* (daughters of the country). Many of these young women, with their flashing black eyes, luxuriant tresses, and radiant complexions, were beautiful; all were vivacious, warm-hearted, industrious, and domestic in their habits. What wonder that they caught the fancy of the newcomers, who were, almost without exception, young, vigorous, ambitious men! As for the señoritas themselves, the blue-eyed, fair-haired strangers were heroes of romance to them, and many of them vowed never to marry any but a man with the admired *ojos azules* (blue eyes). Bancroft says: "It was a happy day for the California bride whose husband was American; and happier still for the Californian husband whose bride was Yankee. In 1847 there lived at the rancho of San Lorenzo two bachelor brothers who once entertained Mr. Bryant for the night. They were men of intelligence and politeness, and their hearts yearned for something to relieve the desolation of their loneliness. They prayed with simple earnestness that Mr.

Bryant should send them two American women, that they might marry, live happy, and die lamented."

Some of these love affairs were conducted under difficulties, owing to the difference in language, for in many cases the young man could speak no Spanish and the señorita no English. But just as "love laughs at locksmiths," so can it get along with few words. An amusing story is told of a certain American who fell in love with a tall and attractive *hija del país* at Monterey. The language of the eyes having brought things to a point where a declaration seemed the next thing in order, the would-be lover found himself at a loss for words in which to express his feelings, so he consulted a better informed friend. "Just say *yo te quiero* (I love thee)," said the obliging friend. So, all the way to the dear one's house the young man kept repeating the magic formula, *yo te quiero, yo te quiero*; but, when he got there, what were his perturbation and alarm when the young lady received his declaration with a slightly surprised look, after which she immediately left the room! After a short wait, during which the lover's feelings may well be imagined, she re-entered, bearing a cup of tea, which she politely offered him! The truth was that in his nervousness and confusion he had transposed the words from *yo te quiero* (I love thee) into *yo quiero te* (I want some tea) the mere change of arrangement making all the difference. But all's well that ends well, and since the marriage took place not long afterwards, it is clear that the embarrassed swain must have found a way to reach her heart.

The young male Californians were naturally not very well pleased with the success of the foreigners among the ladies, and there were some heart burnings even among persons in high places, as we shall see later. Hittell, the historian, remarks: "By degrees the marriageable young ladies throughout the territory began to look upon suitors of foreign blood with more favor than upon those of their own country. There was naturally much dissatisfaction on the part of the young men of native birth with this state of affairs; but the effect was to make better and more deserving men of them; and the general result was to advance the cause of industry, education, accomplishments, and culture."

These international marriages were not confined to men of American blood, for Englishmen, Scotchmen, Irishmen, Frenchmen, and Russians laid their hearts at the feet of the beautiful daughters of California; but the majority were wanderers from the other side of the Rockies. There is no doubt that the strong bond thus formed between the two races of such opposite characteristics and traditions had a powerful effect on later political events. Men naturally had little desire to fight their own fathers-in-law and brothers-in-law, and, besides, the close relationship taught them each other's good qualities.

It is interesting and sometimes amusing to see how soon these first pioneers became thorough-going Spaniards—adopting the religion, language, manners and customs of their new friends. Correspondence was carried on in Spanish, even between English-speaking persons; thus we find Abel Stearns writing to Hartnell in that language. They adopted the rubric, the characteristic flourish of the pen added to the signature by Spaniards as a defense against forgery. Christian names of individuals were often changed to suit the Spanish form; thus John became Juan Bidwell, Johann Augustus Sutter became Juan Augusto, and John Gilroy was turned into Juan Antonio María Gilroy. Their almost forgotten relatives in the east would scarcely have recognized them in their new guise of proud Spanish Dons.

It is estimated that before 1830 there were nearly five hundred foreigners on the west side of the Sierra, a large proportion of them living in the pueblos of Los Angeles and San José. By 1846, according to Thomas O. Larkin's report to the United States government, there were from one thousand to twelve hundred foreigners in California, the majority living on the bay of San Francisco. Three-fourths of them were Americans and most of the other fourth British. It is possible to touch upon the personal story of only a few of these newcomers who formed family alliances with the Californians.

The first one was John Gilroy, a young Scotchman who arrived in 1814. His real name was Cameron, which he changed in order to avoid being arrested and sent back when he ran away to sea. After being baptized in the Catholic faith, he married María Clara de la Asunción Ortega. When the rancho San Isidro was granted to the Ortegas, Gilroy received a league of it, on which he built an adobe house, his home for the rest of his life. Like many another land owner of the time, he had occasion to rue the coming of the Americans. The simple sailor was as helpless in the hands of the land lawyers as the natives themselves, and all his lands and cattle were soon in their hands. He lived to see his old rancho the site of a flourishing town named for himself, but died as poor as when he landed in California fifty years before.

Perhaps the most noted of the foreign residents of the Spanish period was Joseph Chapman, whose introduction into the country was not of the most auspicious, for he was one of the "pirate" Bouchard's men who decided to remain here at the time of the attack on Monterey in 1818. His mechanical talents nevertheless made him a welcome addition to the population, for it was just what the Spaniards themselves lacked. "He built several grist mills, planted a vineyard of some four thousand acres at Los Angeles, built a schooner, served as a surgeon, and did odd jobs at the missions." He married into the wealthy

and aristocratic Ortega family, and spent most of his life at Los Angeles, where he died about 1848 or 1849.

William Hartnell, born in England and educated in Germany, arrived in California in 1822 on the Lima trading ship *John Begg*. He was a scholar, rather than a business man, and has left a reputation as an amiable and cultured gentleman, too generous for his own interests, respected and beloved by all who knew him. In 1825 he married the lady whom Alvarado describes as the "intelligent and beautiful María Teresa de la Guerra"; numerous descendants of this marriage are still living in California, some of whom have given evidences of inheritance of their famous ancestor's scholastic tastes.

In 1829 Alfred Robinson, a native of Massachusetts, then but twenty-nine years of age, arrived on the ship *Brookline*, in the hide and tallow trade. He soon fell a victim to the charms of Ana María de la Alta Gracia Leonora, one of the numerous family of Captain José Antonio de la Guerra y Noriega, which furnished wives for so many of the early pioneers. Young Robinson had previously been baptized under the name of José María Alfredo, and in the early part of 1836 his marriage to Señorita de la Guerra took place at Santa Barbara. This is the affair so graphically described in Richard Henry Dana's *Two Years Before the Mast*. Dana was there at the time as a sailor on the *Alert*, one of the vessels of the Bryant and Sturgis Company, for which Robinson was agent. There was great excitement aboard ship over the projected union of the agent with the daughter of the grandee of the place, the head of the first family of California. The steward was ashore for three days making pastry and cake, and on the ship preparations were made for a salute in honor of the tying of the knot. The guns were ready loaded and run out, men were appointed to stand by each one, cartridges were served out, matches were lighted, and all flags made ready to run up. All waited in suspense for the signal from the shore. At ten o'clock the bride, dressed in deep black, was seen going with her sister to the confessional. An hour later the great doors of the mission church opened, the bells rang out a loud peal, the signal came from the captain ashore, and the bride, now robed in spotless white, came out with the groom, followed by a long procession. Just as she stepped from the church door, a small white cloud issued from the bows of the ship, a loud report echoed from among the surrounding hills and over the bay, and instantly the vessel was dressed in flags and pennants from stem to stern. Twenty-three guns followed in regular succession, and the ship lay dressed in gala colors all day. From this it will be seen that a wedding was a wedding in those days, not the casual sort of affair that it has become in our time. Shore leave was granted to all the sailors in the evening, and, spick and span in their well-brushed uniforms, they went to attend the *fandango* at the house of the bride's parents. A large tent had been erected in the patio in front of the house, where all were expected to come without invitation, and in this were crowded most of the inhabitants of the place, men, women, and children. Inside the house there was a special entertainment for intimate friends of the upper class. The arrival of the American sailors was the signal for loud applause and a hearty invitation to join the dancers in the pavilion. But we will permit young Dana to tell his own story:

"Our sailor dresses—and we took great pains to have them neat and shipshape—were much admired, and we were invited from every quarter to give them an American dance; but after the ridiculous figure some of our countrymen cut in dancing after the Mexicans, we thought it best to leave it to their imaginations. Our agent, with a tight black swallow-tailed coat just imported from Boston, a high, stiff cravat, looking as if had he been pinned and skewered, with only his feet and hands left free, took the floor just after Don Juan Bandini, and we thought they had had enough of Yankee grace." It is only fair to say that Robinson, who was evidently nettled when he read this description of himself written by the irreverent young sailor, says in his *Life in California* that it contains some inaccuracies.

A foreign name which occurs with great frequency in the archives of the Mexican régime is that of Abel Stearns, a native of Massachusetts who arrived in California in 1829. Stearns was a great politician, and became involved in many of the controversies of the time. He was a very ugly man, known sometimes as *Cara de Caballo* (horse face); but he married a woman as beautiful as he was ugly, Doña Arcadia Bandini, thus bringing up the average of the family looks. Through his lands and cattle he became the wealthiest man in Southern California at one time.

William Heath Davis, author of the classic *Sixty Years in California*, came to the coast from Massachusetts in 1831. He became allied to an important Californian family by his marriage to María Jesus, daughter of Don Joaquín Estudillo, and his relations with the relatives and friends acquired by this union were always of the warmest. He left the reputation of being an exceptionally good-natured man, so much so that he was never known to speak ill of any human being. To him every man was an honorable gentleman, and every woman was beautiful and charming—a delightful gift, which must have brought him many friends and added much to his own happiness.

It would be an addition to history to record the full stories of others who engaged in these international marriages—such as William A. Richardson, who came on the English whaler *Orion* in 1822, became the founder of the town of Yerba Buena, took to wife María Antonia, daughter of the comandante of the port, Ygnacio Martínez, and left his name to Richardson's Bay; of John R. Cooper, who came on the Boston ship *Rover* in 1823, and, by his marriage with the "simpática señorita" Encarnación Vallejo, founded one of the leading families of that period; of David Spence, an Englishman, who came from Lima to superintend the packing of hides, tallow, and beef for the John Begg Company, married the "amable" Adelaida Estrada of Monterey and left descendants who still live in that vicinity; of Jacob Leese, who built the first substantial house in Yerba Buena, married the sister of Mariano G. Vallejo and became the progenitor of a family of stalwart sons and handsome daughters; and of many more of those who took part in this "peaceful invasion."

These first-comers, besides the powerful influence which they exerted in binding together the two races by ties of relationship and mutual regard, were the real framers of the constitution of California, for of the forty-nine men who assisted in preparing that document, only eight were Forty-niners. To quote the language of Dr. John Marsh, "These people may be called the true aristocracy of the American occupation of California, if aristocracy may justly be based on character and priority of arrival."

The romance of one of these men has purposely been left for separate telling here, for the reason that it was nearly the only one in which the course of true love did not run smoothly, but was rudely interrupted in a most unexpected way. This story, which concerns an eminent personage, we shall call

The Governor's Revenge

In the year 1825 the people of California were in a state of pleasurable excitement in the anticipation of the arrival of a new governor from Mexico, Don José María Echeandía, if for no other reason than because his coming gave an excuse for the *fiestas* to which they were so passionately addicted. Echeandía reached San Diego in November and was welcomed by the residents with a succession of *bailes*, *corridas de toro* (bull fights), and other entertainments. It is said that the new governor immediately observed a great contrast in point of culture between the people of Loreto and those of San Diego, much to the advantage of the latter. And as for the ladies of that place, they were reported at that time to be the most beautiful in Alta California, and Echeandía was by no means blind to female charms. He has been described as a "tall, thin, juiceless man, possessing but little force of character or enterprise, and much concerned about the effect of the California climate upon his none too robust health." But it is said that the "driest hearts, like the driest grass, are the most inflammable," and it was found, too, that Echeandía could be very firm when his own desires were in the balance.

The joyous anticipations of the people of Monterey, which place had always been regarded as the capital, were changed to anger and suspicion when the new governor, instead of hastening to his post of duty, showed a strange disposition to linger on at the southern city. The citizens of San Diego, on the other hand, were much elated, and began to talk of a transfer of the customhouse and the other branches of government to their town. This proposal raised a storm which was the beginning of the sectional jealousy between north and south, a jealousy which brought on a revolution at a later date, and still has its echoes in our own day. The governor himself gave as his excuses that San Diego was more centrally located for purposes of government, which then included Baja California under the same executive, and that the climate of that delectable place agreed better with his health than that of Monterey. But there were not lacking those who whispered, quite loudly, that other and more frivolous reasons accounted for his determination to remain in the south—no less than the fascinations of a certain lady resident there. Alvarado says, "He was seduced by the blandishments showered upon him by the inhabitants," while Vallejo writes:

"Since he had found such a great contrast between the inhabitants of Loreto and those of San Diego, the young ladies of that place being then considered the most beautiful in Alta California (and Echeandía was not indifferent to the call of beauty), he resolved to remain in that place, which, according to his way of thinking, united all the attractions which make life enjoyable. . . Naturally the Diegueños, male as well as female, were overjoyed when they heard of the decision which virtually translated the capital of the territory to their port; but the Montereyans, when they heard of it, were greatly displeased, and it cost Governor Argüello [the retiring executive] a deal of trouble to prevent them from rising in open rebellion."

Not long after the arrival of the new governor, another person stepped upon the shores of California who was fated to cause great disturbance in the plans and ideas of that dignitary—the young, handsome, debonair American, Henry Delano Fitch, the very ideal to win the fancy of any young romantic girl, particularly one of Castilian blood. Fitch came as captain of the bark *Maria Ester*, belonging to the German, Henry Virmond, a wealthy merchant of Lima. This vessel brought a cargo of mixed goods to exchange for hides and tallow, practically California's only export, and a party of convicts, "sent to California," ironically remarks Alvarado, "to improve the customs of the simple inhabitants." The anger and resentment of the people over this last consignment is another story.

Alvarado goes on to say, "Of all the arbitrary acts of Echeandía, the most iniquitous was that perpetrated on the person of Henry Fitch, who was good in every respect, honorable as far as any man can be, by no means uncultured, and always disposed to cooperate in doing good. While on the coast he formed a friendship with the family of Don Raimundo Carrillo, and by means of his good presence and manners captured the love of Señorita Josefa Carrillo, an angelic girl who won the hearts of all who saw her."

Vallejo tells us that "Captain Fitch was a young man of good presence and the manners of a perfect gentleman. Owing to these notable gifts, he was admitted into the good society of San Diego, and little by little assumed relations with the first families of that place, which then included the Bandinis, the Argüellos, the Arces, the Estudillos, the Carrillos, and many others of the same class. He fell in love with Josefa Carrillo, who returned it; the parents consented; the services of Father Antonio Menéndez were secured to perform the ceremony at the parental mansion, where, as a special luxury, an altar had been erected. But not always do mortals accomplish their purpose, and when everything seemed to be going smoothly an occurrence broke up the golden dreams of loving hearts. The law required that any foreigner wishing to marry a daughter of the country should first secure the permission of His Excellency the Governor, who could not give it unless the groom produced documents proving that he was a Catholic. Fitch had done neither."

Alvarado says the refusal of the governor was based on false premises; and it is certain that sooner or later Fitch became a Catholic, for the archives of San Diego record the baptism of Enrique Domingo Fitch, son of Beriah and

Sara Fitch of New Bedford, Massachusetts. "Malicious tongues," writes José Jesus Vallejo, "ascribed the governor's refusal to his personal ambitions in regard to the fair lady. Josefa Carrillo was a very handsome young woman, who danced extremely well, and Echeandía always singled her out in the dancing." The bitterness of his subsequent persecution of the young couple lends color to this theory, especially as the person most concerned, Doña Josefa, corroborates it in her story, the *Narracion de la Viuda Fitch* (Narration of the Widow Fitch). She says, "At the time, I conceived a great aversion for Governor Echeandía for his opposition to my marriage, which was sanctioned by ecclesiastical and civil laws, but in later years I forgave him with all my heart when I realized that his persecution of me and my husband had been prompted by the despair that took possession of his soul when he became convinced that I had preferred a rival whom he detested." And let it not be thought that Echeandía was a despicable rival, for notwithstanding his forty-eight years, with his tall, slender figure, very white skin and jet-black hair, with the most charming manners, he was personally attractive; and, besides, what young girl in the province would not be dazzled by the prospect of becoming the first lady in the land, the Señora Gobernadora?

But the *ojos azules* won the day against the prestige of the chief executive and the wedding ceremony was actually in progress when a messenger, the bride's own uncle, Adjutant Carrillo, arrived with the governor's orders to forbid the bans. Here we will allow Don Mariano Vallejo to take up the story:

"Adjutant Carrillo arrived when the sala was already full of guests, the bride and groom were facing each other, and Padre Menéndez, dressed in the vestments that the priests were in the habit of wearing on such occasions, was reading the required formulas. Adjutant Carrillo approached the altar, and in the name of the governor ordered the friar to suspend the celebration of the marriage until the documents required by the authorities in such affairs should be presented. The padre feared to incur severe penalties, so he stopped the ceremony, but not without first manifesting to the disconsolate lovers the great sorrow which oppressed his heart on seeing himself prevented from uniting them in the holy bonds of matrimony. The guests departed in very bad humor; the bride turned pale, but spoke not a word; the groom, on the contrary, stormed in Yankee fashion, crying out, 'I shall marry either Josefa or death!' He then left Señor Carrillo's house and went to hold a confabulation with Pío Pico, a young fellow then celebrated through the whole extent of Alta California for his gallantry and great devotion to the fair sex. He expressed great affliction on learning of the interruption which had prevented the realization of the golden dream of Captain Fitch, and without any hesitation promised his assistance, which in affairs of love was equivalent to triumph, for Pío Pico knew the human heart to the bottom, a thing which need not surprise any one, for it had been his principal, I was about to say his only, study. He advised Fitch to go aboard his ship and make all preparations for putting to sea; to prepare a good cabin for the bride, then return to land and spread the rumor that the marriage had been abandoned, and secure his necessary sailing papers for Callao, Peru, adding, 'If you will carry out your commission, I will faithfully do my part, which will be to place the bride on board the *Maria Ester*.'

"Captain Fitch followed the instructions with exactitude, and ordered the anchor raised and all put in readiness for instant sailing. The moment night fell he took his best boat with four strong oarsmen, quickly reached the shore and concealed himself behind a large rock, which even in our days is known as Fitch's rock. There he waited until eleven at night, when, mounted on a spirited horse, Pío Pico arrived, bringing seated before him Doña Josefa Carrillo, whom he had succeeded in convincing with his persuasive talk that the best way to insure her happiness and that of her lover was by embarking with him on the *Maria Ester*, which would reach Chile in two months, where they could be married without any fear of the authorities of Alta California. Fitch, who in one instant had placed himself at the side of his beloved, took her in his arms, ran to the boat where his oarsmen awaited him, took his seat in the prow, and called to the men to row with all speed.

"Urged by the strong arms of the sturdy and no doubt excited sailors, the small boat was at the side of the *Maria Ester* in less than two hours. The ship immediately set sail, and, favored by the wind, which seemed to know it was wafting two lovers to their happiness, reached Valparaiso in less than two months, and the young couple were immediately married by the curate of that metropolis. Captain Fitch made several voyages on the coast of Chile, and from there took a cargo of *panocha* (crude sugar), brandy, and a great supply of woolen and cotton goods for Alta California."

Such is the story of the famous Fitch-Carrillo romance as told by M. G. Vallejo, repeated in practically the same terms by Alvarado. Pío Pico adds that Josefa's parents missed her almost immediately and complained to the governor, who sent a squad of soldiers in pursuit of the elopers, but "all in vain, for the birds had flown." Dr. Platón Vallejo, son of the general, tells it somewhat differently. He says the elopement had New York as its objective, and that the journey was made, with the young lady in the care of a dueña, in the ship *Vulture*, commanded by Captain Barry, and that the pair were married in Baltimore. Notwithstanding the variation in details, the main facts of the story remain the same. It does not end, however, in the traditional fashion, "and they lived happily ever after," as the sequel will show. Revenge, in the person of the implacable governor, still threatened them.

About the end of 1830 the watchman of Point Pinos at Monterey announced the arrival of a brigantine flying the Mexican flag. M. G. Vallejo, then captain of the port, went out to the ship, where he was surprised and overjoyed, when he set foot on the deck of the frigate *Leonor*, to be welcomed by Captain Henry Fitch and his wife, Josefa Carrillo de Fitch, who held in her arms a beautiful babe of three months. After congratulations, Vallejo went ashore and notified the civil and military authorities of the new arrival. When Governor Echeandía heard the name of Fitch he flew into a rage and ordered Vallejo to return instantly and put his old rival under arrest. Much against his will Vallejo carried out these orders, which he thought savored of despotism. To make things as pleasant as possible he put Fitch in his own house and "deposited" Doña Josefa in the care of Doña Encarnación de Cooper. This was in accordance with a custom of the time, which permitted superior prisoners to be incarcerated in private houses. The young couple did not find their imprisonment very painful, for their indulgent jailer allowed the young husband to spend every night with his family, and in the morning brought him back. The whole matter was turned over to the ecclesiastical authorities, who brought Fitch to trial for having carried off one of the daughters of California by force. In the trial she testified that she had gone with him of her own free will, and that no violence was used. It is even quite plainly stated in the record of the *Causa Criminal de Fitch* that the first suggestion of the elopement came from the lady. "Why don't you carry me off on your ship, Don Enrique," said she; whereupon he replied that if she would go aboard the vessel voluntarily he would take her with him. Fitch put up a vigorous defense, in which he denied having broken any law, and complained of the loss to his business through the action and the threatened illegitimacy of his son.

Vicar José Sánchez finally rendered a decision that the accusations had not been substantiated and that the Valparaiso marriage was valid, ordering that the parties be set at liberty and the wife restored to her husband. But the offenders, who had set the whole province in an uproar by their daring act, almost unheard-of in those times, could not be permitted to go entirely unpunished, so the good vicar added: "Yet, considering the great scandal which Don Enrique has caused in this province, I condemn him to give as a penance and reparation a bell of at least fifty pounds in weight to the church at Los Angeles, which merely has a borrowed one." Besides the gift of the bell, the married pair were to present themselves in church with lighted candles in their hands to hear mass for three festival days, and recite together for thirty days one-third of the rosary of the holy Virgin. The kindhearted Padre Menéndez, who had advised the couple to run away, was also hauled on the carpet, but the records say nothing of the penance. Henceforth the couple were allowed to live in Alta California in peace, and to acquire landed property, from which Fitch became very wealthy. Many of the descendants of this matrimonial alliance which had such a troubled beginning are still living in California.

In his account M. G. Vallejo adds a few words more concerning the motives of Echeandía in this persecution. "In the trial of Captain Fitch the governor was impelled by spite. It was known to many of us that His Excellency aspired to the hand of Doña Josefa Carrillo, and it is very natural that, seeing himself slighted, he should cause the weight of the law to fall upon his more fortunate rival. Certainly I do not defend his conduct in that instance, for it is supremely blameworthy. There is no doubt that it would have been much more noble to leave the lovers in full liberty to act as pleased them, but no man is perfect, and to err is the primitive nature of mortals."

Alvarado remarks: "The cause of the governor's action was not in the law but in the heart. He himself had sued for the hand of the lady, but had been refused, and to avenge himself for this slight in his character of lover, he called into play his power as governor. I make these comments in deference to the truth of history, for it is with much pain that I relate this act which so greatly damages the good name and stains the reputation of Governor Echeandía, a person whom I loved and admired. But I am of the opinion that every actor who cuts a figure in history must play the part that corresponds to him, and dance according to his own merits to the sound of his own music."

The Widow Fitch herself adds some details to this romantic affair. She says that on the night of the elopement Pío Pico, who was her cousin, salved his conscience before delivering her to the arms of her lover by saying with due solemnity, "Farewell, Cousin, and God bless you. As for you, Cousin Henry, take care not to give any reason to Josefa to repent having joined her lot with yours!" Fitch promised before God and men that as long as he lived his wife should be happy. Señora Fitch says in her memoirs that this promise was faithfully and loyally kept, and that during the twenty years that she lived by his side he never caused her a single annoyance.

At this point, although it fits in chronologically at a somewhat later period, I am impelled to tell the truth about a certain alleged romance between a daughter of the Dons and a distinguished American. With the reader's permission I shall tell it in the first person, believing that my position as an intimate friend and first cousin by marriage of the lady in question will give more authority to my narrative, which I shall call

Romance Grafted on a Rose-Tree

At the time of the American Conquest Monterey was the social center of California. Especially was it noted for its beautiful and fascinating young women, and among these none was more admired at the *bailes* and *tertulias* that occurred nearly every day in the old capital than Señorita María Ignacia Bonifacio, known to her intimate friends as Nachita. She was the daughter of an Italian father and a Spanish mother, and though she united in herself the attractions of both races, yet I think she possessed more of the mental keenness and brilliant vivacity of the Italian than the soft pensiveness of the Spaniard. It was when she was at the height of her youthful charm that the young American officer, William Tecumseh Sherman, came with the United States troops to Monterey. Out of this combination of circumstances, together with the presence of a certain wonderful rosebush which grew in the garden of the señorita's home on Alvarado Street, some person now unknown, who had a warmer imagination than regard for the truth, manufactured the legend of a sad love affair between these two which keeps constantly bobbing up, despite many denials.

Regard for the truth of history, to use one of Governor Alvarado's favorite phrases, compels me to assert positively that the only true part of the legend consisted in the existence of the two young people and the rose-tree in Monterey at the same period. Otherwise it is made out of whole cloth, for there was not even a casual acquaintance between the Señorita and the American officer, much less any sort of love affair. This she told me with her own lips, adding that she had grown weary of refuting the oft-told fable and finally ceased to contradict it. This contradiction was confirmed by her immediate relatives, who were never pleased with the story. As for the rose which plays so prominent a part in this imaginary romance, it was brought from Santa Cruz by her uncle and was planted by the young lady herself, without any assistance from young Sherman. She used to tell me laughingly how tourists would come and look at it with intense interest, then ask, "And did you really plant it? And is it really a hundred years old?" Considering her miraculously youthful appearance even in middle age, when I knew her, this question was rather absurd. The rose itself, which was of the cloth-of-gold variety, was the object of her tender care, and for many years it unfolded a wealth of golden blooms on the arbor of her garden. If a spot of decay appeared anywhere on its great stem, she carefully scraped it out, applied a healing ointment, then bound it up with a cloth. Through this care it lived long after the allotted years of roses.

I make this contradiction not through any iconoclastic spirit, nor through any lack of appreciation of genuine romance, but through a firm belief that tradition, to have any value, should have some basis in truth. Besides, looked at dispassionately, the story as it is usually told does no credit to either party. It represents Señorita Bonifacio, who, as all her friends know, was a strong, courageous, proud, and high-spirited woman, in the humiliating role of a forlorn and jilted damsel, meekly waiting for the lover that never returned. Nothing could be more contrary to her real nature, for she was not the sort to waste her life in vain regrets for a faithless lover. Had any man in truth ever treated her so cavalierly, she would have tossed her head in scorn and promptly forgotten him. Nor is it right to represent that gallant soldier, Tecumseh Sherman, as recreant to his promises.

Moreover, there is no necessity to make such labored efforts to add interest to the personality and life of this charming woman, for in her true self she possessed attractive qualities that needed no embroideries of false romance. I had the good fortune to spend many a happy hour with her in the immaculately clean rooms of her adobe house, while she told me stories of the old days when she took a leading part in the gayeties of the pueblo. Sometimes, to gratify my youthful curiosity, she would open the camphor-wood chest in her bed-chamber and draw from it reminders of the bygone time in the shape of old-fashioned wasp-waisted dresses with very full skirts, crimson velvets, gray brocades that stood alone, embroidered mittens, tiny slippers, etc. Among other things were two necklaces, one made of a single string of large pearls from the Baja California fisheries, and the other of gold filigree work set thickly with tiny seed pearls from the same source.

In all domestic arts she was wonderfully skilled. In the manufacture of lace, the "drawn work" for which the women of her race are noted, she had few equals, and it was partly by the sale of these filmy creations that she lived in the latter days when, like most of her compatriots, she began to suffer from straitened circumstances. Nor was she lacking in the finer accomplishments, for in the large *sala* stood a harp, whose voice, long since silent, had once responded to the cunning touch of her fingers when she played for the Sunday afternoon dances of her young companions.

Among the interesting and authentic circumstances of her later life was her acquaintance with Robert Louis Stevenson when he was in Monterey. To her house he came to visit his friends who lodged there, of whom I was one, and frequently he walked in her garden and admired the famous rose. He had no Spanish and she no English, but her vivacity and his Scotch wit interpreted for them.

Now that so many years have passed, and most of the actors in her life's simple drama have gone to the silence and indifference of the grave, it seems permissible for me to relate the story of her real romance, so far as I know it. She herself never spoke of it, but her relatives gave me the main facts. In her youth she had, among many others, two admirers who stood apart from the rest. One was an American and the other was a youth of her own race. It happened that her mother favored the American, while she loved the Californian. It was still the custom for young people to give unquestioning obedience to parents, so the young girl never thought of running counter to her mother's wishes, but to consent to marry the man she did not love was more than she could bear, so she made a vow: "*Si no puedo casarme con Pedro, no me caso!*" (If I cannot marry Pedro, I shall never marry.) This vow she kept to the day of her death, and this was the reason why she remained a spinster. Here is romance enough, without resorting to the spurious kind, and, as is usually the case, the true is more interesting than the false. The rose-tree, alas, has been removed; the house through whose spacious rooms Nachita's harp "once the soul of music shed" has been torn down; the adobe wall, with its tile coping which once made the garden a sweet secluded spot, is gone. Nothing is left to perpetuate a charming personality but a false story. If the spirit of Nachita ever comes to hover above the place of her earthly home, she must be saddened by the change.

Chapter VII

CHAPTER VII

Presidios and Pueblos

LIKE THE Indians, the Spanish and Mexican soldiery who took part in the settlement of Alta California have never received the credit that is due them for their indispensable aid. In the colonizing projects of Spain the sword always marched side by side with the cross. The government was wise enough to appreciate the work of the missionaries in subduing the native peoples with the least trouble and bloodshed possible, and it was largely in its own interests that it sent a military force to guard the holy men while they were engaged in this work. But, after all, its chief object was to take possession of the land in the name of the king and establish settlements and fortifications as a defense against foreign attack, for it was an age when all the leading nations were seeking a foothold in the unoccupied spaces of the earth. The forces sent to hold Alta California against England and Russia seem now ridiculously small, but for the time they sufficed, and in point of selection they were eminently well-fitted.

During Spanish domination only men of good character were admitted to the service of the presidial companies. They were physically strong, brave, accustomed to Indian warfare, long-enduring, and loyal to the last degree.

Among them were a number of *soldados distinguidos*, men of good family, who, although they lived in the barracks and did military duty like the others, were entitled to certain privileges, such as the right to the prefix of *Don* to their Christian names and exemption from all menial work. There were some mechanics among them, such as shoemakers and tailors, who practiced their trades when not actively employed in their military duties.

It was such soldiers as these who composed the first expedition under Portolá in 1769, who accompanied Anza in his march from Sonora to the sea in 1775 with the first colonists for San Francisco, and who later opened up the great interior valleys of the Sacramento and the San Joaquín. Without such a military force, inured to the hardships of frontier life, able to go without food or water for long periods and to sleep in the saddle, the occupation and settlement could not have been accomplished; nor could the country have been held against the natives, who, though less warlike than the other aboriginals of America, had enough manhood to engage in a number of serious uprisings against the invading whites. It was, moreover, expected that the soldiers, after completing their time of service, would remain in the country as settlers, thus giving double duty.

Portolá's command included some of the best known names in California history, the pioneers who became the founders of our oldest families—Ortega, Amador, Alvarado, Carrillo, Yorba, Soberanes, and others. The descendants of these men constitute California's real aristocracy, and, just as the ships *San Carlos* and *San Antonio* fill the same place on the west coast as the *Mayflower* on the east, so do these first settlers stand equal to the Puritans of New England. The sufferings of these men, especially those who came by sea, were very great. The ravages from scurvy on the *San Carlos* were so severe that when the ship dropped anchor in the bay of San Diego there were not enough able-bodied sailors left to man a small boat to go ashore, and one had to be sent out to them. The dread disease, for which there was no known remedy at that time, continued to rage after all were landed, and by the time Portolá arrived with the land party less than a third of the soldiers and sailors from the two ships were left alive; the rest were all buried at what is still known as Dead Men's Point (*La Punta de los Muertos*). When will some great poet arise to sing of their deeds of heroism as has been done of the pilgrims who landed on the "stern and rock-bound shore" of New England?

"On July 14, 1769," says Portolá, "I went on by land to Monterey with that small company of persons, or rather say skeletons, who had been spared by scurvy, hunger, and thirst." It was a picturesque troop. The soldiers wore their sleeveless leather jackets and carried on the left arm shields made of two thicknesses of bull hide with which they protected both themselves and their horses from arrow wounds. A fall of leather called the *armas* hung from each side of the saddle to protect the thigh and leg while riding through brush. Their offensive arms were the lance, which they managed with great dexterity on horseback, broadsword, and short musket. Each soldier had six horses for remounts, a colt, and a mule; one horse was kept constantly saddled and ready for use day or night. The engineer, Miguel Costansó, who accompanied this expedition, said of the soldiers, "It is not too much to say that they are the best horsemen in the world, and among the best soldiers who gain their bread in the service of the king."

The trip, through entirely new country, was a hard one; during part of the way a number of the soldiers became so weak from illness and fatigue that they had to be carried on litters swung between two mules. On the way back, it being the winter season, fish and game became so scarce that they were reduced to living on pelicans and sea gulls, which did not make very palatable eating. Finally even these failed, and they were compelled to kill some of the weakest of the mules, which they ate with the most extreme disgust. "The flesh we roasted or half fried," wrote Portolá to a friend in Mexico, "in a fire made in a hole in the ground. The mule being thus prepared, without a grain of salt or other seasoning—for we had none—we shut our eyes and fell to on that scaly mule (what misery!) like hungry lions. We ate twelve in as many days, obtaining from them perforce all our sustenance, all our appetite, all our delectation." "Nevertheless," says Father Crespi, diarist of the expedition, "remembering the object to which these toils were directed, and that it was for the greater glory of God through the conversion of souls, and for the service of the king, whose dominions were being enlarged by this expedition, all were animated to work cheerfully."

After the province passed under the rule of the Republic of Mexico the character of the soldiers deteriorated very much, but still many good men were drafted into the service. In fact practically every man in California was a soldier at one time or another, for each settler, in return for grants of land and other government aid, was required to hold himself, his horse, and his musket in readiness for military service in any emergency. Bancroft says on this point: "Early in the nineteenth century, most of the men in California were soldiers, beginning their career on entering their sixteenth year. The rule was to leave to parents having two or more sons, one, to be chosen by themselves. The rest were mustered into the cavalry or artillery, the choice being left to the recruit. Later in the third decade, when the government called on the alcaldes for recruits, usually the vagrants, lazy or vicious, were summoned. Governor Figueroa called them 'dog killers, saddlers of other people's horses, robbers of hides.' Of course, the industrious and well-behaved were often mustered in from necessity, and occasionally out of spite on the part of the alcaldes to them or their families." Vallejo pays a high tribute to the fidelity of the common soldiers under the most adverse circumstances.

The duties of the military force were to garrison the forts and defend the country against foreign invasion, guard the missions against attacks by natives, conduct explorations into the interior, take the field against Indian uprisings, run down horse thieves, care for the horses and cattle on the king's land, cultivate the fields allotted for their own support, and carry the mails.

Carrying the mails was the hardest service performed by the soldiers in time of peace. The carriers were always Spanish soldiers, never Indians. Carriers were dispatched from either direction between the missions, starting from San Diego at one end and San Francisco at the other. Letters and messages were thus conveyed from one point to another along the entire line, each mission furnishing its share of horses and messengers. People were required to have letters in readiness for the arrival of the carriers, so as to cause no delay. At the military posts the quartermasters were the postmasters; at other places the alcalde received, delivered, and forwarded the mails. The arrangement was primarily for military purposes, but as there was no other mail service in the country, the governor ordered that the citizens "be accommodated by having their letters and papers sent free of expense."

To perform this service, two soldiers started on horseback from San Diego every other Monday, and two from San Francisco at the same time. The two parties, from north and south, met the next Sunday at a rancho about half-way, where they exchanged mails and started back on their respective routes the next morning, arriving at San Diego and San Francisco on the Sunday following. Thus it required two weeks to deliver mails between the northern and southern points. Judged by modern standards this seems very slow, but as compared with other localities at that time it was exceedingly quick work; for instance, in 1843 a mail-bag containing many important communications was found at Mazatlan, where it had been lying since 1837. So no doubt the missionaries and citizens of Alta California congratulated themselves on their up-to-dateness when they could count every fortnight upon seeing the welcome rider dash up on his swift and sturdy mustang with news from the outside world. With a song of Old Spain on their lips, these men of Castile galloped gaily along the Camino Real, from mission to mission on their tireless Arabian ponies, through the summer heat, the winter rain, the flower-spangled fields of spring, and the warm brown hills of autumn, in the new land of California. If night overtook them far from a human habitation, as frequently happened, they simply hobbled their faithful steeds, wrapped themselves in their trusty serapes, and, with the saddle for a pillow on the bosom of old Mother Earth, lay down to dreamless sleep, like the care-free mortals that they were.

The service given by these soldiers in Indian campaigns was far more strenuous than is usually imagined, for the natives put up a much stiffer fight against the domination of the whites than they are credited with by many modern historians. The Suisunes and Sotoyomes in the north, and the Tulareños in the south, were particularly aggressive; the records of the period are full of reports of Indian uprisings and the military expeditions sent against them. The pacification of the country had been practically accomplished before the arrival of the Americans, for which we are indebted to the Spanish and Mexican soldiery.

Discipline among these troops was very rigid, although it may be regarded as certain that the lot of the soldier depended largely upon the disposition of his officers. Among the punishments inflicted upon men in the ranks for serious offences were loss of pay, hard labor in the chain gang, imprisonment, increase of term of service, *carreras de baqueta* (running the gauntlet), during which the culprit had to run between two lines of men armed with ramrods, who struck him as they pleased, and death. Soldiers were liable to the death penalty for what would have been trivial offences in a civilian. Bancroft says, "It was really astonishing how any man escaped the death penalty." Some light is thrown upon punishment by José María Amador, a *soldado distinguido*, who writes:

"Notwithstanding our privileges, Captain Argüello frequently put us in the stocks, the culprit lying on the ground, with no rest for the head, and exposed to the sun. This punishment the captain termed the *pena arbitraria* (arbitrary punishment), and said that he inflicted it because in refusing to assist in loading mules and conducting them from Santa Cruz to the presidio, we gave a bad example to the other soldiers. But as soon as Doña Rafaela, wife of Captain Argüello, saw us in the stocks, she would insist that we should be liberated, many times coming personally to make the corporal of the guard free us. I imagine that she and the captain had an understanding about this, for one day in his presence and that of the officer of the guard, she herself opened the stocks and set us at liberty, after obtaining permission of the officer. The captain merely laughed and called us rattle-brains."

Altogether, the lot of the soldier in the earliest days, while it was certainly not luxurious, was not excessively hard. Such menial labor as tending the crops and cattle he generally turned over to the Indians, who could be hired for a string of beads or a small share of the products. Uprisings happened only occasionally, and attacks by foreigners never but once before the coming of the Americans, that once being when Monterey was sacked and burned by the Buenos Aires insurgents under Bouchard in an attempt to force California into the revolution against Spain. If any foreign nation had really wished to invade California it would have found little opposition, for the forts were allowed to fall into decay and the cannon to rust. Under Mexican rule the force dwindled until in 1835 it consisted of but 307 men, with 22 officers, and the presidial and other companies declined to mere skeletons. All were short of arms and ammunition. All foreign visitors during the Mexican period describe a state of extreme dilapidation at all the presidios.

Before the rebellion of the South American and Mexican colonies against Spain, the soldiers in California, who at first remained loyal to the mother country, at least received their meager pay, about $217 a year for privates, mostly paid in goods sold to the men at advanced prices. Furthermore, supplies came regularly from San Blas on the royal ships. But during the revolutionary years, when the king's ships were prevented from coming by the insurgents, Californians began to suffer great privations. Civilians managed to get along, as we have seen, by trading hides and tallow and furs with the smugglers, but the troops were in the worst plight of all, for they had nothing to sell. They were finally reduced almost to a state of nakedness, and if they did not starve it was owing to the missions, which, though with much grumbling, kept them supplied with food. Even officers had to come to wearing trousers made of deerskin, and, to hide their complete lack of shirts, fastened their collars to the necks of their jackets. Sergeant Amador says that for over eighteen years of service he received no pay, aside from his rations, from either the Spanish or the Mexican government, his only pay, as he expresses it, being the fourteen arrow holes that he had in his body.

The uniforms of the military, when they had any, were very showy. Captain F. W. Beechey of the English ship *Blossom*, who was here in 1826, describes the dress of a California dragoon.

A short round jacket of blue cloth, with scarlet cuffs and collar; blue velvet breeches open at the knees to show white stockings underneath; a wide red sash tied around the body to fill the space between jacket and trousers; deerskin leggings, often richly embroidered in colored silks and tied with silver tassels at the top, reaching from knee to ankle, where they were thrust into shoes of the same material; black hat with very wide brim and low crown, below which hung a profusion of dark hair in a thick queue tied with a ribbon. The feet, armed with a tremendous pair of spurs, were thrust into enormous wooden stirrups, covered in front with a fall of leather almost touching the ground. A long musket, or flintlock gun, was laid across the pommel of the saddle. The sword was fastened to the left hand side of the saddle, under the leg, and generally all carried the Spanish Toledan rapier. The uniforms of officers were distinguished by gold lace trimmings and epaulettes on their jackets.

When on a field campaign the dragoons wore, over all, the *cuera de gamuza*, a garment like a sleeveless sack reaching to the knees, made of several thicknesses of antelope skin stitched together. This garment, which was in reality a cuirass to protect the wearer from arrow wounds, was so much a characteristic of the frontier cavalry that they were usually called *soldados de cuera* (leather-jacket soldiers). On the left arm the rider carried a large shield of several thicknesses of oxhide, varnished, and bearing on the convex side the coat of arms of the king of Spain. This shield was large enough to cover both man and horse, and, with the leather cuirass, gave the troops a quaint resemblance to the crusaders of old. Naturally this armor gave the Spaniards a great advantage over the naked Indians with their bows and arrows, but the latter soon learned to aim high and shoot at the head, with the result that most of the wounds suffered by the Spanish soldiery were in that part.

The trappings of the horse were fully as gaudy as those of the rider, if not more so. Under the heavy saddle, with its high tree to hold the inevitable lasso of plaited deerskin, were three broad sheets or blankets of leather, hanging far over the sides of the horse. These blankets, which overlapped each other, were richly embroidered in silk in figures representing birds, flowers, and other pleasing designs. Through holes pierced in the leather could be seen colored cloth or silk lining. Fastened to the saddle with thongs and lying on the croup of the horse was a semicircular piece of leather or sheepskin called the *anquera*, a sort of tail-piece to the saddle. Upon the *anquera* the rolled-up serape or other baggage was placed and tied, and upon it also sat the horseman when he carried a lady on the saddle in front, as was the usual way, reversing the method followed by American pioneers. On each side of the top saddle blanket was a holster or pocket, which served to carry food or other small articles. The soldier carried everything absolutely needful on his horse when he went on a campaign, and for all else depended on the country. As Portolá said, there never were better frontier soldiers, notwithstanding their many deficiencies, and Americans owe them much for having cleared the way for their coming.

As has already been said, the towns which grew up about the presidios made very slow progress, but all of

Franz Geritz '27

them, San Francisco, Monterey, Santa Barbara, and San Diego, bear present witness to the exceeding good judgment of the Spaniards in choosing sites.

Standing today in the great city of Saint Francis, it is difficult to realize its humble beginnings. It is necessary to picture, in place of the tall buildings and crowded streets in the heart of the financial district, a desolate sandy waste, covered with scrub-oaks and chaparral. This spot was known as *El Parage de Yerba Buena* (the place of the good herb), from a little aromatic vine with medicinal qualities which grew there in profusion. The importance of this place, which lay about three miles from the presidio, consisted in the good anchorage for ships furnished by the little cove in front of it. It was better sheltered from winds than the port at the presidio, and for that reason it gradually became the rendezvous for shipping; so this circumstance of nature decided the actual site of California's famous city. Roads ran from it to the presidio and mission, mere narrow bridle paths, where the rider had to take constant care to save his person and clothing from injury by the bushes and trees. At first there was no thought of a town there, and up to 1834 all was in a state of nature but for the presence of a party of foreign boat-builders for a time. In 1833 there was not a single inhabitant of what is now known as the city and county of San Francisco outside of the presidio and mission. The shores of the bay were a solitude, where forest animals roamed at will. But it had a wild charm, as Richard Henry Dana relates in his description of the scene as his vessel left the harbor in 1835:

"Great numbers of deer overrun the islands and hills of San Francisco Bay. The tide leaving us, we came to anchor near the mouth of the bay, under a high and beautifully sloping hill, upon which herds of hundreds and hundreds of red deer, and the stag, with his high branching antlers, were bounding about, looking at us for a moment and then starting off, affrighted at the noises which we made for the purpose of seeing the variety of their beautiful attitudes and motions."

So wild, indeed, was this spot that bears and mountain lions, as well as deer, haunted it by day and by night, and even after people were living there boldly committed depredations. One night in 1840 a lion, which had been observed for several days prowling about the settlement, seized and carried off an Indian boy eight years old from the yard of Jacob Leese, at the spot marked later by the corner of Clay and Dupont streets. In the same year, Captain Phelps of the Boston ship *Alert*, which then lay at anchor at Yerba Buena, sent his second officer with a boat's crew to cut firewood at Rincon Point. Leaving their provisions in a firkin in the fork of a tree, the men set to work; but imagine their surprise and chagrin when they went for their dinner to find a mother grizzly bear and her cubs gathered around the firkin and heartily enjoying its contents. "Not relishing the air and manner of the matron, the sailors beat a hasty retreat, and, rushing down to the beach, made for the ship as soon as possible." This scene occurred not far from the place where Folsom Street wharf was situated in modern times.

Yerba Buena was first laid out as a town in 1839 by order of Governor Alvarado. A public plaza[1] was measured off first, then the rest of the level ground was divided into streets, the place thus taking on the character and form of a regular town. The growth of the little settlement was very slow, and in 1844 it contained only about twelve houses, and not over fifty permanent inhabitants. In January, 1847, by the alcalde's order, the name of Yerba Buena was changed to San Francisco, as Vallejo says, "So that presidio, mission, and town, might come under the same appellation." Don José Arnaz, who came

[1]*Now known as Portsmouth Square.*

to California as supercargo of a trading ship from Peru in 1840, gives an interesting description of society in Yerba Buena at that time:

"The spirit of addiction to amusements was spread all over the coast, and in San Francisco, when it was desired to give a dance, the ships anchored in the port sent out their boats and launches to different ranchos of the *contra costa* (opposite coast). The owners of these ranchos, the Estudillos, the Castros, Martínez, Peralta, and Richardson of Sausalito, all gladly came with their beautiful wives and daughters to attend these dances, coming to Yerba Buena in these boats and returning in the same to their houses. They were frank and affable in their manners, but had not had the same opportunity to acquire culture as persons at other points. The most important family was that of Don Ignacio Martínez, of Pinole. In character he was courteous, lively, and a great dancer, in spite of the fact that he was at that time past fifty. To arrive at the rancho and attend a fandango in the evening was one and the same thing. . . During one of my voyages to San Francisco, I believe in 1842, there came to the port a Russian frigate, bringing the governor of all the Russian possessions in North America and the comandante at Ross. A banquet was given on board the frigate and we were invited to it. The banquet was followed by a dance on board, for which the decks of the ship were cleared. I observed that here and there were brasiers in which perfumes burned; for, so they told me, without this precaution it would have been very disagreeable to breathe the air, because of the fetid odor proceeding from the crews of Kodiaks and other individuals of those regions, the effect of the excessive use of the oil of whales and fish, which they take as we do coffee or tea. The gayety was great, the concourse numerous and brilliant, above all the women, among whom there were many beauties. The enthusiasm was such that even Padre Lorenzo took part in the dance, changing clothes with me, he putting on my frock coat and I his habit, making the girls laugh heartily. The dance lasted all night, and in the morning the guests departed."

The place continued to be a mere village until nearly the end of the '40's, with its inhabitants dancing away the idle hours, but with the political events leading up to American occupation it made a sudden move forward. Bancroft gives a lively picture of its condition at the end of the decade:

"The beginning of 1848 saw at the cove a thriving seaport town, which, with the surrounding shrub-clad hills and valleys, presented from Signal Hill[1] a view of thirty-five adobe public buildings, well-stocked warehouses, stores, and dwellings, and 160 snug frame buildings, with their respective out-houses and enclosures, glittering in whitewash and fresh paint. Builders now began to think of permanence, and put heavier timbers and better material into their houses. More wharves were built, on which, as well as on the beach and temporary landings, were stacked and strewn bales, boxes, and barrels of merchandise, and the usual paraphernalia of commercial industry. Whalers and coasting vessels entered and departed through the Golden Gate."

This was a great change since the day in 1775 when Captain Ayala slowly and cautiously felt his way in the dusk of the evening through the uncharted entrance of the great "arm of the sea" discovered by accident by the men of Portolá, and the astounded natives rushed to the water's edge to gaze upon the *San Carlos* as she rested at anchor, the sole craft on the quiet waters of the lonely bay.

As to Monterey, another of the presidial towns, it has always had a peculiar fascination for visitors since the day, December 16, 1602, when Sebastián Vizcaíno sailed

[1] *Now known as Telegraph Hill.*

into the beautiful blue bay and became so enamored of the place that he wrote almost too enthusiastically to the king concerning its advantages as a port. Just 233 years later, in 1835, a man of a different race, Richard Henry Dana, wrote of it also in terms of praise:

"We came to anchor within two cable lengths of the shore, and the town lay directly before us, making a very pretty appearance; its houses being of whitewashed adobe, which gives a much better effect than those of Santa Barbara, which are usually left of a mud color. The red tiles, too, on the roofs, contrasted well with the white sides, and with the extreme greenness of the lawn upon which the houses—about a hundred in number—were scattered about irregularly here and there. There are in this place, and in every other town that I saw in California, no streets or fences (except here and there a small patch might be enclosed for a garden), so the houses are placed at random upon the green. This, as they are of one story, and of the cottage form, gives them a pretty effect when seen from a little distance. . . As it was now the rainy season, everything was as green as nature could make it—the grass, the leaves, and all; the birds were singing in the woods, and great numbers of wild fowl were flying over our heads. . . Coming to this place from a long voyage, it seemed almost like coming to a home."

From a social viewpoint all early writers place Monterey at the head of all the towns of California. Don José Arnaz, an educated Spaniard, noted that there was greater learning in Monterey. This he ascribed to the fact that the seat of government was there, with the customhouse, treasury, etc., and hence there was necessarily more contact with strangers and people from the outside, whose customs, style, and manners were acquired by the citizens of the town. Ships of all nations, especially war vessels, came often to the port, and their distinguished officers served as models in deportment. Consequently the people of the better class in Monterey had finer manners than those of any other town, not even excepting Los Angeles, where there was at that time a very select society. Although there was much gayety at Monterey, with frequent dances and picnics to the pine woods, punctilious order was observed, and there was a distinct separation of classes. The houses of Don Juan Cooper, Don José Amesti, and Don José Ábrego were usually the centers of family reunions, and at one or another of them on days of *fiesta* there would be an informal dance in the afternoon or evening. These home affairs were given without ostentation or expense, but at the public balls, in which Monterey and Los Angeles surpassed all others, elaborate refreshments were served, including the finest wines and dishes. This refers to the better class. There were, of course, entertainments of a different sort for the rougher floating population generally to be found in a seaport town. Dana, whose tastes as a wild young sailor did not always lead him into the best society, says Monterey was a great place for cock-fighting, gambling of all sorts, fandangos, and various kinds of knavish amusements. Trappers and hunters from over the Rockies with valuable skins and furs, sometimes belonging to themselves and sometimes to their employers, were often entertained with amusements and dissipation until their money was gone and they were left to go back stripped of everything, but no doubt they would have been disappointed had it been otherwise. Let us quote from Walter Colton, who lived for three years in Monterey in the most intimate relationship with the people and serving as their chief municipal officer:

"It is no wonder that California centered her taste, pride, and wealth here, until the vandal irruption of gold hunters broke into her peaceful domain. . . I have never been in a community that rivals Monterey in its spirit of hospitality and generous regard. Such is the welcome to the privileges of the private hearth that a public hotel has never been able to maintain itself. . . Generous forbearing people of Monterey! There is more true hospitality in one throb of your heart than circulates for years through the courts and capitals of kings."

In 1842 Monterey was at the peak of her prosperity during the Spanish-Mexican period. To use the words of one of her own daughters: "It was the social center sought by every one, and the mecca of all travelers. Including the military, the white population numbered about one thousand." For such a small community it was extraordinarily cosmopolitan, including, besides the families of Spanish and Mexican extraction, those of foreigners from England, Germany, France, Ireland, Scotland, South America, and especially from the United States.

Bayard Taylor, who visited Monterey in 1849, gives a pleasing picture of life there at that time: "With the exception of Los Angeles, Monterey contains the most pleasant society to be found in California. There is a circle of families, American and native, residing there whose genial and refined social nature makes one forget his previous ideas of California." Domestic life in the capital was very strictly regulated, at least as far as the women and children of the better class were concerned. Brigida Briones says in her reminiscences that in 1827 ladies were rarely seen on the streets except early in the morning on the way to mass. They went to church attended by servants, who carried small mats for them to kneel on, as there were no seats. The church floors were cold, hard, and damp, and every young lady embroidered her own rug to alleviate the discomfort. The dress worn by the women in the mornings at church services was very plain—a rebozo, wrapped around the head and draped over the shoulders, and a petticoat of cheap black stuff. All classes wore the same, for the priest said that all ranks of men and women were the same in the presence of their Creator. For home wear and company the more well-to-do had expensive dresses—silk, velvet, and laces, often imported, but sometimes of home making. There was much rivalry in dress among the beauties, and those of small means often underwent privations to equal the rich. Relations with servants were agreeable, much like those between the families of the southern states of the Union and the negroes in the days of slavery. The Indians were faithful, good-natured, and easy to manage. They often slept on mats on the earth floor, or in summer time in the courtyards. There was the same easy familiarity in their relations with their masters as in the case of our southern slaves, and when they waited at table they often held conversations with the company and joined in the laughter without restraint. It was said that a good servant was one who knew when to be silent and when to put in his *cuchara* (spoon).

Great efforts were made to regulate public morals. Liquor was not to be sold on feast days nor after drum-beat at night. Gambling and the carrying of offensive weapons were prohibited. No person was allowed to be out of his house after *la queda* (curfew) except for urgent necessity, nor to have company in his house after that hour except by consent of the council. Entering dwellings or taverns on horseback (a habit sometimes practiced by reckless young men) was strictly forbidden. Idle persons were put on public works.

The citizens of Santa Barbara were noted for their respectability, and for their grave and serious character, being less addicted than those of other towns to the pleasures of the dance and such frivolities. This gravity of disposition, so thinks Señor Arnaz, was in imitation of their comandante, Captain José de la Guerra y Noriega, a blue-blooded Castilian who was exceptionally religious and a great friend of the friars. The inviting climate and fertile lands in the vicinity of this place, had, moreover, attracted a superior class of settlers. Alfred Robinson gives an interesting description of the town as he saw it on his arrival in 1829:

"Seen from the ship, the presidio or town, with its charming surroundings and neat little mission in the background, all situated on an inclined plane, rising gradually from the sea to a range of verdant hills, three miles from the beach, have a striking and beautiful effect. Distance, however, 'lends enchantment to the view,' which a nearer approach somewhat dispels; for we found the houses of the town, of which there were some two hundred, in not very good condition. They are built in the Spanish mode, with adobe walls and roofs of tile, and are scattered about outside the military department, showing a total disregard of order on the part of the authorities."

Many of the most important families of Alta California resided at Santa Barbara—the de la Guerras, the Carrillos, the Pachecos, the Arellanes, and others; the tombs of some of them, the de la Cuestas and others, are still to be seen in the old cemetery at the mission.

San Diego, with its good harbor and its exceptionally fine climate, might have become the metropolis of Alta California, it is thought, had the country immediately surrounding it been as fertile as the valleys of Santa Barbara and Los Angeles. As it was, the other presidial towns soon outstripped it in civil and military importance. As we have seen, one of the governors, Don José María Echeandía, thought so favorably of its climate, or, as has been told, of one of its beautiful daughters, that he tarried on there long enough to arouse the fears of Montereyans lest the capital should be moved to the southern town.

Señor Arnaz writes that the people of San Diego were

extremely gay, and especially fond of the fandango. He relates an incident occurring in 1841 as an illustration of their great predilection for amusements. Don Miguel Pedrorena, supercargo of the ship *Juan José*, gave a dance which lasted three days and nights. It was the best that had ever been given there, and was the talk of the town. Piqued by this, Captain Walker of the *Clarita* and Don Elogio Célis invited Señor Arnaz to contribute to a dance that would outshine the one given by Pedrorena. By their combined efforts the three succeeded in providing an entertainment which lasted eight days. At night they danced in the pueblo, by day they climbed into their *carretas* and went to the beach and from there boarded the *Clarita*. Dinner was served on board, and after a short rest for sleep, they danced again, afterwards returning to the pueblo to continue the dance all night. Every day for the whole eight that the affair lasted the same program was kept up. Arnaz remarks that nevertheless it cost very little.

In addition to the presidial towns there were three civic pueblos—Los Angeles, San José, and Branciforte. As has been already stated, the last-named passed out of existence so soon as to need no further comment. San José de Guadalupe was the first of these pueblos to be established. Its inhabitants, perhaps because their origin was from a lower social stratum, or because the place was more accessible to the rough hunters and trappers of the plains, were in a more backward social state, says that excellent observer, José Arnaz, than those of other points on the coast. This was noticeable in their manners, and especially in their fiestas and diversions. The merrymaking then sometimes took on the boisterous quality of the frontier camp; men would ride their horses up the steps of dancing pavilions, and make them curvet on the floor. Women threw their rich embroidered China shawls, valued at 200 or 300 pesos each, under the feet of the dancers to serve as a carpet. The better families kept aloof from such wild affairs, however, and small home dances were given among exclusive circles, usually at the houses of Don Antonio Suñol, Don Antonio María Pico, and Señor Bernal.

The population of the place in 1835 was about 600; its inhabitants raised wheat and cattle, and traded in the skins and tallow of deer, which were abundant in that vicinity. Alfred Robinson described the town as containing about 100 houses, a church, courthouse, and a jail, under the rule of an alcalde and two *regidores* (councilmen). The town had already laid the foundation for its modern name of the "city of gardens," for there were many little orchards of fruit trees attached to the houses, besides fine fields of wheat and corn. The pueblo was then connected with the mission of Santa Clara by the famous alameda, shaded on each side by large and stately willow trees, planted by Father Maguín de Catalá for the benefit of his flock, who had to make the journey of three miles between the two places to attend mass. On Sundays and feast days all the townspeople, gaily attired in silks and satins, might be seen mounted on their finest horses, proceeding in a leisurely way up the road. There were no carriages, and though there was less pomp and splendor than in the larger cities of the Mexican Republic, we have Robinson's word for it that in one respect the scene excelled them all, that is, in the display of female beauty. "No part of Mexico can show so large a share of bright eyes, fine teeth, fair proportions, and beautiful complexions." And lest an unfair impression should be given of the social beginnings of this lovely city of the plain, it is but right to repeat Robinson's statement that "there are perhaps few places in the world where, in proportion to the number of its inhabitants, can be found more chastity, industrious habits, and correct deportment than among the women of San José."

We now come to Monterey's principal rival in the south, the pueblo of the lengthy name—*Nuestra Señora la Reina de los Angeles de Porciúncula*. From the time when the Indians raised their wolf-like howl in greeting to Portolá and his party at this spot, the place occupied a position of great importance in the annals of California. From its beginning as a settlement made up of outcasts from Mexico of the lowest class, it grew to be the chief center of culture in the south. The choice lands in its vicinity drew to it the most influential of those who came to the country, and in 1835 it was the principal pueblo, with a population of about 1,500.

Too much stress has been laid by superficial observers upon the bad manners and morals of the lower element of Los Angeles society in early days, and too little credit has been given to the better class. Sir George Simpson described it as a "den of thieves, the noted abode of the lowest gamblers and drunkards in the country," but Don José Arnaz, who had the advantage of intimate acquaintance with the best people in the place, gives us a very different picture. He says the residents of Los Angeles, generally speaking, were a moral people, very zealous in religious observances. One of their pleasing customs was to give thanks to God from their open windows at the break of day; one person would speak first in a loud voice, and the rest would follow with their responses. They were, in general, affable in their manners and free from ostentation. Society was at the time of the arrival of Arnaz very much mixed—rich and poor, respectable women and those of a different sort, associating together freely in their diversions, a custom which was very puzzling to strangers. At a later date an attempt was made to establish an exclusive circle of decent people. The upper class had their *tertulias* (social parties) at the houses of prominent citizens, most often at that of the American, Don Abel Stearns. The leading citizens of the pueblo at that time were Captain Santiago Argüello, Don Manual Requena, Don Juan Bandini, Don José Antonio Carrillo, Don Vicente Sánchez, Don Tiburcio Tapia, Don Antonio del Valle and his son, Don Ignacio.

At the time of the American Conquest Los Angeles was a town of adobes, surrounded by a mud wall for defense against the Indians, who were numerous and predatory if not bloodthirsty. Fifty years after the first settlement Indian scares were still frequent, and a guard was kept on duty at the *cuartel* on the eastern side of the old plaza. J. M. Guinn tells us that:

"By the beginning of the nineteenth century the town had grown beyond the walls, and as it grew it straggled off from its nucleus, the old plaza, in an irregular way, without plot or plan. The builder of a new house built it wherever it was most convenient to him, without regard to streets. If the house did not align with the street, the street could adjust itself to the house. A half century after the founding of the pueblo there was not a regularly laid out street in its limits."

The architecture of the houses was, with few exceptions, always the same, square-walled, flat-roofed, one-story structures, looking, as one writer says, "like so many brick-kilns ready for the burning." It is a mistake to speak of the "quaint tiled roofs of Los Angeles," for it was the custom there to cover them with asphalt from La Brea pits in the vicinity. Only a few of the aristocrats had tiled roofs. The houses were comfortable enough and especially well suited to the climate, but they were built for utility rather than for beauty. The people made the outdoors their real home, with the blue sky for its roof and the flower-spangled fields for its adornment. Houses were used chiefly as shelters from the rain and storage places for necessities. The old pueblo was not particularly pleasing in appearance, with its crooked streets and clay-colored houses, with no glass in the windows, no lawns in front, no sidewalks, and no shade trees. Yet the owner enjoyed some advantages that will be appreciated by citizens of modern times; there were no taxes to be paid on the property, and no rent to be paid, for every man lived in his own house. The real estate agent and the tax collector were unknown in the land. Quoting J. M. Guinn again:

"The streets were ungraded and unsprinkled, and when dashing *caballeros* used them for race courses dense clouds of yellow dust enveloped the houses. There were no slaughter houses, and each family had its *matanza* in close proximity to the kitchen where bullocks were converted into beef. In course of time the ghastly skulls of the slaughtered animals formed a veritable golgotha in the back yards. The crows acted as scavengers, and when not employed in the street department removing garbage, sat on the roofs of the houses and cawed dismally. Like the dogs, they increased and multiplied until the 'plague of crows' compelled the council to offer a bounty for their destruction. There was no legendary hearthstone and fireside, and the pleasing fiction of Santa Claus coming down the chimney with toys on Christmas Eve would not have been understood by the youthful Angeleno of long ago, for there were no chimneys in the old pueblo. The only means of warming the houses was a *brasero* of live coals set on the floor. . . The furniture was meagre, mostly homemade—a few benches or rawhide-bottomed chairs to sit on, a rough table, a chest or two to hold the family finery, and a cheap print or two of saints on the wall. The bed was the pride of the housewife; sometimes a snowy counterpane and lace-trimmed pillows decorated a couch whose base was a dried bullock's hide stretched on a rough frame of wood."

Naturally the above description applies to the houses of the ordinary citizen; some of the well-to-do had comfortable and commodious dwellings. *The Palacio de Don Abel*, as the natives called Abel Stearns' house, covered a whole block, and was luxurious in its inner appointments. So was the Carrillo house, the *casa* of Alvarado and others, but even these were not elegant or imposing externally.

Some of the ordinances for the government of the pueblo were as quaint as those at Monterey. Ordinance nineteen required that a license of two pesos should be paid for all dances except for weddings, and for even the latter permission had to be obtained from the alcalde. "The festive lover who went forth to serenade his lady without a permit from that official was subject to a fine of one peso and a half; if he tried it a second time, the fine was doubled, and a third offense landed him in the calabozo."

By the simple expedient of requiring each citizen to perform his part in city work, the different departments were most economically run. Every house owner was required to sweep every Saturday in front of his house as far as the middle of the street, his opposite neighbor doing the same on his side; so the street was cleaned without expense to the city. Every owner of a house of more than two rooms was required to hang a lantern in front of his door at night, from dark to eight in winter and to nine in summer, at which hours it is assumed that all good citizens were supposed to be in bed. Every Monday was set apart as dog-catcher's day, and it may be said that the official was as heartily detested by the small boy as now. There was no need for a fire department in the old pueblo, for the houses, with their clay walls, earth floors, and rawhide doors, were nearly fireproof, especially as the cooking was generally done out-of-doors or in separate outhouses. There was no paid police department; every able-bodied young man was subject to military duty and had to take his turn standing guard. The guards policed the city without pay. Most of the city officials were paid in the glory of holding office, which was no mean prerogative, for great deference was shown to them by all classes.

The above notes make it clear why the Angelenos of that day were able to administer their municipality so efficiently and economically; the public spirit of the citizens and their willingness to serve without compensation made it possible.

With some slight local variations, life and customs were much the same in all the towns, both presidial and civic. Everywhere there was the same care-free existence and irresponsibility. Pleasure before business was the reversed order in which they read the old motto. J. B. Dye, a Kentuckian trapper and scout who came to the country in 1832, gives an entertaining description of the people and their habits: "The Californians were the happiest people on earth. Their time was spent in one continual round of feasting and pleasure, gaiety and happiness. If any person was so poor that he had no horse to ride, some friend, relative, or *compadre* would give him a splendid charger, another a saddle, bridle, reata, and spurs; a third a milk cow, another a bullock for beef, and so on, leaving no want unsupplied. Thus it was that no one suffered, all had plenty to eat and drink, were provided with ample stock and clothing; never in want, never required to labor for a living, they would skim across the plains or over the mountains, perhaps catch a grizzly bear, bring him into the settlement and have a bull and bear fight, and give a fandango every night."

Chapter VIII

CHAPTER VIII

Life on the Ranchos and in the Missions

THE SPANISH GOVERNMENT was very jealous about issuing land grants to individuals, only about ten or twelve being ceded during that period. Among them were the holdings of the Nietos, Verdugos, Domínguez, Tapias, and Zúñigas, names which have come down to our own times. The largest grant ever issued in California was that given in 1784 to Manuel Nietos by Governor Fages. It extended from the Santa Ana River to the San Gabriel, from the ocean to the mountains, and contained about sixty-eight square miles, something over 300,000 acres. Later it was reduced at the request of the padre in charge of Mission San Gabriel.

It was during the Mexican régime, however, that most of the large grants were made, and especially toward the latter part of the period, when it became evident that California would pass to the control of the United States. In 1824 an extremely liberal policy was adopted, under which any Mexican of good proven character, or any foreigner willing to become a naturalized citizen of Mexico and accept the Roman Catholic faith, might acquire for the asking eleven square leagues of land—one league to be irrigable soil, four dependent on rain, and six for grazing, and with it freedom from taxes for five years. A league comprised a little more than 4,438 acres, quite a sizable farm in itself. Ranchos were always spoken of in terms of leagues, never of acres, and one of four or five square leagues was considered comparatively small.

Boundaries were loosely defined by some well-known landmarks, such as a chain of hills on either side of the grant, a lagoon, river, or ravine. The limit of one of them was marked as "the place where Don Bernardo Yorba sits on his white horse," referring to the habit which the gentleman named had of riding over his rancho on his white horse and pausing on a certain eminence to look over his broad domains. It was little more slipshod than the method practiced in the early days of New England, where farms were marked by a certain stone fence, a tree, or other sometimes temporary landmark. In California the tract was measured off by a horseman galloping at full speed with a fifty-foot reata trailing behind him, beginning at some definite point, generally marked by a pile of stones called a *mójonera*. The quantity of land was roughly estimated or guessed at, the convenient phrase *poco mas ó menos* (a little more or less) being used to cover any deficiency or excess, which sometimes amounted to double the number of leagues contemplated in the grant. It will be readily understood that this vagueness of description caused much trouble and litigation when these properties fell into the hands of American òccupants, whose titles are founded upon the original Spanish land grants.

In time almost every Californian had his rancho, large or small, and some had several, each with its herds of cattle and horses. By 1830 there were fifty of these private ranchos in existence, fourteen of them being in the Monterey district, with nearly 400 persons living on them. Having obtained the land, it was an easy matter for the settler to stock it by borrowing horses and cattle from

Franz Geritz 21

the missions, returning them when the increase permitted. The period of the greatest prosperity of the ranchos was from 1828 to 1846, when their owners found a ready sale with the English and American traders for the hides and tallow. Many of the rancheros became very wealthy, and it was then that social life reached its highest development during the whole Spanish-Mexican period.

Each rancho had its distinguishing name, in much the same way as the great country estates in Europe. These names were various in their origin. Some were religious, such as *La Sagrada Familia* (the Holy Family); *Natividad* (the nativity of Christ); *Las Virgenes* (the virgins), etc. Some were based on an event in their history, such as *Pinole*, referring to a time when a party of Spanish soldiers were saved from starvation at that place by the *pinole* (gruel) given them by the Indians, or *Sal si Puedes* (get out if you can), in reference to an occasion when an exploring party was lost in its maze of ravines and hills. Others referred to the topography of the location, or some natural phenomenon, such as *Las Ciénegas* (the swamps), *Agua Caliente* (hot springs), *La Brea* (the asphalt springs). Many were of Indian origin—*Sotoyome*, *Buri-Buri*, etc. Still others implied a facetious reference to some experience, amusing or otherwise, such as *Las Pulgas* (the fleas), which commemorates an occasion when the Spanish discoverers were nearly devoured by these insects in an Indian village. Many of these names survive, playing an important part in the romantic nomenclature of California.

Enough has been said to show with what a prodigal hand Mexico parceled out the land it claimed by right of seizure from its aboriginal owners. A California rancho of the first class was about equal in extent to a German principality, while some were content with a modest holding of one, two, or three leagues. John A. Sutter enjoyed the full complement of eleven leagues, sixty miles long, well stocked by the favor of his California friends. The sites now occupied by the large and flourishing cities of Oakland, Alameda, and Berkeley are only a part of what was once the Rancho San Antonio, the property of Don Luís Peralta, which furnished pasture for 8,000 head of cattle, 2,000 horses and mares. It was perhaps fortunate that the Americans took over the province in time to prevent the division of its entire territory into great principalities, for in that case agrarian troubles might have arisen like those which have caused so many years of strife and bloodshed in Mexico. William Heath Davis is authority for the statement that 1,045 grants were made by the governors of California of ranches of all sizes, about 800 of which were stocked, averaging 1,500 head of cattle to each rancho, making a total of 1,200,000 head. He adds: "I make the assertion, without fear of contradiction, that the department of California, previous to and after the ruin of the missions, in proportion to the population, was the richest country under Spanish dominion inhabited by citizens of Castilian extraction." In considering this side of the subject it should not be forgotten that the Indians not only furnished the land, without any compensation, but did practically all the manual labor of its development.

Many a foreign resident who became rich on the land owed his fortune to the generosity of Californians, who gave him a rancho without money and often without request. John Bidwell says: "Many old Californians made a distinction between 'Gringo thieves' and the manly pioneers who were good neighbors. A volume could be written about the unsolicited gifts of land—fifty acres here, a hundred there—made to Americans to whom the rancheros had taken a fancy, or who had rendered them a service. 'Take the land,' said Señor Alviso to a man from

Connecticut in 1849, in Alameda County. 'You can keep it. I can not.'" Would that it could be truthfully said that this generosity was always met in the same spirit!

Many restrictions were placed upon the ranchos in the way of provisos against sale or mortgage, but these were ignored by the Californians, who sold or hypothecated their lands at their pleasure. These regulations, though regarded as burdensome by the land owners, were humane in their object, being designed to prevent their estates from being gambled away by the reckless or encumbered by the thriftless, to the disadvantage of widows and orphans, who were always tenderly protected by Spanish law.

The establishments of the wealthier rancheros bore many resemblances to the feudal estates of the Middle Ages in Europe, each with its over-lord, his mayordomo, or steward, and his large band of retainers. The mayordomo of J. J. Warner, one of the American beneficiaries of California generosity, said he could raise for his master 300 fighting men in a few hours. There were many things in common, too, between the great ranchos of California and the plantations of our southern states during slavery times. Both had large bodies of unpaid laborers to bear the burden of the work, for the Indians of California were hardly less enslaved than were the blacks of the South. On the plantation there was the "negro quarter" in the rear of the "big house" where the white folks lived; in California there was the "Indiada," as the horde of natives gathered about the mansions of the Dons were called. Some rancheros supported whole tribes. General M. G. Vallejo, once the richest man in the province, maintained a small army of Indians in the fields besides about fifty house servants. When asked by a visitor how employment could be found for so many, Señora Vallejo replied:

"Each child [of whom there were sixteen] has a personal attendant, while I have two for my own needs; four or five are occupied in grinding corn for tortillas, for so many visitors come here that three grinders do not suffice; six or seven serve in the kitchen, and five or six are always washing clothes for the children and other servants; and, finally, nearly a dozen are employed at sewing and spinning. The Indian generally learns very few things; she who is taught to cook will not hear of washing clothes, while a good washerwoman is insulted at being asked to sew or spin. All our servants are very much attached to us. They do not ask for money, nor do they have a fixed wage; we give them all they need, and if they are ill we care for them like members of the family. If they have children we stand as godparents and see to their education. If they wish to go to a distant place to visit a relative, we give them animals and escorts for the journey. In a word, we treat our servants rather as friends than as servants." This description calls to mind a story of old plantation days. A mulatto girl, being asked after the war of secession what vocation she was fitted to follow, replied, "I'se de fanner." "What's that?" asked the surprised questioner. "Well," said the girl, "I fans Massa and Missus and little Massa when dey's asleep."

The life was patriarchal, and, although the Indians performed practically all the labor, they were by no means unhappy, for the Californians were not hard task-masters; they recognized the necessity of distributing the work among a large number, so that it might not fall too heavily upon individuals. All that had to be given to the Indians was their food and a few articles of coarse clothing. According to Spanish custom, servants addressed their masters and mistresses by their first names, but always with the prefix of Don or Doña. Thus General Vallejo was Don Mariano and his wife was Doña Francisca, much as the southern negro would say, "Marse Henry," and "Miss Mary."

It goes without saying that not all Californians lived in this luxurious way, for though there was no real poverty there were always degrees of affluence. Some of the larger ranches had over a hundred Indian retainers, usually under white mayordomos, although occasionally an Indian of uncommon intelligence was chosen to serve in that capacity. It was observed that Indian foremen were much harder on those under them than white men; they seemed to take a special delight in punishing offenders of their own race. The work of vaqueros and house servants was generally done by civilized Indians, while the wild, or "gentile" natives were employed in the fields, making another analogy with plantation life in the southern states of the Union, where the less intelligent were used for outside work.

The ranch houses were very similar to those in the towns—low, square or oblong buildings of adobe, with thatched or tiled roofs, according to the means of the owners, and varying in size and inner fittings for the same reason. At first they were built on high, open ground, devoid of trees and shrubbery, which it was feared might serve to mask the approach of marauding Indians; but as this fear passed away, fruit and shade trees were planted, as well as flowers of all kinds, which, in that favoring climate, flourished exceedingly. No ranch house had locks on its doors, for there was nothing to steal and no thieves.

The Californians inherited from their Spanish ancestors a certain austerity in regard to the adornment of their houses, which, with their small deep windows, sometimes barred, and simple furniture, had a rather bare look. Usually about the only adornment of a ranch house was a print or wax figure of the Virgin and infant Jesus, before which was set a vase filled with wild flowers. The chief care and expense of furnishing was lavished on the beds, which often had coverlets and pillowcases made of satin trimmed with costly lace. Bare floors were the rule even in the best houses, for carpets and even rugs were considered insanitary and troublesome, an idea to which we have gone back in modern times.

The better houses were designed with a view for the entertainment of guests; the principal room was a large hall for dancing, the universal amusement. It was no unusual thing for the owner to invite enough people to make a dancing party to remain several days, sleeping accommodations being found for them somehow, and they did very little sleeping anyway.

Life on the ranchos was of pastoral simplicity. Very early hours were kept, the *patron* and *patrona*, as the master and mistress were called, often rising at four or even three, while the birds were singing their matin song, for although the Californians were not laborious, they were not slothful. The day was opened by the recital of the *alba*, the prayer of the dawn, in which thanks were given for the safe passage of the night and a plea made for aid in all dangers that the day might bring forth. The whole household, including the Indian help, joined in the prayer. In some places the charming custom prevailed of singing a morning hymn from the open windows.

A horse was always kept saddled and bridled at the door for the *patron*, and after a light breakfast of a cup of chocolate and a *tortilla*, he was up and away to look after his flocks and herds and to see that his army of Indian retainers did their duty. It is said that one of these rancheros used to ride out with his sixteen sons, all over six feet in height.

The *patrona*, on her part, busied herself in setting the host of Indian girls at their various tasks—sweeping, sewing, cooking, and making lace and embroidery, in which they became expert under the tuition of the Spanish ladies.

With the setting of the sun all assembled for the evening meal, and after the long day spent mainly in the open air, everybody was abed by eight o'clock, except perhaps some young lover, who touched his guitar and raised his voice in song beneath his lady's window:

> "Fly not yet, 'tis just the hour
> When pleasure, like the midnight flower,
> That scorns the eye of vulgar light,
> Begins to bloom for sons of night,
> And maids who love the moon."

In the quiet domestic routine of ranch life there was no lack of entertainment; in fact, so much were amusements a part of the serious business of life, both on the haciendas and in the pueblos, that they have been left for consideration in a separate chapter.

It was a life almost primitive in its simplicity, in which ambition and material progress had little place, but all early American writers agree that California, during the period before foreign "invasion" had made its deteriorating influence felt, was the happiest community, the most free from care, in the whole world. Walter Colton tells us that:

"There are no people that I have ever been among who enjoy life so thoroughly as the Californians. Their happiness springs from a fount that has very little connection with their outward circumstances. There is hardly a shanty among them which does not contain more genuine gladness of heart, more true contentment, than you will meet with in the most princely palace."

Relieved of all care for the morrow, saved from exhausting toil by a numerous band of ready-made servants, rejoicing in abounding health, blessed with the love of a devoted wife and respectful children, situated in a rich and beautiful land where Nature poured out her bounty at his feet almost unasked, far from the turmoil of a wrangling world, the California ranchero led his simple pastoral life in his Eden undisturbed by the ambition that in other lands tortures men's souls.

At first thought it would seem that the missions should not be included as elements in the social life of the community, but in the earliest times, at least, conditions were such that the missionaries acted not only as religious arbiters, but also as hosts to foreign visitors and people of their own race who found it necessary to travel through the province. For many years the missions were the only inns, and in them travellers received an open-hearted hospitality, without money and without price. The friars were well fitted to play this part, for most of those of Spanish birth were highly educated men, able to converse with the most polished of their visitors on all intellectual subjects. The infrequent calls of such persons were their only social diversion, their only escape from the society of the barbarous natives, and one may well imagine how welcome was the sound of clattering hoofs on the camino real in the ears of the lonely monks! Even for the mails they had to wait for chance couriers until Governor Neve established a regular service. All early travelers speak in the most enthusiastic terms of their entertainment by the fathers at the various missions, where they had set before them not only the best the country afforded in the way of food for the body, but also enjoyed a "feast of reason and flow of soul." In the narrative of the French navigator, La Pérouse, we read of his visit at Carmel Mission:

"As we drew near the collection of grass-covered huts in the Carmel Valley, for they were little better, the mission bells rang out a joyous welcome. We were received like lords of a parish when they make their first appearance on their estates; the president of the missions, clothed in his cape, the holy water sprinkler in his hand, waited for us at the door of the church, which was illuminated the same as on their greatest festivals; he conducted us to the foot of the high altar, where the *Te Deum* was sung in thanksgiving for the happy outcome of the voyage. The fathers at the mission were as kind to us as the officers, and acquainted us with every detail of the management of the missions, the Indian manner of living, their arts and customs, in fact, all that might interest travellers."

The Russian von Langsdorff and the Englishman Vancouver both describe the most delightful visits with the priests at Santa Clara Mission. Captain Beechey, who came in 1826, also visited the same mission, where the visitors were surprised to see the bountiful repast served on silver dishes, with cups and spoons of the same metal. After doing full justice to this repast, they stretched themselves upon couches of bull hide, "as tough and impenetrable as the cuirass of their dragoon escort," and soon fell asleep, thanks to excessive weariness, and slept as soundly as *las pulgas* (the fleas) would let them. At San Juan Bautista jolly Padre Arroyo was so touched by the references of the visitors to having been in Seville, his native place, that he burst into a patriotic song at the table, and afterwards led them to their beds to the tune of *Malbrouk sa va t'en guerra* set to Spanish words. Harrison Rogers, American trapper, who came overland with Jedediah Smith in 1826, speaks of the friars as "gentlemen of the first class, both in manners and habits."

Many social affairs, such as weddings, etc., took place at the missions, and for them the padres laid out their best, but they themselves were bound by vows of poverty as required by the Franciscan Order, and lived in a state of such abstinence from all luxuries or even comfort as to astonish the visitors from abroad. The church was the principal building, and upon it was lavished the greater part of the wealth of the new community. The friars, who could own no personal property, purchased from their slender stipends pictures, images, and other ornaments for the house of God. Scarcely a penny was ever expended for any other purpose except for the simple clothing required for themselves or their converts and medicines for the sick. The result was a startling contrast between the splendor of the church and the humble, almost squalid dwellings of the priests and others.

As an illustration of the simple living of the priests, let us relate the story of the breach of the rule by Father Viader of Santa Clara which once scandalized his superiors in the church. The usual method of locomotion among the padres was by horse or burro back, when not afoot, but Father Viader, who was a very large man, found himself unable to get about by this means in his old age; so the Indians set to work and made him a special carriage. It was a unique contrivance, with a narrow body only wide enough for one person, mounted on a pair of very low wheels. The shafts were so long that the mule or horse was too far ahead to be managed by reins, so it was led by an Indian who rode ahead on another animal. The seat of the vehicle was well stuffed with lamb's wool, and the body was covered with brown cloth. Sometimes two vaqueros rode on each side with lassoes tied to the axle-tree, by which means they assisted the mule up steep places. Attended by two or three servants, and followed in the rear by a number of Indian alcaldes, the good father's procession was quite imposing, if somewhat comic. But when news of this unheard-of luxury reached the College of San Fernando, headquarters of the Franciscans in Mexico, the whole place was thrown into a flurry. Members of the order of mendicant friars riding in state like titled nabobs! The very thought of such a thing could not be endured, and orders were at once sent that all such wagons should be sold and their use at the missions discontinued. Poor old Father Viader was compelled once more to entrust his great bulk to his trusty mule, no doubt to the sorrow of the over-burdened animal.

Cheap watches bought from Boston ships caused another reprimand. Their use had to be given up, and the fathers had to depend upon the sun as before for the daily routine of meals, mass, and prayer. Their lives were indeed abstemious, bare of the commonest comforts. La Pérouse writes on this subject:

"At present the friars, more occupied with the interests of heaven than temporal welfare, have greatly neglected the introduction of the common arts; they are themselves so austere that they have no chimneys to their chambers, though winter is generally very severe there. Even the greatest authorities have never led a more edifying life."

Later there was a change, and Governor Micheltorena, who came in 1842, complained to the bishop that the clergy of California had abandoned the ways of the missionaries of old. "The early padres slept on the ground with an adobe for a pillow, and a hide for a blanket; while now the padres Real, Jimeno, Quijas, Mercado, Santillan, and others have luxurious beds adorned with curtains, and provided with good mattresses. Formerly they punished the padre who carried a silver watch, but today all the priests go with gold watches and chains." It seems in every era there are these wailers for the "good old times," and critics of changing customs.

In the matter of food they were well provided for; as the years passed their granaries overflowed with the grain reaped by their Indian farmers, and their herds increased to such an extent that it is said the Indians of the missions were better supplied with meat than most laborers in the thirteen states of the American Union.

In the days when the missions were the only taverns,

a servant was kept at the door day and night to take and unsaddle the horses of the guests who might arrive without notice. The table was soon spread and a meal set forth with the best the establishment could afford. But let not the reader paint a picture of luxury or even common comforts as we understand them in our day, for the missions were not overly supplied with such things. There were no stoves or fireplaces, and if the traveller arrived wet or cold he must needs dry or warm himself as best he could. There was no glass in the windows, and the floors were of earth or rough puncheons. The adobe walls were sometimes whitewashed, and were often damp. The scanty furniture consisted of strong unpainted chairs, table, and benches, made in the simplest designs by an ordinary carpenter. It was from these pieces, the product of necessity rather than of art, that the modern vogue for "mission furniture" had its rise. Tallow candles furnished the only light, but, as retiring hours were very early in those days, and the guest was usually very weary from a hard day's ride, the absence of good lights mattered little. The bed was but a well-dried cow-hide stretched in a corner a short distance from the floor, fastened to the wall on two sides and supported at the outer corner by a stout post fixed in the floor. Some of the coarse blankets woven by the Indians were spread over the hide, making it a fairly comfortable bed for a tired man, at least preferable to the hard ground by the roadside, especially on a rainy night. Pillows and sheets were entirely wanting, but if fleas and other pests permitted, a good night's rest could be enjoyed on this rudest of beds. The fathers themselves were utterly indifferent to physical comfort, and the Indians were not good housekeepers

There was little inducement to the traveller to linger long at the mission, for after the resources of conversation were exhausted there were few ways of passing the time.

If the weather was pleasant one could sit in the arched corridor across the front of the building and watch the throngs of Indian children, generally naked and dirty, playing in the patio, or the performance of ordinary household duties in public view by the women. All the laundry work, basket-making, and even much of the cooking was done in the open square. In the center an immense pot was kept boiling with the atole which made up the chief part of the food of the Indians. At meal times each came with his dish, often but a curved piece of bark, into which was poured his portion, about three pints. La Pérouse was interested in the native method of roasting the grain before it was ground into meal. "As the women have no vessels of pottery or metal for this operation, they perform it in large baskets made of bark, over a little lighted charcoal; they turn these vessels with so much rapidity and address that they effect the swelling and bursting of the grain without burning the basket, though it is made of very combustible material; and we can testify that the best roasted coffee does not nearly equal the exactness with which these women prepare their corn."

If the mission guest possessed the rather rare accomplishment of being able to read, he might spend an hour in the library, but he would find there only such books as the lives of the saints, sermons, or other religious and edifying books.

Of the life that went on in one of these community centers La Pérouse gives an excellent description. At sunrise the angelus summoned all to mass. After an hour at worship all took their breakfast of atole, made of barley which had first been roasted and ground, cooked without salt or other seasoning. Then men and women joined their respective bands and proceeded to their regular tasks for the day. Some went to turn up the earth with their rude ploughs made of forked limbs of trees shod with iron; others to the work-shops; everyone was employed in some useful occupation. The women had the care of housewifery and the roasting and grinding of the various grains, an interminable task when done with their hand mortars.

Between eleven and twelve the midday meal was taken. It consisted of atole again, but diversified this time with vegetables or sometimes mutton or beef. Milk was reserved for the sick or the aged, but as a matter of fact the repugnance of the Indians for this food was so great that they could seldom be induced to touch it. A rest period followed until two o'clock, when labor recommenced and lasted until five. During the heated hours of summer afternoons a mule laden with buckets full of sweetened vinegar and water—a real luxury—would be sent around the fields to regale the thirsty workers. After the day's work was finished the evening meal was served, once more of gruel. But let it not be thought that the diet of the neophytes was restricted to this monotonous round of gruel. They were permitted to raise chickens around their huts, to go hunting and fishing, and to gather wild fruits and nuts. The products of these excursions were always shared with the padres.

At sundown the angelus bell called the faithful to prayers; neophytes, workmen, missionaries repaired to the chapel or church, where the beads were told, the litany sung, and the evening blessings imparted. One hour after supper all girls and women whose husbands were absent were put under lock and key in the *monjerio*, or nunnery, from which they were not permitted to come out until after daylight. The girls were guarded during the day by matrons, sometimes elderly and trustworthy Indian women, sometimes wives of the soldiers. During this time they were taught to sew, cook, spin, weave, and to practice other housewifely arts.

Upon the whole the life was not hard; the tasks were not made too heavy for people who had been accustomed to a wild, free life, and who had not known the meaning of regular work. Yet the ceaseless round of religious and industrial duties sometimes became irksome to those who had never before known restraint, and they would run away to their wild life in the woods, from which remembrance of the regular meals at the mission often brought them back repentant.

The missionaries very sensibly permitted the Indians to retain such of their ancient usages as did not conflict with their new religion. In the evenings and on holidays they were permitted to engage in their native games and dances and other social diversions. So great was the security in which the fathers lived among these lately barbarous people that their doors were never even shut at night. La Pérouse says the Indians believed the missionaries held immediate communication with God, and for this reason they were held sacred.

A system of simple rewards was employed to encourage good behavior, usually consisting of small distributions of grain, which the native women made into small cakes, baked on hot coals. For great festivals, rations of beef were given out. Many ate it raw, especially the fat. "They skin the animals with the greatest address," says one writer, "and when they are fat they make, like the ravens, a croaking of pleasure, devouring at the same time the most delicate parts with their eyes."

As time went on the employments of the converts became still more diversified. They learned to be good farmers, herdsmen, blacksmiths, weavers, and builders. Most of the actual manual work on the massive piles, whose ruins are California's greatest historic treasure, was done by the natives themselves, directed by the padres or experts brought from Spain or Mexico. The missions became veritable hives of industry, in which the fathers instructed their charges, so lately won from savagery, in manual trades as well as in the doctrines of the church. Speaking of this phase of mission activity, Bolton says:

"Every mission was almost as much a school as a church. The chapel was the most conspicuous feature of any mission and the pride of the padre's heart. But the church was the smaller part of the mission plant, for every well-developed mission was a great industrial establishment at the center. It was not the up-to-date twentieth century educator who first devised the manual training school in America. Two or three hundred years before him the Franciscan and Jesuit missionary had made a successful beginning in this kind of instruction over two-thirds of the western hemisphere."

It has come to be recognized that the missionaries were wise in their judgment that the only way to civilize barbarous nations with hope of permanent results was by slow development on a natural basis, through pastoral, agricultural, and industrial stages. No other system has ever come so near accomplishing the reduction of barbarous races to a state approaching civilization as that of the padres of California. To quote Blackmar, "The result of the occupation of the province for the short period of sixty years by a handful of monks, laboring under many disadvantages, with little substantial aid from civil or military authorities, is little short of marvelous."

In the personal character of her first missionaries California was singularly fortunate. In the great process of civilizing the dark places of the world there have been few similar bodies of men who were their equals in moral purity, mental vigor, and single-hearted devotion to the cause which they espoused. Judge Dwinelle, who, as one of the earliest of the American arrivals, had excellent opportunities to form a reliable opinion on the subject, writes:

"It was something, surely, that over thirty thousand wild, barbarous, and naked Indians had been brought in from their savage haunts, persuaded to wear clothes, accustomed to a regular life, inured to such light labor as they could endure, taught to read and write, instructed in music, accustomed to the service of the church, partaking of its sacraments and indoctrinated in the Christian religion; and that this system had become self-sustaining under the mildest and gentlest of tutelage; for the Franciscan monks, many of whom were highly cultivated men, who had been soldiers, engineers, artists, lawyers, and physicians before they became friars, always treated the neophyte Indians with the most paternal kindness, and did not scorn to labor with them in the field, in the brick-yard, the forge, and the mill. . . When we view the vast construction of the mission buildings, including the churches, the refectories, the workshops, the granaries, the materials for which were sometimes brought for many miles on the shoulders of the Indians, we cannot deny that the Franciscan missionary monks had the wisdom, sagacity, and patience to bring their neophyte pupils far forward on the road from barbarism to civilization, and that these Indians were not destitute of capacity."

For the enrichment of her history by their half century of devotion California owes the missionaries an incalculable debt. It is largely to the ruins of the old missions that she owes that pensive air of romance which sets her apart from every other state in the Union, and they have been the inspiration of some of our finest literature.

Chapter IX

CHAPTER IX

Education

EDUCATION, in the modern sense of the word, hardly existed among the Californians. The reasons generally advanced for this state of affairs are the neglect of the governments of both Spain and Mexico to supply funds for the support of schools, and the general indifference of the people themselves to such matters. Vallejo and Alvarado add to these causes the opposition of the friars, who held that education, except in the industrial trades, was bad, not only for the Indians, but also for the less mentally developed of the whites. A reason for the lack of interest among the people was the absence of any practical motive for study in a country where the learned professions were not in demand. Since there were no openings for doctors, lawyers, professors, teachers, engineers, etc., why spend long years with one's nose in a book in a land where all nature invited to an outdoor life? What need had a cattle raiser for a knowledge of the classics or logarithms? "Of what avail was learning in this lotus land? There was in it neither health, wealth, nor happiness, and besides it was a great waste of labor." Under the circumstances there could be but one motive—a personal taste for exercise of the mental faculties—and, as we shall see, this motive operated in the case of a small handful of intellectuals. For the rest, they blew their pipes like Pan and danced away the merry hours in the flowery meads of California.

Not even for social purposes was book education really needed, for such was the native talent of the Californians in the use of language, and such their grace of manner that persons who could not read or write had an air of culture. They came of a race noted for dignified courtesy of manners, and had about them a sort of old-world polish which made many an American visitor conscious of his own crudeness. Josiah Royce writes of them in this wise in relation to education:

"The Californians had of course little opportunity for cultivation, and they had generally few intellectual ambitions. But, like the southern peoples of European blood in general, they had a great deal of natural quickness of wit, and in their written works often expressed themselves with ease and force. Their women were fascinating conversers, even when not at all educated. Their more noteworthy men, such as Alvarado, Vallejo, Bandini, and others, were often persons of very marked intelligence, and even of considerable reading. The curiously unequal aesthetic sense of the people always puzzled the American observer. They spoke and gestured with what seemed to our dull eyes wonderful grace. They appeared to be born musicians, and, quite without training, they sang finely and played their guitars skillfully and spiritedly. They dressed with true southern taste. All their movements, on foot, or on horseback, were easy and picturesque; and their keen perception of beauty was in some ways marvelous."

Bayard Taylor, speaking of the people of Monterey, says: "In spite of the lack of cultivation such as only the priests were competent to give, the native population possesses a natural refinement of manner that would grace the most polished society."

The almost universal aptitude for music, inherent in the Latin race, went a long way in making up for the want of education in other directions. In every house the sound of the guitar and of the voice might be heard at almost any hour of the day or night. Many of the young men played the violin with skill and taste, although none had any scientific or technical instruction, and they were not ashamed to use this means publicly to win the hearts of coveted fair ones. The serenade was an institution of the country which lasted until long after American occupation. Nearly every evening some love-lorn swain raised his plaint beneath his lady's window, no doubt often to the disgust of elderly neighbors whose courting days were over.

If the boys received little education, the girls fared even worse, for if they were able to dance gracefully, to play the guitar and sing with taste, to attend devoutly to their religious duties, to sew and embroider, and to perform other household tasks, they were thought not to need any further instruction. Bancroft writes of female instruction as it was practiced in that early day as follows:

"In the towns the daughters of some of the prominent families assembled at the house of the mother of one of them, who taught them to read and write, in the same way that the boys were taught, although not to the same extent. They also learned to weave in hand-looms the gaudy rugs which, spread upon the floor of the church, served them as seats. Or seated on the floor of the school-room, or of the inner corridor of the house, each child with her hoop-like embroidery frame upon her knees, they slowly wrought with the needle in cotton stuff not over fine, the simple embroidery intended for the embellishment of valances and the like, which ultimately were to form part, frequently all, of the maker's dower. The simple cookery known to Californians and the care of children each girl learned at home."

Manuel Torres, who came from Peru in 1843, complained of the lack of learning among the women, what he politely called their "inexpertness," which he ascribed to the fact that they were allowed to read only religious books, when they could read at all, and were kept secluded from association with persons from the outside world. One writer remarks that, "although hospitable, the Californians seldom allowed strangers in their private family rooms. In the houses of the wealthy there were rooms for strangers, but they were not allowed to enter into familiar conversation with the young women." Yet their natural vivacity made them charming social companions.

It is said that the education of the children in many cases consisted of little more than learning to recite their prayers at their mother's knee. That child was fortunate indeed whose parents were able and willing to instruct him to the extent of reading in a halting way and writing a badly spelled and expressed letter. "Occasionally some woman," says Bancroft, "fortunate among her sisters, with a mother's love imparted to her little ones her own scant store of knowledge, while at times the *amiga*, as she was significantly called, performed the same duty toward a neighbor's child, or taught to the ambitious soldier the simple accomplishments necessary to his promotion." José María Amador says that in his childhood—he was born in 1794—there were no schools; and what little instruction he, as well as his brothers, acquired he owed to his mother, María Ramona Noriega, who also instructed the children of some of their neighbors. She, moreover, taught a few soldiers, who were desirous of becoming corporals, to read and write.

As for the teachers, in such schools as were maintained at spasmodic intervals, their qualifications seldom extended beyond reading, writing, and a little figuring, and even such as they were hard to get. More often than not they were old, invalided sergeants, who, by some strange chance, had picked up a smattering of these branches of learning, and were paid an infinitesimal sum for imparting it to the youngsters by dint of much flogging and scolding. In 1834, with the Hijar colonists, a better class of teachers came, and some of the schools were fortunate enough to secure their services. The name of Ignacio Coronel is honorably remembered among these to this day. Prudencia Higuera relates that the Spanish gentleman who taught the school near where the town of San Pablo now stands "told us many things for which we remember him with respect; but when he said the earth was round we all laughed aloud, for which we were much ashamed."

Some of the governors made earnest efforts to remedy this backward condition and tried to introduce education into benighted California. Governor Borica, an intelligent and conscientious ruler, did what he could, but conditions were against him. First, he was under the necessity of creating funds for the schools, and was confronted by the want of qualified teachers. In December, 1794, he inquired of the comandantes of the presidios and the *comisionados* of the pueblos whether in their respective jurisdictions there were any persons who knew how to read and write, and were otherwise fitted to become instructors of youth.

Notwithstanding the overwhelming difficulties in his path and the wall of indifference on the part of the people which faced him, Borica did succeed in establishing a system of public schools, which, crude as it was, may fairly be regarded as the forerunner of the present magnificent public institutions of learning in the state. Some time in

1794, Manuel de Vargas, a retired sergeant, opened in the public granary of San José the first primary school in California. The only schoolrooms available were these empty granaries or similar places; books and utensils were almost wholly lacking.

All children over seven and under ten were required to attend, with time off allowed for aiding their parents in the work of the household and farm. After a time it was noticed that the attendance was falling off rapidly, and neither arguments nor threats on the part of the governor made any improvement; the parents said they needed the assistance of the children in supporting the family, and that in the sort of lives they led no book knowledge was necessary, anyway. Why learn to read in a country where there were no books upon which to exercise the accomplishment? Why learn to write when they never received or wrote letters, and could always get the public clerk to make out any necessary documents? It cannot be denied that there was some logic in their arguments.

A blight thereupon fell on education in California, and nothing much was done to lift it during the rule of Arrillaga, a kindly but apathetic man. But when Sola arrived he had great ideas about the elevation of California, and at once set about the revival of the schools. Among other things which he did to arouse the interest of the young, who had never had anything to read but the catechism, was to present to some of the more advanced pupils at the capital a copy of *Don Quixote*, promising more when this should have been carefully perused, thus opening to them a realm of delight of which they had never heard. By great efforts he caused the reopening of the schools at various places in the province, and out of his own means founded at Monterey a school for boys and one for girls. Punishment was ordered for such short-sighted parents as refused to send their children to school. In a letter to

Franz Geritz '21

Comandante Argüello at San Francisco, the governor writes: "Do not accept any excuse from parents who refuse to send their children to school; for, if the young are not educated, the country, in place of making progress, will necessarily be forced to retrograde, a thing which it is the duty of the authorities to prevent at all costs."

Sola, the last of the Spanish governors, was sincere in his desire to uplift the country which had been placed in his care, and even planned a system of real education for the Indians; but when he found himself opposed by the friars and the people themselves, and crippled by the entire lack of funds in the public treasury and utter indifference on the part of the central government, even such enthusiasm as his cooled, and he abandoned the hopeless struggle. Nevertheless, it was during his time that the schools were at their best. Just how they rated as compared with modern institutions of learning may be seen from General Vallejo's feeling description of the one which he attended in his youth:

"The room itself was long, narrow, badly lighted; with walls unadorned save by a huge green cross or the picture of some saint, generally the virgin of Guadalupe, suspended over the master's head, or to one side of his table; dirty everywhere, and in places dilapidated. Around its walls were ranged roughly made benches. At one end there was a rude platform, sometimes with a railing, but more frequently without, on which was placed a table covered with a dingy black cloth. Behind this table sat the teacher, generally a poor, broken-down old soldier with a sour countenance, and wearing fantastic clothing, only remarkable for being always torn and greasy. The first thing the pupil did on arriving was to advance and kneel before the image of the saint and repeat the *Bendito* aloud, then to go trembling to the *maestro* and offer his hand, with a stammering *buenos dias*, in answer to which salutation he generally received only a surly growl. Lessons were then assigned to the children, which they studied at the tops of their voices, until the veins on their necks stood out."

What most attracted the frightened eyes of the children was the *disciplina*, a sort of cat-o'-nine-tails made of hempen twine with iron points, which generally lay in plain sight on the corner of the teacher's desk, as constant visible warning. This instrument of torture was not allowed to grow rusty from disuse, for such terrible crimes as dropping a blot of ink on a copy lesson, laughing loudly or running in the street on the way to school, or failing to recite the catechism correctly, were enough to cause each little guilty wretch to be stripped of his poor shirt, often his only garment, stretched face downward on a bench, and lashed with a dozen blows on his bare back.

The only reading book was a catechism written by one Father Ripalda, a writer whose very name became an object of consuming hatred to all the pupils as long as they lived. "The catechism of Father Ripalda!" writes Vallejo. "Who among the surviving elders of the native Californians is not acquainted with Father Ripalda? Who among them possessed of a glimmering of reason, and the least desire for liberty of conscience, does not detest that monstrous code of fanaticism?"

And did the blessed Saturday give the little sufferers any relief? Not at all, for this was the day of the worst torture, when the children would rather have been ill in bed with the cholera than go to school, for it was then that they had to repeat all of Ripalda they had learned during the week. Any slight failure was regarded as a heinous crime, to be severely punished by the *disciplina*.

So great was the dread of the children of the school that when it was time to start in the morning, after prolonging the frugal breakfast as long as possible, pale and tearful, they begged their parents to be let off. This their tender-hearted mothers would gladly have done, but their fathers stood by the teacher, and, saying, "As I was ground, so be thou ground," took away all hope. With sad, drooping faces and lagging steps they went toward the hated school, which they themselves had to keep clean, making their own brooms of twigs from the woods, tied with twine to sticks. If the sweeping was not well done, another bout with the cat-o'-nine-tails awaited them. Any complaint made against the teacher received the same punishment.

After reading these descriptions one is no longer surprised to hear that education was not very popular in early California. Vallejo winds up his harrowing tale with the following bitter indictment of the schools of his boyhood days:

"The *escuela antigua* (old school) was a heaping up of horrors, a torture for childhood, a punishment for innocence. In it the souls of a whole generation were inoculated with the virus of a deadly disease. . . There opened, black and frightful, the tomb of thought, and the school, which should be the gilded vestibule carpeted with roses, by which the human family enters the sanctuary of civilization, in the time of the viceroys and the earlier governors of California was but the gloomy and harmful passage which swallowed slaves for the future use of monarchy. In my mind there rise up such painful emotions, such bitter remembrances of the sad consequences due to the education which our masters gave us, that the mere recollection is absolutely painful. Recalling to mind these things is like the dream of the escaped victim who sees arising from the depths the spectre of his hated executioner. The old school should have been called the school of servilism, since it was the torture chamber wherein was done to death the sentiment of dignity which perished amid a thousand torments, physical and moral, encompassing the martyrdom of the body, and extinguishing the light of reason in the new-born man."

Nevertheless, in judging the California schools of that day, it must not be forgotten that it was an era all over the world when the belief was firm in the old adage about sparing the rod and spoiling the child. Nor is it true that the spirit of the children was entirely broken by this treatment, for tales are told of rebellions against the hated master equal to any in our own lawless day. On one occasion the pupils, in their haste to get down to the beach and see an incoming ship, the *Princesa*, neglected to close the *gatera*, or hole cut in the door for the passage of the cat. In their absence a number of hens took advantage of the forgotten opening, came in and caused dire destruction, upsetting ink bottles over the neat new copies. Great was the terror of the guilty children when the master entered and took in the situation at a glance. With an angry growl he seized the *disciplina*, ordering two of the larger boys to hold the first victim. To his stupefaction, they flatly refused, and even proposed to the others to apply a dose of his own medicine to the preceptor, who wisely took to his heels. This desperate affair was reported to the commissioner, who, perhaps because some memory of his own school days came up before him, pardoned the offenders on the ground that their excessive joy at the arrival of the *Princesa* so affected their minds for the moment as to render them irresponsible agents. This little story indicates that the modern "alibi" of temporary insanity was not altogether unknown to our predecessors.

The friars took no part in public instruction, all the more surprising when one considers that they were all men of good education, some of them highly cultured. Yet they did teach, privately, and as though for their own pleasure, their favorites among their military guards, or the few white children who lived at the missions. A story is told of one friar who became so interested in his soldier pupil that he arose at all hours of the night to instruct him while on sentry duty, and with the ramrod of the man's musket traced in the ashes of the guard-house hearth the letters of the alphabet. It reminds one of the stories of Lincoln's early life, doing his sums on a shovel by the light of the fireplace, except that the poor California soldier never came to fame.

Governor Echeandía came to California in 1825 with great ideas for reform in educational matters. He held that learning was the corner-stone of a people's wealth, and its encouragement the chief duty and greatest glory of a governor. He indulged in dreams of education for rich and poor, Indians and *gente de razon* alike, and made the most earnest efforts to bring about the realization of his dreams. It was not long, however, before he found himself against the same stone wall of opposition by the friars and indifference of the people. When the authorities complained that it was useless to hire teachers when not a single child attended school, the governor called upon the comandantes at the presidios to compel parents to send their children. This measure had some effect, and the alcalde at Monterey voluntarily acted as master of a school of which the sole equipment consisted of a covered table, one arithmetic, and four primers.

Echeandía reported to his government that the schools had been paralyzed by the lack of funds and the impossibility of obtaining suitable teachers. He therefore called on the supreme government for aid. But the interest of local authorities was short-lived; no money came to the treasury; the friars continued to oppose general education; and, worst of all, the people themselves cared as little as ever about it. So Echeandía, like his predecessors, abandoned the struggle, and the cause of education again declined.

It is useless to continue the relation of how Figueroa, Alvarado, Micheltorena, Pico, one and all went through the same experience. All earnestly strove to bring the light of knowledge to their beloved California, but one and all were defeated in turn by the same obstacles—want of funds, lack of competent teachers, indifference on the part of parents—which made their efforts fruitless.

Naturally, there was a great scarcity of books in California. During the early years of the missions they had been furnished with certain approved religious and historical works; but fear of the great wave of "free thought" which was then sweeping all over the world, especially in France, caused the Inquisition to prohibit the introduction into California of any but what were regarded as "safe" books. Notwithstanding that the friars kept close watch on the baggage of foreigners who visited the country, a few were smuggled in by the Boston skippers and supercargoes. A number of books received by one of the Carrillos from the American bark *Volunteer* were burned by the missionaries, who obtained permission after much argument from Echeandía. The missions, at the time of their secularization, had about three thousand volumes, and the Hijar colonists brought with them a few. In 1846 there were several libraries in California besides those at the missions: M. G. Vallejo's at Sonoma; Hartnell's, which had cost him a good sum and from which he generously lent to his friends; Francisco Pacheco's collection of bound periodicals and books on Mexican history; Captain de la Guerra's scientific and religious works; the fine library of Dr. John Marsh, from which he lent books to others. These books would make a valuable and interesting addition to Californiana if they could be found and collected, but, according to Bancroft, they have been almost hopelessly scattered. Vallejo's were burned; Hartnell's were divided among his descendants; Pacheco's went into the possession of his brother-in-law, Mariano Malarin, of Santa Clara; De la Guerra's were probably scattered among his sons and their descendants. The recovery of these books, some of which were no doubt old and quaint, would be a very suitable task for one of the historical societies of the state.

It was not until the members of one native born generation grew up in California and had children of their own that the most ambitious, when they could afford it, sent their sons abroad to be educated. The sons of Hartnell, Pacheco, Spence, and others received their training in the Sandwich Islands, as they were then still known. Señor Suñol sent his to Paris, while Vallejo's eldest son went to Valparaiso and the others to the United States. But when Vallejo and Alvarado were young themselves the great difficulty about sending them out of the country for their schooling was the shortage of ready cash for the expenses, for there was only about $25,000 in actual money in all California. As we have seen, business went on by barter, hides and tallow being the principal medium of exchange with the trading ships for manufactured articles.

Such being the very backward state of education at that time, how can we explain the fact that both Vallejo and Alvarado, with some others, exhibit in their writings some familiarity with the classics, as well as other evidences of culture? This was due to the presence in the country of a certain number of well-educated persons from various parts of the world—the Spanish priests, some of whom were doctors of philosophy; military officers, and English and American college graduates. Notable among these latter were Dr. John Marsh, who had a good library and allowed free use of it to the seekers after learning, and William Hartnell, who was an accomplished scholar and linguist, speaking French, Spanish, German, Italian, Hebrew, Russian, Greek, and Latin. Hartnell generously passed on his knowledge to the sons of his friends, and it was to him that more than one young Californian owed a liberal education.

As so often happens in such cases, the greater the difficulty in acquiring an education the greater was the thirst for it among the few who had such inclinations. Among this small coterie were three youths: Mariano Guadalupe Vallejo, afterwards the most distinguished of all the Californians; Juan Bautista Alvarado, destined at a later date to become the first native born governor of the province, and José Castro, prominent actor in all the political upheavals which subsequently occurred. These three, Vallejo and Alvarado being uncle and nephew, were inseparable friends; with them it was the same as with the famous three musketeers of Dumas—"all for one and one for all." And they longed for books far more than for gold.

All of the above leads us naturally to what happened in San Francisco on a certain dark night in 1831, a story which may be aptly called

The Bootlegging of the Books

Out on the still waters of the bay a frigate, the *Leonor*, just up from South America, Captain Fitch, and supercargo and owner Virmond, swung gently at anchor. There were no signs of life aboard the vessel; it was plain that the crew were all asleep. Presently a small boat might have been seen creeping cautiously out from the shore. As it reached the ship's side, a slender, agile figure, clothed in governmental uniform, leaped lightly to the deck. It was none other than Lieutenant Mariano G. Vallejo, one of the hungerers after learning mentioned above. Having heard that a spiteful or fanatical sailor from the ship had come ashore and informed the ecclesiastical authorities that the *Leonor* had aboard some boxes of "bad books," and that the friars were about to take steps to confiscate them, he was hastening out to warn the captain and owner of the vessel of their danger. But let us hear the story in Vallejo's own words:

"I did not lose a moment, but, although it was now an advanced hour of the night, ordered my boat made ready and went aboard the ship, where Virmond and Fitch, unaware of the peril that threatened them, were sleeping soundly. Having sent a sailor, who was on watch, to awaken them, I went down to their cabin, and there, in the bosom of confidence, I told them of the rumor that was running around on shore, and offered to save them. I can scarcely describe their joy, which took the place of the fright which seized them when I informed them that the missionaries knew of the existence of the prohibited books on board the *Leonor*, when I offered to buy the contraband from them. They even offered to give them to me, but I did not accept this offer, and in exchange for four hundred beef hides and ten kegs of tallow I became the owner of the best library that up to that time had existed in California. After the sale had been made, Captain Fitch selected six of his most trustworthy sailors, ordered the boxes of books loaded on the large launch, and this same night all were unloaded at a designated spot on the shore."

By five o'clock in the morning the treasure was safe in Vallejo's house, and he remarks, "I can say in all sincerity that at that epoch I would not have exchanged it for the presidency of the republic." As he says, he and his friends had hungered to learn what was being thought and written by men of knowledge and intelligence in the Old World. They had made every effort and sacrifice to that end, but all their plans had been thwarted by the vigilance of the missionaries, who "kept guard over all the ports and bays of California, like Saint Peter at the gates of heaven, to prevent the entrance of books of a liberal tendency." And their troubles were not yet over!

With a heart swelling with pride and joy, the young man sent a messenger post haste to Monterey to inform the other two of the triumvirate that the newly acquired library was at their disposal. Castro, as soon as he heard the joyful news, saddled his horse and started off to San Francisco to inspect what he called "our bonanza," for what belonged to one of the three belonged to all. After examining the lot, he selected a few to carry back to Monterey to read, and by so doing brought down heavy trouble upon himself and his friends. It happened, not very strangely, that at this time he had a *querida* (sweetheart). This young lady, like most of the women of her day and place, was devoutly religious, and went often to confession, where she thought it her duty to report not only her own sins but those of her lover. So she told the priest that the young man was spending an unconscionable time with his nose in some very suspicious looking books. The priest, good old Father Esténega, hastened to do his duty in his turn by reporting the whole nefarious affair to his superior, Father Durán, prelate of the missions, who at once issued an order of excommunication against the three young men, for it was soon discovered that all were concerned in it. Let it not be thought that the penalty was a light one. All persons were ordered to cease communication of any kind with the offenders. The women of their acquaintance all fled from them, which, to young fellows of their natural gallantry, was in itself a hard penance. Their own mothers and sisters were in despair, and spent most of their time on their knees praying for pardon for the three desperate sinners.

Meanwhile, the three went right on with their reading,

although in secret, and there is no telling how much longer this state of affairs might have continued had it not been for a plan of escape from their predicament evolved by Alvarado, who was already beginning to show that astuteness which later made him the leading politician in California. While in Los Angeles about that time, he was entrusted with a large sum of money by some merchants to be delivered to Father Durán for the use of the church. When he stood face to face with the reverend father, the audacious young fellow said, after the usual courteous salutation, "Father, I have a large sum of money here in my bag for your mission, but, since I am excommunicated and every one who holds any dealings with me will suffer the same punishment, I cannot deliver it to you. So I will be going." With that he took a few steps toward the door. Padre Durán, who was himself a broad-minded man, and not destitute of a sense of humor, saw the situation. The church needed the money, Alvarado had the whip-hand; so, with a quizzical smile, he called the young man back, and said:

"Listen, Juanito; thou hast misunderstood what Padre Sarría said. What thou sayest applies only to persons under excommunication major, and you young men are only under the minor. I have power to annul the sentence, and even more. From this time thou and thy companions are absolved, and I give you permission to read the prohibited books, even Voltaire, Telemachus, Rousseau, etc., and even the Protestant Bible, with the sole condition that they shall not be placed in the hands of irresponsible or non-intelligent people."

All was now good feeling between the two; the father ordered refreshments brought in to celebrate the peace, and their friendship was cemented anew in a bottle of good wine and a plate of savory tamales, of which Alvarado records that they left not a drop nor a crumb. The good news of the lifting of the excommunication was received with the utmost joy in Monterey, where it was celebrated with dances and fireworks. When Vallejo heard it in San Francisco he caused the bells at Mission Dolores to be rung. We find him writing to his betrothed at San Diego: "It is now permitted to me to improve my education without incurring the danger of being stigmatized as an excommunicated heretic." Alvarado says: "Notwithstanding that Father Esténega caused me all this trouble, I never stopped loving him, and realized that he was only doing his duty to his superiors in what he believed to be our wrong-doing." He remarks that Father Durán seemed to enjoy the little tilt with him, and that from that time on both the friars assisted the three young men in all their undertakings.

In his *Historia de California* Alvarado writes in heartfelt gratitude and generous appreciation of the change for the better in educational matters after American occupation:

"In my youth an invalided soldier, sometimes ignorant, was the one who taught the children to read and write; today, the best and most accomplished professors in the known world fill the chairs in our schools, colleges, and universities; and youth has, without the need of being a burden upon parents, the privilege of learning all the known sciences. I am of the opinion that the improvements introduced by the North Americans in the branch of public instruction ought in themselves alone to be sufficient for the Californians to celebrate with enthusiasm the anniversary of the day on which Mexican rule was abolished forever in this state."

When M. G. Vallejo became a man of means, one of his first acts was to send abroad for a library of select books, many of which were on classical subjects. His studious tastes are reflected in the Christian names of his children. He was reading the works of Plato when one of his sons was born, so he called him by the Spanish equivalent of the name of the great Greek philosopher, Platón. Another son came along when the father was deep in Plutarch, so he was named Plutarco. Andrónico came on the scene while his father was engrossed in the drama *Titus Andronicus*, by the immortal William Shakespeare. He was reading the life of Napoleon when his son Napoleon arrived, and to make sure that all would know it was the great Corsican and not his lesser descendant whom he had chosen, he called the boy Napoleon Primero (Napoleon First). And so on down the line. In this way Vallejo secured very illustrious names for his family. He, too, speaks generously of the change for the better in matters educational after the American Conquest. Here follows what he has to say about it:

"The inhabitants of California have nothing to complain of in the change of government, for, even though the rich saw themselves robbed of thousands of horses and cattle, the condition of the poor has been improved. Formerly an ordinary education was obtained with great difficulty, while today it would be hard to find any place where educated people do not abound. How splendid it would have been if the superior culture which the North Americans brought to California had not perverted our patriarchal customs, and relaxed the morality of youth; for, much as it pains us, we cannot deny that our descendants have relegated to forgetfulness a great part of the wholesome maxims that were taught to us. This relaxation of the principles of moral sanity must be attributed to the association which they have had with unscrupulous people who emigrated in such numbers to California in the first epoch of the discovery of the rich gold placers which caused such joyful surprise to the ends of the universe."

To appreciate fully the magnanimity of this man's character, and his intense regard for education, one must recall that he himself was one of the rich who lost heavily by the coming of the Americans, besides having suffered the humiliation of a wholly unjust imprisonment. He speaks truly when he says: "The old Californians had generous souls, and were little addicted to vengeance."

Chapter X

CHAPTER X

Health and Medicine

HEALTH AND MEDICINE; the first-named abounded in early California, and as a natural corollary there was little need of the second. But even in this Eden there was occasional illness, and almost no medical means for its alleviation except at the capital and in its near neighborhood. For the exceptional health of the Californians there were some excellent reasons. A highly favorable climate, where the human body is not called upon to endure extremes of heat or cold, had much to do with it. When Governor Borica came to take possession of his office in 1794, he wrote to a friend in Mexico:

"To live long and without care come to Monterey. This is a great country; climate healthful, between cold and temperate; good bread, excellent meat, tolerable fish, and *buen humor*, which is worth all the rest; plenty to eat; but the most astounding is the general fecundity, both of rationals and irrationals [Indians and whites]. The climate is so good that all are getting to look like Englishmen. This is the most peaceful and quiet country in the world; one lives better here than in the most cultured court of Europe."

The conditions of the life led by the people at that time

were also a great factor for good health. Cattle raising and farming, which were their chief occupations, took them into the outdoors more than usual, and the doors of their houses were never closed. Walter Colton ascribed their almost complete freedom in the earliest days from tuberculosis to this life in the open. He was so impressed by this fact that he said if he had his way he would drive every young person in the United States out into the open air, to live like the Californians. "They were probably as healthy and athletic," says Bancroft, "as any people in the world. These characteristics were theirs by inheritance, for in the instructions of the viceroy to Captain Rivera it was ordered that the head of each family desiring to emigrate to California should be a hale country laborer, without blemish, physical or moral. Recruits for the presidios, selected with even greater care, were to be of not less than eighteen nor more than thirty years of age, at least two *varas* (five and one-half feet) in height, and of healthy color and good presence, without marks of any kind on body or face." It is true that later and less wise viceroys attempted to turn California into a penal settlement, but this practice met with such a fierce resistance from the people that it had to be abandoned.

The habits of the people in those early days were conducive to good health. Their food was simple, but nourishing. They knew nothing about the famous American "pie," but ate beef for breakfast, dinner and supper, with plenty of fat and vegetables. On this plain diet, with constant horseback exercise, the people kept robust, agile, fresh-colored, and lived to a good old age. Certainly their example holds little comfort for the vegetarian faddists of our day. They often retained all their teeth in perfect condition to the end, while a grey head was seldom seen and a bald one almost never. The excessive use of liquor was not usual among them, and, although wine was made and used in the country, the table drink was generally water, even coffee and tea being reserved for special occasions. Richard Henry Dana says, "I do not remember having seen one of them intoxicated," and William Heath Davis makes the assertion that "the people were sober, and did not drink to excess; it was a rare occurrence to see an intoxicated person among the early Californians, but they deteriorated after the coming of the Americans."

All of these factors, added to the fact that the Californians kept their white blood purer than did the Mexicans or South American Spaniards, had a very decided effect upon the personal appearance of the people. Physically they were vastly superior to the people of the other Mexican states, being tall, muscular, and well-featured, often with red and white complexions. "Many of the women," says Bancroft, "were as fair as those of New York and had rosy cheeks, contrasting with their jet-black hair, eyebrows, and eyelashes. Their beauty was by no means of an inferior order. Both the men and women had small feet. Particularly was the *hijo del pais* well-formed, graceful in his movements and athletic. Spending his life in manly pursuits, roaming his native hills, breathing the pure air of the Pacific, the horse his companion, the lasso his weapon, he carried about him and into all life's commonplaces the chivalrous bearing of the cavaliers of old Spain . . . Vischer saw in San Diego and Santa Barbara the cradles of California society, the classic type, Greek or Roman, running through whole families, with a frequent occurrence of the oriental and Gothic."

Bayard Taylor, writing in 1846, says:

"The Californians, as a race, are greatly superior to the Mexicans. They have larger frames, stronger muscles, and a fresh ruddy complexion, entirely different from the sallow skins of the *tierra caliente*, or the swarthy features of those Bedouins of the west, the Sonorians. The families of pure Castilian blood resemble in features and build the descendants of the Valencians in Chile and Mexico, whose original physical superiority over the natives of other provinces of Spain has not been obliterated by two hundred years of transplanting." William Heath Davis says: "I distinctly remember the Californians and how they impressed me when I first saw them, as a boy in 1831 and 1833—a race of men of large stature and of fine, handsome appearance."

The fecundity of the race was remarkable, families of twelve, twenty, or even more being not uncommon. The even dozen may be said to have been the regular-sized family, and in 1828 the ratio of births to deaths was three to one. "A native was pointed out to me," says Taylor, "as the father of thirty-six children, twenty of whom were the product of his first marriage, and sixteen of his last. Another, who had been married twelve years, already counted as many heirs." José María Martín Ortega was the oldest of twenty-one children and himself the father of twenty-one, while one of his sisters had twenty-two. The wife of J. A. Castro had twenty-six children, and Mrs. Hartnell had twenty-five. During the journey of the Hijar colonists to San Juan Bautista, one of the carts containing women and children was at a certain point upset; when righted, it was found that two more colonists had been added to the number, apparently as strong as any of them. In 1848 there were born in Sonoma, then a hamlet consisting of some forty families, no less than nine pairs of twins and one set of triplets. This productiveness was by everyone attributed to the climate, or to the virtues of some particular spring. In San Francisco there was a spring called Polin which was said to have the quality of bringing offspring to the childless. When Mrs. Benjamin Hayes, who was an invalid, came to Los Angeles in 1850, the native women expressed surprise that she had no children. "But never mind," they said in their kind-hearted efforts to comfort her, "*California es muy fertil!*" And so the good woman soon found it to be. The above examples, quoted from Bancroft, are but a few of the stories that might be told to prove that California was as prolific in human as in plant life.

"They were moreover a long-lived people. Eighty or ninety was common, and many reached the age of one hundred or over. In 1858 Guadalupe Romero died at the age of one hundred and fifteen; Crisóstomo Galindo was living in 1875 at the age of one hundred and three; María Marcelina Domínguez, on whose land the famous grapevine of Santa Barbara grew, died in 1865, aged one hundred and seven. Eulalia Pérez, who died in 1878, at the time of dictating her recollections in December, 1877, laid claim to one hundred and thirty-nine years, but did not present any proofs; careful study of the evidence would seem to indicate that she was born not before 1760, but even that would make her 118 years old at the time of her death." One of the factors in this length of years was undoubtedly the extreme quiet and non-exciting nature of the life led by the Californians.

As Bancroft says, "Like Kentucky, Missouri, and all virgin lands where there are present no counteracting causes, California bred a fine race," and, looking back upon the start which they had, it seems probable that if they had been left to continue as they had begun, far from the deteriorating influences of other peoples, favored by an extraordinarily benign climate, freed from exhausting labor in securing sustenance, living a life of pastoral simplicity, unspoiled by destructive habits, they would have developed a distinct race, peculiar to California, notable for its physical perfection and its gaiety of spirit.

But even here bodily ailments sometimes came to trouble the inhabitants, and the very beginning of its history as a white settlement was marked by a desperate struggle with that devastating scourge, the scurvy. Altogether ninety soldiers, sailors, and mechanics belonging to the Portolá expedition of 1769 died of that dread disease, at sea on the way up and after arrival at San Diego, leaving only one-third alive of the original colony intended for Monterey. The hero of this frightful affair was the surgeon who accompanied the party, Pedro Prat, a native of Barcelona in Spain and a graduate in medicine from the university of that city. To quote Dr. George D. Lyman's excellent monograph on the subject of *The Beginnings of California's Medical History*: "And so the medical history of California goes back to the cradle of the new Spanish province; the sword, the cross, and the scalpel proceeding hand in hand, and had it not been for the presence of Pedro Prat, it is probable that the projected province would have miscarried and never withstood the travail of its birth."

A tent hospital, the first in California, was constructed ashore, and to it the sick and dying were removed from the ships. Then followed a harrowing time, when the physician, assisted by the padres and such of the men who could stand up, did what they could, in view of the lack of any real knowledge of the cause and cure of the disease at the time, for the unfortunate sufferers. One of their hardest tasks was to drive off the marauding Indians, who tried to steal the very sheets from under the sick and yet were shrewd enough to refuse offers of the white man's food, to which they very wisely ascribed the horrible affliction which they saw before them. The terrible experiences at this place made such a profound impression on the mind of Pedro Prat that later, when he had become Surgeon-general at Monterey, he became demented, and was unable to classify and label the large assortment of drugs he had brought with him. Within a year he died and was buried in the mission at Monterey. Surely, among the pioneers of California to whom honor is due should be included the name of Pedro Prat, first resident physician in California and a martyr to her first settlement.

Afterwards there was always a surgeon attached to the Monterey presidial company, but most of them remained in this remote province unwillingly, for as men of education, accustomed to refined society, they found the isolation from their kind unendurable, and not even the offer of fifty per cent increase in pay was sufficient to retain them. Dr. Pablo Soler, also a graduate of the University of Barcelona and the most noted of the Spanish Surgeons-general in California, wrote in 1798 to the king of Spain, "complaining of his sad fate in being thus confined within the walls of a remote presidio surrounded by Gentiles and comparatively deprived of society, and begged to be relieved."

Bancroft is mistaken in saying that "none of these surgeons except Benitez possessed professional skill," for several of them were graduates of the best medical institutions in Spain, and the records prove, not only that they performed some remarkable feats in surgery, but that they were far ahead of their time in recognition of certain medical facts which are regarded as modern discoveries. The chief of these was belief in the infectious nature of tuberculosis, years before the discovery of the bacillus by Dr. Robert Koch, the great German bacteriologist, in 1882. Lyman remarks that "Spain and Italy were the only countries in the earlier part of that century which believed that the great white plague was contagious and could be imparted one to another." It cannot be doubted that Dr. Juan Morelos, surgeon at Monterey from 1800 to 1802, shared this opinion. When Comandante Hermenegildo Sal died at Monterey in 1800 of tuberculosis, Morelos gave orders for the roof, doors, and windows of the house to be removed and burned, the bricks of the floor to be taken out, and the plastering on the walls to be scraped off. The furniture and clothing of the dead man were also burned. This was done because the disease was considered to be contagious. Under the medical régime of Dr. Manuel Quixano, when a certain wealthy Spaniard died of consumption his furniture and clothing were ordered burned, and in the excitement of the occasion his jewels and money were lost or stolen. As the deceased had left his property to the "pious fund" pertaining to the California missions, the president of the college of San Fernando, headquarters of the Franciscan order, brought suit against the authorities of the province of the Californias for the full value of the property destroyed. This was not an exceptional case, for a few months later, two women having died of phthisis at Santa Barbara, the governor directed that their clothing should be burned, the walls picked, the lock and key of the door cleansed by fire, and the places where they had slept fumigated. The belief was shared by the people in general, who always destroyed all articles used by a tubercular patient, even in cases where this procedure worked a great hardship on the very poor.

To the Dr. Quixano mentioned above belongs the honor of having performed the first recorded autopsy in California, and in doing so he cleared up a mystery. It was in the case of Father Quintana of Santa Cruz Mission, who was thought to have died of natural causes until the autopsy performed by the doctor two years afterward disclosed that the unfortunate priest had been cruelly and hideously murdered by the Indians.

It is recorded that Dr. Soler performed the most difficult operations upon patients, in a time and region when anesthetics and sterilization were unknown. In the archives of Mission San Carlos there is the following item concerning him:

"Dr. Don Pablo Soler is a great physician and a great surgeon. Had not his humanity prompted him to give his profession to the service of the California colony he would have been renowned in Spain, but he gave the best years of his life for the welfare of the people, travelling many miles to minister to officers and soldiers, to settlers, rich and poor, to the missionaries, and to the Indians, to all with equal kindness."

Bleeding was much thought of in the treatment of nearly all diseases at this time, not only in California but all over the world. Many of the Spanish soldiers who came to California had licenses to practice this art, which was finally taken up by barbers, until in 1799 Governor Borica issued a "bando" prohibiting them from continuing it.

It was indeed fortunate for the lone doctor who, during the fifty years of Spanish rule, was supposed to cover the entire province, with no means of getting about except by horseback, over roads that amounted to mere bridle trails, that the general health of the people was remarkable. In 1802 California's white population was estimated at 9,000, in 1822 at 16,000, and in 1831 at about 23,000, scattered from San Francisco to San Diego. The Surgeon-general at Monterey was required to visit distant missions, ranchos, and pueblos; Dr. Soler complained that sometimes he had to travel as far as forty leagues to visit a sufferer, and he had only his faithful horse to carry him there.

Under the circumstances it is clear that the services of the solitary physician could not always be secured. In fact, with the exception of Monterey and the region within a reasonable distance about it, the province was absolutely without skilled medical attendance. At the three other presidios, the twenty other missions, and all the pueblos, sick and injured persons had but three recourses—the friars, the Indian *hechiceros* (witch doctors), or wandering foreigners who set up, often falsely, to have some medical skill. If the sick person was fortunate, he sent to Monterey for the one surgeon, or the medical officer from some visiting man-of-war or trading-ship. Any American or Englishman who happened to be about was likely to be called in, for any Anglo-Saxon in those days was supposed to have some mysterious power of healing.

The same thing is experienced in our day by American mining men who go to Mexico, for they are supposed to know how to treat every human ailment, from relieving a babe in convulsions to assisting another into the world. Alfred Robinson, who came to California in 1829, found himself a full-fledged *medico* before he knew it, merely through having prescribed a few drops of laudanum to relieve a poor woman's colic. Robinson tells the story of an American sailor, a deserter from a ship, who set himself up as a physician at Santa Barbara, where he met great success with his concoctions, which resembled some of the patent medicines of our own day in that the principal ingredient was aguardiente. It is said that much harm was done in California by these American and British quacks, and it is not surprising to read that a general prejudice arose in the country against doctors, for the people were not able to discriminate between the true and the false. So great did the evil of this quackery become that in 1844 the governor decreed that any one pretending to practice medicine or surgery should produce documentary proof of his qualifications before receiving a license.

The friars were supposed to minister to the bodies as well as the souls of their converts, and most of them had a certain amount of medical knowledge and surgical skill. Each mission had its infirmary, consisting of but one room, with mats instead of beds for the patients to lie on, and each padre had his small supply of drugs and a set of simple surgical instruments. One of these medical and surgical kits is still to be seen among the relics at San Juan Bautista. It is recorded that one of the padres amputated the arm of an injured Indian, "doing it so cleverly that years afterwards its success was attested by one of the friars of San Juan Buenaventura." When all else failed, prayer was resorted to, and, as the fathers claimed, often with marked success. In 1802, about the close of the rainy season, an epidemic appeared at Monterey, Soledad, and San Luís Obispo, characterized by symptoms strongly resembling the modern influenza—cough, pains in various parts of the body, and fever. This disease, which was fatal in many cases, in the opinion of ecclesiastics and laymen alike yielded to prayer rather than to human remedies.

The friars were wise enough, too, to adopt such of the Indian remedies as experience and observation showed were really useful. It is interesting to read that several of the valuable standard remedies now in general use by the physicians of modern California were the discoveries of the despised Indian. There is the *yerba santa* (holy plant), which was used by the medicine men in afflictions of the respiratory tract. Then there is the *cáscara sagrada* (sacred bark), sold everywhere today in the drug stores as a useful cathartic. The *yerba buena* (good herb), from which the village which first stood on the present site of San Francisco was named, is an aromatic vine for which the Indians found many medicinal uses, especially in the treatment of infants' disorders. As there was usually but a scant supply of drugs kept at the presidios and missions, the people came to depend in general upon the vegetable remedies whose beneficial qualities they had learned from the Indians. Every Spanish woman was a natural born nurse and an adept in the use of the simplest of herbs, which she always had ready to hand, growing in her garden.

Like people in many other parts of the world at that time, the Californians sometimes put their faith in remedies that would now be regarded as absurdities. General Vallejo had a little book which had been brought from Cádiz, called *Botica General de los Remedios Experimentados*, which he regarded highly enough to publish a reprint of it in 1838. Some of the items which follow, quoted from Bancroft, read queerly in our day, but it is true, nevertheless, that some of the old-time prescriptions once scoffed at are now being found to contain the germ of a useful idea:

"For impaired eyesight, do as the swallow does—bruise the leaves of swallow-wort and anoint the eyes with the juice. For constipation, imitate the ibis, and use a clyster of salt water. An agreeable remedy was a decoction of red wine and rosemary, which was prescribed for weakness, and was said to be very comforting, while as a wash it preserved beauty and banished wrinkles. A glassful of sugar water, with the unimportant addition of a like quantity of aguardiente, whenever one felt inclined, gladdened the heart, purified the blood, was exceedingly good for the head and stomach, cleansed the spleen, and opened the appetite. The toothache was cured by carrying in the mouth the eye-tooth of a man, or that of a black dog. Cancer yielded to a wash distilled from wine in which rosemary leaves and flowers had been boiled. A remedy that should be recorded in letters of gold was the following: Take a radish cut in four pieces, and two drams of powdered broom seed; put them in half a pint of white wine to which a few drops of lime-juice have been added, and leave them there for twenty-four hours. This draught would dissolve a stone in the bladder, though it were as big as a lemon. Chicken stewed in wine cured the catarrh and eggs boiled in vinegar the dysentery. That the colic may never return, drink for several successive days a decoction of mint, and be bled at the wane of the moon in May, or drink daily some aguardiente with a fresh egg in it. For the bloody flux, use a clyster of the blood of a sucking pig. For kidney complaints, eat four ounces of fresh butter, and immediately afterward drink half a pint of white wine. Scorbutic tumors were dissolved by the application of cloths moistened in a liquor distilled from vipers. For erysipelas, sprinkle the face with the fresh blood of a black hen, and tie to the neck a twig of broom. For jaundice, eat radishes and sugar, and place over the heart a poultice of the same in a cloth dyed with cochineal; this is also a cure for melancholy. For excessive vomiting apply to the pit of the stomach a cataplasm of roast pork and veal. Wash the swellings produced by chilblains with water in which sardines have been cooked. Powdered soot, sage, and salt, mixed with the white of an egg and bound around the wrists, will prevent a continuance of fever and ague. Powdered mustard seed, well sifted and used as snuff—in moderation, though, for the habit grows upon one—will enable the user to comprehend more in an hour than others, who do not know the remedy, can in a day." The last might be recommended to college students.

Some of the sanitary precautions against cholera were peculiar, though others seem well judged enough. The wearing of a small plate or medal of copper next the skin was advocated in the government regulations as a guard against infection. Cleanliness of houses, streets and public buildings was made obligatory. Houses were to be fumigated and bonfires lighted. The use of fat meats and watery vegetables was prohibited; food was to be served in vessels of clay; the rations at the presidios were to be of rice, beans, vermicelli, mutton, and veal; lime or charcoal to be thrown into the sinks; every night the quarters to be fumigated by burning a mixture of salt and vinegar; the men were warned against liquor; all offal to be burned. No one was to be out of doors after eight o'clock at night save in case of necessity; and those found at balls, or frequenting taverns or like resorts, should be condemned to four days' labor on the public works. Under a penalty of six dollars for disobedience, liquor could be sold only between the hours of eleven in the morning and three in the afternoon.

One of the remedies supplied by nature, the mineral springs with which the state is liberally sprinkled from Siskiyou to San Diego, was strangely ignored by the Indians. Having seen dead birds in these springs they held them in fear, and in fact never used these medicinal baths until they saw the Spaniards using them without hurt.

The Indians, seeing the white men afflicted with frightful diseases with which they seemed unable to cope, clung strenuously to their own remedies, stubbornly resisting the offices of the padres. In their illnesses they had two resources—the medicine man and that peculiar institution the *temescal* (sweathouse). There is no question that the *hechiceros* had some real curative skill, which they used in combination with their sorceries in treating the sick. They had a knowledge of the effects of certain plants which defied the understanding of civilized doctors. "Once when an Indian was arraigned in the city of Mexico on the charge of quackery he asked his judges to smell a certain herb, which immediately produced a severe nose bleed, and then invited them to check it. Seeing that they were unable to do so, he administered a powder which at once had the desired effect." In 1802 a number of the padres at Mission San Miguel were attacked with a strange sickness from which they died. It was believed they had been poisoned by the Indians, but, although Dr. Morelos made

Franz Geritz 27

an autopsy, he was unable to ascertain the nature of the poison. Contrary to what one might expect of a primitive people, the natives were much given to "doctoring," and as soon as they felt ill immediately sent for the medicine man, in whom they had profound faith. On the arrival of this very clever "faker," who put on a fantastic head-dress for the occasion, he proceeded to give the patient a thorough examination, then generally announced that the illness had been caused by the entrance of some animal—lizard, frog, snake, or what not—into the body of the sufferer. Then, with a great hocus-pocus of waving of hands and muttering of incantations, he took out the hollow tube or pipe which was the instrument of his office, and after blowing through it upon the afflicted part, placed his mouth upon it and sucked it, soon producing a dead lizard or some other small animal, which he said he had sucked out, but which of course he had previously concealed in his mouth. By the power of suggestion, supplemented by the use of herbs possessing genuine curative qualities, the patient frequently recovered. Father Boscana relates a case of an Indian woman who was lying apparently at the point of death, notwithstanding all that the friars could do for her, and after treatment by the medicine man the father saw her working as usual the very next day at her task of gathering seeds in the fields. Boscana admits that the case passed his understanding.

The Indians had great faith in the temescal in the treatment of bodily disorders, but the Spaniards regarded it with much disfavor, and the friars made strenuous efforts to put a stop to its use. It was a sort of half-cellar and half-house, for it was partly excavated, then roofed with heavy timbers and covered with earth, so that it was hermetically sealed except for one small opening for entrance and exit. In the treatment of disease, a fire was built inside the mound-like structure, the patient entered, and the entrance was closed. When the sick one, after a sufficient stay in the steaming, fetid atmosphere, was in a dripping perspiration, he rushed out with a shout and plunged into the cold waters of the neighboring stream. This heroic method, while no doubt effective in some diseases, was apt to be fatal in others, particularly those brought by the white men, such as smallpox. So determined was the opposition of the civil authorities, as well as of the missionaries, to the use of the sweathouses that they were ordered to be destroyed; but the Indians only reconstructed them in secret places, so that finally a compromise was effected, by which the neophytes were allowed to use the temescal in the presence of a watchman, who prevented the subsequent plunge into cold water, and in doing so perhaps neutralized whatever benefit lay in the treatment.

The *gente de razon*, being witnesses of the occasional successes of the medicine men, often called them in for themselves. These native "doctors" sometimes haughtily refused their services, and could be induced only after much persuasion to grant them. Apropos of this disposition on their part, José de Jesus Vallejo says:

"The northern part of New California was continually exposed to attacks of the Indians, and we had no other physician than the Indian Petronío, who cured his friends and killed his enemies. The scarcity of doctors among us was so great that, as far back as 1844, when, near my estate, a soldier named Francisco Soto accidentally shot himself, I sent two Indians to Sonoma to escort Doctor Petronío to San José; but the proud infidel refused to accede to my request, and sent me word that he would not move one inch unless Castro should come in person to solicit his assistance. My emissaries returned to San José, reported to Castro what Petronío had said, and that officer without delay mounted his horse and rode to Sonoma to beg the Indian to come and cure his wounded soldier and relative. Petronío at first refused, but after a while he acceded to the petition and returned with Castro to San José, where he restored health to the wounded man by means of herbs whose virtue was known to him only."

Bancroft says that "even as late as 1844 these Indian practitioners were in great demand, and were, no doubt, for the most part as good as any." In the case of arrow wounds especially the whites depended entirely upon the skill of their Indian dependents. José María Amador, a noted Indian fighter, had during a certain expedition received four arrow wounds, which were both dangerous and painful. The Indian who treated him brought from the woods a root, red in color and some eight inches long, called *yerba de jarazo* (herb for arrow wounds); another of about the same size, but of a yellowish color; and a third which was long, delicate, and fragile. After chewing the red root, the Indian applied it to the wounds, at the same time telling Amador to chew the third root and swallow the juice. He did so, and at once blood began to flow very freely from the wounds, which had been opened and enlarged by the application referred to. The Indian then removed the arrow heads, which had remained in the wounds, with pinchers, a very painful operation which caused the wounded man to swoon. The yellow root was then applied as the *yerba de jarazo* had been, and in a month the patient was entirely well of his hurts. Bancroft adds that "if left alone he might have been well in two weeks," but there is no certainty of this.

If the lone doctor who covered the whole province during Spanish days had no sinecure, in the Mexican period conditions became very much worse, for the foreigners who began to pour in brought with them those scourges of civilization, smallpox, measles, scarlet fever, and even cholera. Epidemics of these diseases occurred at intervals, causing frightful destruction both among the Indians and whites. Smallpox, which is more responsible than any other factor for the rapid disappearance of the natives of California, made its first appearance in 1798, and in 1834 there was an outbreak in which 12,000 Indians are said to have perished. In 1838 the disease was brought down from the Russian settlement at Ross, and spread with fearful rapidity among the wild Indians, many thousands of whom died. It is estimated that fully three fifths of the savage population of the Sacramento Valley were swept away at this time. The great Suisun tribe, said by General Vallejo to have numbered at least 40,000 persons in 1835, was during the three years that this outbreak lasted reduced to barely two hundred. It is now extinct. So fatal was the type and so swift the deaths that it was impossible to dig graves for the dead, and General Vallejo had them interred in trenches, often so shallow that the corpses were barely covered with earth, where they fell an easy prey to the hungry bears and coyotes. Dr. Platón Vallejo tells a grewsome story of an Indian who, in the general haste, had been buried before the breath of life had quite departed, and was awakened by a grizzly bear, which succeeded in partly devouring one leg before his agonized cries brought help. It speaks well for the health and strength of the Spanish Californians that many of them escaped contagion entirely, even though they mixed freely with the sick. As is usual in such cases, the Indians were the worst sufferers.

The pueblo of Los Angeles, being in the route of overland travel, had periodical smallpox scares. At such times the *ayuntamiento* acted as a board of health, issuing a set of rules to be observed by the people while the epidemic lasted. The proclamation embodying these regulations, some of which sound rather odd now, was read before each house. The horrors of the plague were painted in vivid colors to frighten the people into obeying the rules. All were ordered to refrain from eating red peppers and spices and unripe fruit, were required to bathe and cleanse themselves once in eight days, and to burn sulphur in the houses. All travellers on inland roads were quarantined four leagues from town for three days, during which time they were required to wash their clothing. As soon as vaccine could be obtained vaccination was enforced. The friars were instructed to do what they could to allay any unfounded prejudice against it. It was in 1828 that that peculiar character, James Ohio Pattie, a young trapper and trader from Kentucky, made his famous vaccinating tour of California. On a charge of having entered the country unlawfully, Pattie had been thrown into jail at San Diego, and in exchange for his liberty offered to vaccinate everybody in California where an epidemic was then raging. The offer was accepted, and, taking the vaccine which he fortunately had with him, he made the trip as far as Fort Ross, vaccinating all the way, to the number, he says himself, of 22,000 persons. For this great service he received his liberty, one hundred dollars in cash from the Russians, and the offer of five hundred cattle and five hundred mules, with land to pasture them on, from the Spaniards, but only on condition that he embrace Catholicism and become a Mexican citizen. This offer he angrily refused.

In 1834 and 1849 there were outbreaks of cholera which wrought great havoc. In the last outbreak Dr. John Townsend, one of the earliest and most noted of the American physicians who came during the Mexican period, and his wife, fell victims.

Mingled with the steady flow of foreigners who began to come in during the latter part of the rule of the Republic of Mexico there were naturally some men of the medical profession. As might be expected from the circumstances, these men were generally eccentric personalities, adventurous world wanderers, who made in themselves a picturesque chapter in the history of California. There is room here to speak of but a few of the most noted among them, many of whom married into leading California families and became an integral part of the life. Prominent among them is the famous Dr. John Marsh, pioneer of 1836, who married an *hija del pais*, became wealthy from his land grants, and ended his adventurous life in 1856 when he was murdered by "road agents" near Martínez for money he had received from the sale of cattle. Marsh was a splendid looking man, six feet two inches in height, large in proportion, and very powerful. He was a graduate of Harvard University, distinguished by high intelligence and varied accomplishments. For years he was the only physician in the San Joaquín Valley, which compelled him to travel long distances to visit the sick. Although there were none but wild Indians in that part of the country, "they never molested the Señor Doctor because on various occasions he had treated some of the Indian women who were suffering from maladies that the native doctors did not know how to cure." His home in the valley became a little center of culture, for he had a fine library, from which he lent books to others. He had not a very agreeable personality, and his brusque and taciturn manners prevented him from becoming a general favorite. If the hints let fall by some historians are true, his faults of temper were due to a broken romance in early life, for, like many another in that day, it was said that he came west to forget.

Among the Californians Don Juan Marsh was highly respected, not only for his services as a physician, but for invaluable aid in taking the field with them against Indian horse thieves, who became the scourge of the whole country from Sonoma to San Diego after the fall of the missions. Vallejo says of him: "Dr. John Marsh has now gone to a better life, but the recollections of his fine qualities will remain eternal in the memory of all of us who were eye-witnesses of his philanthropy and good characteristics."

Another interesting and romantic figure among these first *medicos* from the outside to settle in California was Dr. James L. Ord, assistant surgeon of Company F, Third United States Artillery, who arrived in 1847. Soon afterwards he married one of the beautiful daughters of Captain de la Guerra y Noriega of Santa Barbara. Added to the distinction acquired by his marriage into this highborn Spanish family, he is said to have had blue blood in his own veins through direct descent from King George IV and his morganatic wife, Mrs. Fitzherbert (married while he was Prince of Wales), of which union Dr. Ord's father was the offspring. Dr. James Ord was a native of Maryland; a number of the descendants of his marriage with Doña María de las Angustias de la Guerra are still living in California, some of them united by intermarriage with the wealthiest and most influential American families of the present day.

Then there is the truly resplendent figure of Dr. Richard Somerset Den, known affectionately to the Californians as Don Ricardo. This cultured Irishman, graduate of the University of Dublin, came to visit his brother Nicholas in Santa Barbara in 1842, and immediately fell a victim to the charms of "lotus land." Resigning his position as surgeon of a passenger ship bound for Australia, he settled down as practicing physician at Los Angeles. What a striking personality his was is vividly set forth in the following description by Newmark:

"He was seldom seen except on horseback, in which fashion he visited his patients, and was, all in all, somewhat a man of mystery. He rode a magnificent coal-black charger, and was himself always dressed in black. He wore, too, a black felt hat; and beneath the hat there clustered a mass of wavy hair as white as snow. In addition to all this, his standing collar was so high that he was compelled to hold his head erect; and, as if to offset the immaculate linen, he tied around the collar a large black silk scarf. Thus attired and seated on his richly caparisoned horse, Dr. Den appeared always dignified, and even imposing." This man of mystery, although he was "at all times dressed as though he were going to a wedding," remained a bachelor. He won great fame in the mining camps as a physician, receiving sometimes as much as $1,000 a day for his services.

The first Anglo-Saxon resident physician at Monterey was a young English surgeon named Edward Turner Bale, described as "a man of good education but quarrelsome." He married María Ignacia Soberanes, a niece of General Vallejo, and is said to have been so insanely jealous of his beautiful wife that he fought a duel with swords with her uncle, Salvador Vallejo, impelled thereto by his resentment of her exhibition of natural affection toward her relative. Unfortunately for the jealous husband, Captain Vallejo was the most accomplished swordsman of his day in California, and defeated his opponent as he might a child armed with a stick. Enraged at this, the doctor attempted to shoot the victor, with the result that he was thrown into jail. Some turbulent characters, including the notorious Kelsey brothers, attempted to rescue him, and for a time there was wild excitement in old Monterey. This fire-eater later cooled off somewhat and went into the lumber business, in which he accumulated considerable wealth.

The complete story of these doctors of the later Mexican period, including some of Spanish blood, would fill a book. Through the mental picture of old California they ride—for their practice over such a wide space of thinly populated country required them to become as expert horsemen as the Californians the heroes of many adventures and often victims of violent deaths, a picturesque cavalcade about whose members might be woven a hundred romances.

Chapter XI

CHAPTER XI

Family Life

FAMILY LIFE among the Spanish pioneers was full of dignity and ceremony, but was at the same time accompanied by a warmth of affection that awakened the admiration of foreign visitors. The Russian, von Langsdorff, speaks of the "simple, artless attachment" shown by the Argüello family for each other. "There was strong affection," says Bancroft, "and never a happier family than when the ranchero, dwelling in pastoral simplicity, saw his sons and his sons' sons bringing to the paternal roof their wives and seating them at the ever-lengthening table. Additions were sometimes made to that most comfortable of buildings, the family abode, and, whatever else might be lacking, happiness was always present."

Intermarriage occurred to such an extent among the always small population of the province that finally nearly everybody was related to everybody else. They called one another cousins even though no relationship existed. When families met at a house every woman went about the household duties as though she lived there. On returning from church they often remained at the first rancho belonging to one of the party for the night. The men went to kill a fat calf, and the women set about the work as though they were at home. After eating there was music, singing, and dancing. Neighbors regarded the property of one another to some extent as common, and none cared whether the other slaughtered one of his bullocks or took one of his horses. Even when there was no blood relationship certain customs of the country produced special bonds of friendship. Sepúlveda, writing of the old days, says:

"There was one link in the chain of society of those days which contributed to keep in a strong and affectionate unison the social relations of men and women. It was the relation of *compadre* and *comadre*. Whoever stood godfather or godmother to a child was the *compadre* (co-father) or *comadre* (co-mother) of the infant. Always treating each other with respect and affection, and having the child as a living token of their esteem, it was rare to see these pleasant relations disturbed. It no doubt added much to the harmony of society."

When men were bound by special ties of friendship, based upon mutual respect and confidence, they designated each other as *valedor* (defender). So, when a man referred to another as *mi valedor*, he meant to say, "The one who will stand by me through thick and thin"; and seldom was his trust misplaced.

One of the customs that contributed much to the solidity and permanence of families was that of the eldest son becoming the head on the death of the father. The younger brothers always looked up to the elder with the greatest respect, and placed complete trust in his decisions and advice. It was a beautiful custom, and had an excellent effect in holding families together.

Birth, courtship, marriage, and death—the great events in the private lives of the people of any land—made up the placid cycle of their days, and each epoch was met with respect and even veneration. The birth of a child was always heralded with great joy; it mattered not what might be the circumstances of the parents or how many brothers and sisters may have preceded the newcomer. Each little stranger, even though twelfth or twentieth on the list, received the same warm welcome and had the same joyous fiestas in its honor. Months before the arrival the *padrinos*, or god-parents, were chosen, and began to make preparations according to their means. It was considered a great honor and mark of confidence to be selected as padrino.

Baptism was a solemn but at the same time a happy occasion. When the babe was but fifteen or twenty days old, or even younger, it was taken to the parish church to be baptized. On the way to the house to take the infant to church the padrinos played on musical instruments, for seldom it was that one lacked this art. They were received at the door by the whole family, who then joined the procession to the church, the music continuing the whole way. When the baptismal party emerged from the church it was met by others who had waited outside, with the firing of rockets, the ringing of bells, and more music. All now joined together for the return to the house of the parents, including the good padre. Once arrived there, refreshments, consisting of *panecito*, a sort of bread made especially for the occasion, slices of watermelon, or other light comestibles, were served to the whole company. Money was given to the padre and his assistants, and presents were distributed by the padrinos. Then began a baile which lasted one or two days. The nearest relatives were expected to attend the christening without invitation, but others were invited. Baptisms usually took place at night, but those who lived at a distance from the mission had it done on Sundays after mass. Speaking of baptisms from the ranchos, one writer says:

"The moment a child was born and the nurse had had time to dress it, it was given to a man on horseback, who, with its future god-father and god-mother, rode post-haste with it to the nearest mission and presented it to a priest for baptism. The ceremony concluded, the party, full of glee, started on their return. From that time hardly a day passed without the little newcomer being on horseback. He literally rode from his cradle to his grave."

A custom probably brought from the old world was that of bestowing a great number of Christian names upon an infant. For instance, the full name of the heroine of the famous Fitch-Carrillo romance was María Antonia Natalia Elijia. One is not surprised to hear that her god-mother forgot the names on her return from church and thought one of them was Josefa, and so the child was always known by that name, which was not rightfully hers. A fondness for some particular name sometimes caused a curious repetition in the same family. For instance, Juan Antonio Hernández had three sons named José, with the addition of another to distinguish them; thus, José Basilio, José Fernando, and José Antonio, while two of his daughters were named María.

The attachment between parents and children was very tender, but nevertheless the young were taught great respect for their elders; indeed, this trait was almost a part of their religion. Mothers were indulgent, but fathers preserved a strict discipline, although the punishment was often mental rather than physical. Nothing was more wounding to a sensitive young sinner than to be compelled to kneel before a stool in the corner on which was placed a coarse earthen plate, tin cup and wooden spoon, while the rest of the family enjoyed their meal comfortably at the table in the same room. "It was a thousand times worse than flogging," says Alvarado, "as I know by frequent experience; but we never used to increase the shame of it by laughing at the culprit. And as soon as the father went out, mother and brothers and sisters always hastened to the one *en penitencia* and gave him all the choice food that he could eat, besides their sympathy."

Obedience from children was sternly required, even after the years of maturity. A boy could not take his first shave without permission from his father, who seldom gave it before the age of twenty-two, which was considered the age for marriage. Vallejo laments:

"In our day a boy would have been buried in the bowels of the earth rather than appear before his father with a cigar in his mouth; but now it is common. Before the Americans came, our sons, meeting us on the street, came up respectfully, and with hat in hand, said, '*Señor padre, he salido de su casa con ánimo de ir con Fulano á dar un paséo. Me permite Vd. que continúe divirtiendome?*' (My father, I came from your house with the idea of going with so-and-so for a walk. Will you permit me to go on amusing myself?) If we consented, he saluted again and went away; but if we refused he obeyed without a word."

So great was the respect for parents in California that a young man would never dance in their presence until permitted; and the dances were always opened by the married and elderly, while the young people waited their turn after the elders became weary and retired. A young man was not allowed to take part in a ball before the age of twenty. The authority of the father ceased only with his death. It was the privilege of any elderly person to correct young people by words, or even by whipping, and it is not recorded that anyone so chastised ever made a complaint. No son, even if fifty or sixty years of age and a father of a family himself, dared to smoke, or sit, or wear his hat in the presence of his father, and fathers not infrequently chastised grown sons with the lash. Pío Pico says, "Until I was twenty-six I was in complete subjection to my mother, my father being dead. My lady mother, who was very rigid with me, never permitted me to be out of the house after eight at night, and even at twenty-five years of age I observed the same rules." Arnaz has to say, "I saw more than once in the north and south an old man lashing his son, who was married and had children of his own, the son humbly kneeling to receive the blows." Walter Colton, who was appointed alcalde of Monterey in 1846, tells of a case which came before him for settlement:

"A California mother complained to me that her son, a full-grown youth, had struck her. Usage here allows a mother to chastise her son as long as he remains unmarried and lives at home, whatever may be his age, and regards a blow inflicted on a parent as a high offense. I sent for the culprit; laid his crime before him, for which he seemed to care but little, and ordered him to take off his jacket. Then, putting a reata in the hands of his mother, whom nature had endowed with strong arms, directed her to flog him. Every cut of the reata made the fellow jump from the floor; twelve lashes were enough; the mother did her duty, and as I had done mine, the parties were dismissed; no further complaint from that quarter." But let us dwell no longer on this subject, which must seem like a tale of Munchausen to modern parents.

Death was a cause of poignant grief among these people, for their family attachment was exceedingly strong, but the passing of a young child was an occasion for rejoicing rather than of mourning, for it was believed that they were translated directly to heaven to become little angels, and that it was therefore wrong and selfish to grieve too greatly over their going to that land of bliss. The little body was dressed in purest white, to represent an angel, usually the patron saint of the child. Eating and drinking, the firing of rockets and muskets, and even dancing often followed the death and burial of a small babe. So, far from being heartless, this custom only indicates the perfect sincerity of the people in their religious beliefs. As Colton says, "The child was borne to the grave as if it were to be laid at the open portal of heaven, and few were the tears which fell upon that threshold of immortal bliss." Tenderness for children was a very marked trait among the Californians. To quote again from Colton, who was a wise and sympathetic observer:

"There is no need of orphan asylums in California, for the amiable and benevolent spirit of the people hovers like a shield over the helpless. The question is not who shall be burdened with the care of an orphan, but who shall have the privilege of rearing it. Nor do numbers or circumstances seem to shake its spirit; it is triumphant over both. A plain, industrious man, of rather limited means, applied to me today for the care of six orphan children. I asked him how many he had of his own. He said, 'Fourteen as yet.' 'Well, my friend,' I observed, 'are not fourteen enough for one table, and especially with the prospect of more?' 'Ah,' said the Californian. 'The hen that has twenty chickens scratches no harder than the hen that has one.'"

The custom of wearing black for the dead was so universally observed by the Californians, even for cousins of the third degree, the smallest children being required to wear the robes of grief, that in a community where nearly everybody was related to everybody else, many families never went out of mourning at all. This custom must have been a hard penance for a people who were by nature fond of bright colors and the gayer side of life. Funerals were attended by relatives of the remotest degree, and each was expected, following the priest, to throw a handful of earth upon the coffin after it had been lowered into the grave.

But let us move on from this sad subject to one better suited to the light-hearted Californian—courtship and marriage.

"It was considered very improper for a girl to receive a proposal of marriage," writes Guadalupe Vallejo, "before her parents had been consulted by the lover or his parents. Old maids were scarce, and very much thought of. If a lady did not marry in those days it was not for lack of suitors, but from choice, for, indeed, white women were very much in demand; and therefore she was very much admired and venerated. I have an aunt, a sister of my mother, whose parents died; being dissatisfied with her life at her uncle's, she formed the determination of accepting the first offer that should be made to her. She was then fourteen years of age, and they lived at a ranch a few miles from Santa Barbara. Very soon a letter came to her uncle with proposals of marriage for his niece from a young gentleman of San José. She was told of it, and, although she had never set eyes on the suitor, she accepted. Arrangements proceeded for the wedding; the bridegroom soon arrived, and indeed it required all her moral courage and strength to sustain herself in her determination, for she had never seen such an uncouth person before; she was totally unprepared to meet her fate with such a face. Nevertheless she kept her word and rode on horseback, accompanied by her friends, to Santa Barbara to be married. She says that she wept bitterly all the way; her face, all tear-stained, was more like that of one going to a funeral than that of a happy bride. He died after they had been married fifty-nine years, and she was at last liberated from her unhappy fate, at the age of seventy-three!"

Girls were often married at as early an age as thirteen or fourteen, a custom which prevailed also at that time in the middle western United States. A man wishing to

Franz Geritz '27

marry sent his father to open negotiations with the father of the girl, for it was not considered proper for him to make the proposal in person. The poor fellow was then kept on the anxious seat for eight or ten days while the elders took their time in coming to a decision. If this was favorable, the parents then made all the arrangements for the wedding with the priest, who proceeded with the publication of the bans. But let it not be thought that the lovers had not learned the state of each others' hearts long before this, for despite stern parents and watchful dueñas there were ways of conducting courtship. One way was by *haciendo el oso* (playing the bear), that is, for the lover to plant himself under the desired one's window with his guitar and pour forth his plaint in song, accompanied by many sighs and languishing glances. Many a happy marriage of that day had its beginning in the serenade, which was a regular institution of the country. Then there was the whispered word in the dance, the flashing exchange of love messages through the eyes at the church door or on the *paseo*, and through the language of flowers. For this last the lovers of California were indebted to their own Governor Chico, who interpreted it in this way:

"Yerba Buena, I wish to be useful; white Indian cress (nasturtium), I wish to be a nun; red Indian cress, my heart is dripping blood; tuberose, I wait for thee; red rose, thou art the queen of thy sex; white rose, thou art the queen of purity; passion flower, hatred and rancor; hundred leaves, I am dying for thee; turnsol, I cannot bear the sight of thee; dahlia, I love only thee in this world; jasmine, thou art a coquette; red pink, I am justified in feeling jealous; hortensia, I wish to marry thee; violet, modesty; geranium, I will always love thee; evergreen, my love will be eternal; the winter gillyflower, I sigh for thee."

The serenade was sometimes perverted from its proper

use, as is illustrated in a humorous story from the records of the courts:

A wife once summoned her husband before an alcalde for having serenaded another woman.

"Bring us the culprit," said the judge, "and let him play to us as he played before the woman he wished to captivate."

When this was done the judge asked: "Is that the tune you played?"

"Si, Señor."

"Is that the best you can play it?"

"Si, Señor."

"Then I fine you two dollars for disturbing the public peace."

Elaborate descriptions of wedding ceremonies in those days have been left by various writers, both Spanish and American. José María Hijar, who brought a colony of superior settlers from Mexico in 1834, describes them in substance as follows:

"The bridal party marched silently to church, without music; but after the ceremony, friends received them at the door with music, and bore them home in triumph. If the pair lived at a distance in the country, another band of musicians met them half-way, and all proceeded to the rancho, where an arbor had been prepared for the dance, which lasted sometimes a week or more.

"The wagons of the party were adorned with colored coverlets, and silk hangings, branches and flowers. The men were all on horseback, and so were some of the women, who sometimes had a man seated behind them on the croup of the horse. A special table was generally set for prominent guests; the others feasted beneath the trees, by the creek or spring, cooking their own steaks. Most of the men knew how to play on some musical instrument, so that they could take turns in relieving the musicians.

"Usually the happy pair were richly dressed for the occasion, but sometimes they wore their ordinary apparel, the bride adding only a crown of artificial flowers, sometimes white, but usually variegated. Often the fathers would not allow the pair to meet until after the feast. The padrinos were selected by the parents of both."

Another account relates that:

"When the marriage contract is agreed on by the parties, the first care of the bridegroom is to get, by buying, begging, or stealing, the best horse possible, and also a saddle and a silver-mounted bridle; the overleathers of the saddle must likewise be embroidered. These articles are deemed indispensable to a wedding, no matter how poor the parties might be. The bridegroom must furnish the bride with not less than six articles of each kind of women's clothing, and provide everything necessary to feast his friends for one, two, or three days.

"The wedding day being come, the fine horse is saddled, and the bridegroom takes up before him on his horse his future godmother, and the future godfather takes up the bride before him on another fine horse, and so they gallop to church. The ceremony over, the newly married couple mount one horse, and the godfather and godmother the other, and so they gallop back to the house of the bride's parents, where they are received with rockets and a salute of muskets. Before the bridegroom has time to dismount two persons who are in readiness seize him and remove his spurs, which they keep until he redeems them with a bottle of aguardiente or the money to buy one. The couple then enter the house, where the near relatives are waiting in tears to receive them alone. They kneel down before the parents and ask a blessing, which is freely bestowed. Then the bridegroom signs to some one near him, whereupon the guitars and violins strike up and the dance is soon in full swing, to last for three days or sometimes a week."

Here is the way in which a rich young man of Los Angeles was dressed on his wedding day, in 1842:

"Yellow hat of vicuña wool, with a heavy string of glass beads around the crown; the under part of the brim nearly covered with silver lace. The jacket easy fitting, of green satin, with large flaps of the same material, its buttons being of Mexican *pesetas* with the eagle stamp on the outside. The waist-coat of yellow satin with the pocket flaps buttoned up with gold dollars. Wide breeches of red velvet to the knees, where they were fastened with silver buckles. A buckskin legging of the natural color, tied around the knee where the breeches ended with green silk ribbons forming a flower, and with tassels from which depended little figures of cats, dogs, puppets, etc., made of seed-glass beads, interspersed with gold and silver thread. Where the deer-skin leggings ended began the shoe, which was sharp-pointed and turned upwards. The *manga*, or serape, was of sky-blue cloth of the finest quality, with red lining, the opening for the head faced with black velvet, and edged all around with fringed silver galloon. The long hair, braided in a queue, hung down upon the jacket, where the queue was tied with a large flower of green ribbon. To light his cigarette he used a *mechero*, or cotton twist burnt at one end, with a steel piece and flint-stone weighing about an ounce; from the *mechero* hung an ornament of beads, beautifully made. The *mecha*, or tinder, was perfumed with Peruvian balsam.

"The bride, who was almost eclipsed in gorgeousness by the groom, wore a dress of yellow satin, trimmed on the skirt with green ribbons; white satin shoes with upward turning points, flesh-colored stockings, a black handkerchief around the head, a three-cornered shawl, and artificial flowers."

It was a pretty custom for the bridegroom to make with his own hands the white satin slippers worn at the wedding by his bride. Guadalupe Vallejo gives us a pleasing description of a California wedding party:

"Nothing more attractive can be imagined than a wedding cavalcade on its way from the bride's house to the mission church. The horses were more richly caparisoned than for any other ceremony, and the bride's nearest relative or family representative carried her before him, she sitting on the saddle with her white satin shoe in a loop of gold or silver braid, while he sat on the bear-skin covered apron behind. The groom and his friends mingled with the bride's party, all on the best horses that could be obtained, and they rode gaily from the ranch house to the mission, sometimes fifteen or twenty miles away. In April and May, when the land was covered with wild flowers, the light-hearted troop rode along the edge of the uplands between hill and valley, crossing the streams. Some of the young horsemen, anxious to show their skill, would perform all the feats for which the Spanish-Californians were so famous. After the wedding, when they returned to lead in the feasting, the bride was carried on the horse of the groom. One of the customs which was always observed at a wedding was to wind a silken tasseled string or sash, fringed with gold, about the necks of the bride and groom, binding them together as they knelt before the altar for the blessing of the priest."

William Heath Davis gives us an interesting account of some of the customs in weddings of the day:

"A gentleman who carried a lady before him on a horse was considered as occupying the post of honor, and it was customary when a bride was to be married in church for a relative to take her before him in this fashion to the church where the ceremony was to be performed. On the occasion of my marriage, in 1847, the bride was taken in this way to the church by her uncle, Don José Martínez. On these occasions the horse was adorned in the most sumptuous manner, the leather coverings being beautifully worked with ornamental devices in gold and silver thread. The bride rode on her own saddle, somewhat smaller than that of the gentleman, and without stirrups, in place of which a piece of silk—red, blue, or green—perhaps a yard wide and two or three yards long, was gracefully hung over the saddle, puffed like a bunch of flowers at the fastening, and hanging down on one side of the horse in a loop, in which the lady lightly rested her foot."

One thing to be said for marriage among the Californians is that it was always based on love, never on interest. Such a thing as a marriage settlement, of money or property, was utterly unknown. And it was generally permanent, for divorce was almost unheard-of. One curious custom of the church in connection with marriage was the extension of the bar of relationship even to cousins of a deceased wife or husband. For instance, in 1825 J. A. Yorba, of Santa Barbara, wished to marry a first cousin of his first wife, who was fond of his children, but the request was refused by the padre president.

Marriage of the military, either privates or officers, was hedged about with even more difficulties than that of civilians, for they had to obtain the consent of the authorities in Mexico before they could take the momentous step. And thereby hangs a tale, the romantic story of the marriage of the most distinguished of all the Californians, Mariano Guadalupe Vallejo, which we will relate under the title of

Betwixt Love and Duty

When Don Mariano was scarcely more than a boy, only twenty-four years of age, although he was already an officer in the military service of Mexico, he happened to make a trip to San Diego. While there he met and instantly fell in love with the beautiful young Señorita María Francisca Felipa Benicia Carrillo, a daughter of one of the oldest and most aristocratic Spanish families in the place. The attraction was reciprocal; in fact, Vallejo writes that he had never seen a young lady "more earnestly in love." The parents on both sides were more than willing. For once it seemed that the course of true love would surely run smoothly, but, alas for the hopes of the young pair, there was one powerful obstacle, which could only be removed by long time and patience. "This incident touches me very closely," writes the chief actor in this old romance, "but I consider that it should be known by my readers, for it will give them an idea of the vicissitudes to which were exposed in the beginning of this century the military men who watched over the safety of the inhabitants of Alta California."

At that time the rules of the Mexican army were tightly bound up in red tape. One of the regulations was that no officer might marry until he first received permission from the War Department in the city of Mexico. Violation of this rule by any officer meant, Vallejo says, that he would be deprived of his rank, his legal rights, and of his wife, but without any of the privileges of widowerhood. The only thing to be done was to prepare a humble petition for permission to contract marriage with Doña Francisca Carrillo, "a spinster of fifteen years of age, legitimate daughter of Don Joaquín Carrillo and Doña María Ygnacia López, of honorable family," and send it to the city of Mexico, there to be acted upon by the War Department.

This was all very well, but unfortunately there were no steamships, airplanes, or even railroads then, and the only means the impatient lover could find for getting the all-important missive through was by slow burro express. As neither the burro nor the messenger was particularly interested in a wedding that was none of theirs, they made no haste, creeping at a snail's pace down the peninsula to La Paz, where a wait had to be made for a vessel to transport them to the mainland. Arrived at Mazatlán, there followed the hard climb over the high Sierra Madre to Durango, and then came the slow tramp across the broad table-land to the city of Montezuma. Here the long and cold-blooded delays of the law had to be encountered before the petition, freighted with the prayer of two loving hearts, could reach its turn to be presented. After giving it serious consideration, the council of grizzled old soldiers at last decided that no great harm could result to the state if the petition of young Vallejo to be permitted to espouse Señorita Carrillo were granted. No sooner was it done than the messenger, now armed with the precious document, started back on the same long journey, and we may be sure that he made many a stop on the way to visit old friends and refresh himself and his faithful burro. In consequence the round trip took nearly a year and a half, at least so says M. G. Vallejo, although his son Platón puts it at two years and a half. In any case it was a long and irritating delay, and the feelings of the waiting lovers in California may well be imagined. The prospective bridegroom raged in helpless fury, and even in his old age still speaks bitterly of the affair:

"Whatever may have been the motives in my individual case that induced the President of the Republic to keep me in suspense for seventeen months, I do not thank him for them; for I am of the opinion that in such cases the betrothed persons are the ones best fitted to judge of the propriety of their union, and if their parents are not opposed I do not see why the government should intervene."

As for Señorita Carrillo, like the well-reared Spanish girl that she was, she concealed her feelings in public, but no doubt shed many a tear in private. But, to quote an old Spanish proverb, "there is no ill that lasts a hundred years," so at last the joyful day came when Cupid's long-delayed messenger ambled in on his footsore burro. Young Vallejo received the welcome *permiso* on the sixth of March, 1832, at the Mission San Juan Capistrano, twenty-three leagues distant from San Diego. "My readers," says he, "will readily believe that I lost no time in hastening to that city and celebrating my marriage, which took place with great ceremony, in the presence of Governor Echeandía and all his staff besides many of the most distinguished persons in the place."

All was now going as merrily as the traditional marriage bell, and the governor added to the *éclat* of the occasion by making a flowery speech of congratulation and drinking to the health of the happy couple in a glass of wine. Then, to the stupefaction of all present and the utter horror of the bridegroom, he set down his glass and addressed the young man in these words:

"My young friend, times of disturbance are not the most suitable for marriage. News which I have just received makes imperative a rapid movement to the north, and you must accompany the expedition. I have already positively arranged it, and it is now impossible for me to change the measures I have taken. I feel in my heart the necessity of snatching you from the company of the dear one, but matters of public service take precedence over all others."

At these words the young man shuddered, and all the company turned inquisitive eyes upon him, as though to ask whether he would obey the orders which separated him from his bride at the moment of their union. Both the young people, however, maintained their composure under this scrutiny, and allowed no one to see the affliction of their hearts.

Notwithstanding this dampening news, the festivities which always attended a wedding were at once inaugurated, and dancing was kept up until six the next morning, the music being furnished by musicians from the presidio and a full Indian band from Mission San Luís Rey. By the custom of the day the bride and groom were compelled to remain until the concourse was dismissed. Just as the morning sun began to peep into the banqueting hall, a messenger arrived with sealed orders for Vallejo from his commander-in-chief. Sustained by the hope that his superior officer might have taken pity upon his situation and at the last moment designated him for guard duty at San Diego, he hastily tore open the document.

"How soon," says he, "were all my hopes dissipated when I saw that the paper contained my appointment as field adjutant, with strict instructions to present myself at once before the comandante general! My reader, does not my situation at that moment inspire your pity? For compassion's sake, lay aside the book and stop to consider. Transport yourself mentally to those times, to those moments! Twenty-four years of age, full of dreams, an ardent soul, abounding health! Alas, just when I thought myself freed from all the obstacles that embitter the lives of mortals, when I believed that there did not exist on this terrestrial globe a more enviable being than I, when I dreamed that I was the elect of the elect, a cruel hand broke the cup from which I was about to drink the nectar of my happiness, and substituted for it one full of gall!"

For a moment he wavered between love and duty, and even thought of resigning the career of arms, which at that instant seemed to him so extremely despotic. But almost immediately he recalled the fact that the country was just then in the throes of one of the numerous revolutions which kept it unsettled during the whole Mexican period, and that the governor needed every arm for its defense. Animated by these thoughts, which even the image of his lovely young bride could not dissipate, he seized his arms, and, after one last embrace, sprang into the saddle and was away. Here he interpolates in his memoirs his last farewell expressed in verse; and let the reader not be astonished at this, for it was one of the peculiar customs among the Californians to break into impromptu poetry upon any and all occasions.

. . . . Francisca,
Ven y estrechame; no apartes
Ya tus brazos de mi cuello.
No ocultes el rostro bello,
Tímida huyendo de mi.
Oprimanse nuestros labios
En un beso eterno, ardiente,
Y trascurran dulcemente
Lentas las horas asi!

Of which a literal translation follows:

. . . . Francisca,
Come and embrace me; do not take
Thy arms from my neck,
Do not hide thy beautiful face,
Timidly fleeing from me.
Let our lips meet
In an eternal, burning kiss,
And thus will pass sweetly
The slow hours away.

It was eight months before they met again. Vallejo had then become comandante of the presidio of San Francisco, and director of colonization for all the territory north of the mission lands of Santa Clara, with unlimited authority in all that region. To this was added later by the government of Mexico the title of general in its army. As his duties were peremptory, he sent his brother Salvador, with an escort of twenty troopers, to bring home his bride. Dr. Platón Vallejo, one of the sixteen children with which this union was blessed, tells us in his memoirs of the home-coming of the young woman:

"My mother never wearied telling of this journey. The soldiers were all young, very striking in their new uniforms. An easy-paced jack, an animal then much prized, was assigned for her to ride. She was seated on a sort of pillion, and, instead of a stirrup, her feet rested on a board suspended along the jack's side. It was no more tiresome than sitting in a rocking-chair. One of the soldiers held the bridle, and, except at night, never relaxed his grasp from San Diego to San Francisco. When the party started on the long journey the mission bells were ringing, and all the people of San Diego turned out to bid the bride Godspeed, and to strew the street with flowers. It was in the springtime. All the country was carpeted with blossoms, and the soft air, laden with perfumes, joined with the prospect of great happiness, induced a sentimental mood. Sometimes they stayed over night at the missions, welcomed by the kind padres and joyous chimes. But more often they camped by some limpid stream, and in a sylvan bower she listened to the music of the ocean until lulled into forgetfulness and sleep by its measured cadence; and in the morning she was awakened by the birds singing their own wedding march."

Never did a bride have a more beautiful wedding journey, even though she had to take it alone. It was in fact a fitting prelude, as Don Platón continues, to a long life of love and devotion on either side. For more than sixty years they lived as husband and wife, and, looking back over half a century, they could recall no incident of their union that they could have wished different.

Chapter XII

CHAPTER XII

Amusements

THERE WAS never a people fonder of amusements than the Californians. With them the old adage was reversed, and became "pleasure before business." "Firmly enough," says Bancroft, "they held that pleasure, up to a certain point, must be classed among the utilities, as well as ploughing and sheep raising, for without enjoyment the race would speedily degenerate. Idleness there did not seem to visit the people with its usual curse." Fortunately for their physical health and their morals, most of their amusements were of the active, energetic sort, frequently carried on in the open air. Horse riding and racing, dancing, hunting, cockfighting, bull and bear fights, were the favorites, and to them the people devoted themselves as earnestly as though they were the chief business of life.

Any excuse was seized for a fiesta. Even rodéos, which were in reality part of the work of cattle raising, always ended in a grand ball, attended by rancheros with their families for leagues around. The coming of a new governor from Mexico, even though he might not be altogether welcome, could not be resisted as an occasion for gaieties. So the arrival of Micheltorena at San Diego with his ragamuffin army was heralded by the townspeople with many festivities, though when their chicken roosts began to suffer they were quite as glad to speed the parting guest as they had been to welcome him. On the other hand, the enforced departure of Gutiérrez from Monterey was celebrated with dancing and fireworks. The entrance of a foreign ship in any of the harbors inaugurated a season of festivals, picnics, and balls, all of which were heartily returned by the visiting officers. When Vancouver was in Monterey Bay the hospitalities of the Spaniards were returned by a dinner aboard the *Discovery*, followed by a picnic in the garden of the presidio especially for those of the ladies whose sea legs were not of the best. The festivities ended with a grand display of fireworks on the beach furnished by the visitors, to the delight of the Spaniards and the astonishment of the Indians. One is not surprised to read that there was profound regret on both sides when the English vessels sailed away.

Even when Commodore Jones made his famous mistake and raised the American flag too soon in Monterey Harbor, which he afterwards repaired by re-raising the Mexican colors, the settlement of the affair was celebrated by general and reciprocal festivities. A brilliant ball was given aboard the *Savannah* to the people of the town, and this compliment was returned by a grand function at the customhouse which was attended by the select of Monterey society. So the affair, notwithstanding its potentialities for ill feeling, ended as merrily as though there had been no question of conquest, and everybody was happy.

"Ah, what times we used to have at San Diego in 1825!" sighed an aged lady in recalling the old days. "Every week to La Playa aboard the trading ships—silks! officers! rebozos! dancing! frolic! Days of primitive simplicity, its traces not yet all gone among the descendants of the founders. The summer labors and harvest and their cattle filled most of their wants. The missionaries drew a heavy trade from abroad that supplied many luxuries in exchange for the products of individual industry. The arrival of a ship was more than a sensation; its date served the memory to reckon ordinary events thereafter. And cold the heart not to relish the gayety and enjoyment that followed the dropping of the anchor at La Playa! Liberality on one side, unbounded hospitality on the other, contributed to gild and prolong the festive hours."

Dr. Maxwell, writing in 1843, says:

"We, the officers of the squadron, gave a ball at the government house. At that time the female population of Monterey had never tasted cake, mince-pie, or anything of that sort, and the stewards of our messes were set to work making all kinds of delicacies of the kind for the supper. . . These people had the most extraordinary customs. They would come on board ship and dance all day, and we would go ashore and dance all night. At the ball were a number of American hunters, who had come to town because of our presence there. Captain Armstrong's dancing was very vigorous, and the perspiration rolled down his cheeks. The natives called him Brazos Fuertes (strong arms)." What unwonted indigestion they must have left behind them!

The inseparable companion of the Californian, both in work and in play, was the horse. The system of cattle raising developed a race of famous cavaliers. All observers testify that there were few such riders in the world as the Californians, not even excepting the Cossacks of Tartary. All were expert horsemen, could throw a lasso and shoot unerringly, even the women. They were said to be almost born in the saddle, for at only four or five years of age, when their little legs hardly reached halfway down the animal's sides, they were put on horseback and taught to ride at a breakneck pace. It is said that those who were not killed in the beginning became expert riders. As soon as a boy was strong enough, he would go out to the fields, lasso a wild colt, halter and mount it, and then let it run flying over the open country until it was exhausted. If the colt fell in jumping a ditch, or rolled over in order to get rid of its burden, the boy had to look out to keep on top. It was the favorite sport even in babyhood to whirl the lariat and cast it over anything that came in the way. One writer of the day says:

"The men are always on horseback; horses being as plentiful in the country as dogs and chickens are in Juan Fernández. These animals are never stabled, but are allowed to run wild and seek for pasture where they please; they are, however, branded, and attached to their neck is a long green-hide rope, called a lasso, which trails behind them, and renders them easy to catch when wanted. One is generally caught in the morning, a saddle and bridle is thrown over him, and he is used for the day; at night he is turned loose, and another takes his place next day. There are no better riders in the world than the Californians. From childhood they are so continually on horseback that they may be said to have grown there. They can hardly go from one house to another except on horseback, there being always several of these animals standing tied to the door-posts of the little cottages. When a cavalier wishes to show his activity, he makes no use of the stirrups in mounting, but, striking his horse sharply, he springs into the saddle as the animal starts, then, with a prick from his long spurs, he dashes off at a full gallop." The use of these spurs, which were very cruel instruments with four or five rowels, each about an inch long, generally dull and rusty, was the worst thing in the treatment of these true and faithful servants by the Californians.

The vaqueros acquired all kinds of fancy tricks, which they were proud of showing off in public. It was very easy for one of them to pick up a coin or handkerchief at full gallop, and their skill with the lasso won the admiration of all foreign visitors. They often took their meals in the saddle, and could light a cigarette at a gallop. The story goes that a horseman of San José won a wager that he could start at full speed with a salver of a dozen wine-glasses filled to the brim, and after fifty rods stop suddenly and hand down the salver without spilling a drop. Young fellows would often remove the reins of their horses and guide them merely with blows of the hat on their heads. At times they would lasso some animal, cast away the lasso, follow it, and pick it up at full run. Bonifacio López, weighing three hundred pounds, used to ride his horse at full speed up and down a breakneck trail near San Diego, to the great wonder even of his countrymen.

For hard work, strength, and agility, the Californians surpassed the famous gauchos of the pampas of South America. Unhorsed, a Californian considered himself but half a man, and he who was not a skilled rider was looked upon with contempt. Everything possible was done on horseback, even firewood being lassoed and dragged to the door in this way. An American carpenter used to tell a story about an apprentice who left him because he could not shove a jack-plane from the back of his horse. John Bidwell said it was a proverb that a Spanish-Californian would not do anything unless he could do it on horseback. It was one of Walter Colton's jokes that the reason fish was seldom seen on the tables of Californians was because the sport of fishing had to be carried on afoot. "If they could go to sea on their horses and fish from their saddles they would often be seen dashing through the surf, but to sit quietly in a boat is entirely too tame a business."

Horseback was the universal mode of travel, even the women preferring the back of a fine animal to the clumsy, springless carretas, and there were consequently no wagon roads, only bridle paths. This period may very appropriately be called the equestrian era of California, when a man's home was the back of his horse. "Leave him this home, and you might have the rest of the world." The attachment of the Californian to his steed was as great as that of the Arabs, and the strongest token of friendship between man and man was the gift of their best horse. Californians were probably capable of riding for longer distances and longer hours than any other horsemen in the world. Speaking of José Castro, Alvarado says, "It is my belief that Castro possessed a constitution of iron, for on occasions he was in the saddle for thirty-six hours, yet when he alighted he appeared as fresh as though he had just arisen from his bed."

As to the horse himself, it is strange that *mustang* should ever have been a term of contempt, for he was a beautiful creature, of pure Arabian lineage, and retained nearly all the fine points of his aristocratic ancestors. Small in size but finely formed, full-chested, thin-flanked, with unusually small head, feet, and ears, large, full eyes, flowing mane and tail, he was full of fire. In color he varied from black or white to grey, dun, spotted or *pinto*, bay, or what was most admired, a golden cream, with silver-white mane and tail. These last were called *palominos*, and were great favorites for wedding cavalcades. These horses were broken only for the saddle, and when Governor Micheltorena arrived in the province bringing with him a wheeled wagon, he was compelled to attach saddle horses, each with a rider, to the shafts.

These horses always traveled at either a full gallop or a walk; they had no medium gait, what Dana called a "genteel trot," and they could keep their hard pace up all day long without apparent fatigue. Their extraordinary intelligence made them invaluable assistants in cattle herding and lassoing, in which they exhibited almost human sagacity. They would stop instantly when going at full speed, brace all four feet, lean over and pull on the lasso. By this means they could stop and hold grizzlies and elk, notwithstanding the superior strength of those animals.

The mustang lived to a greater age than the horses of other countries, many reaching the age of twenty-five years. They were free from the usual equine diseases, and their only enemy was the puma, which destroyed many young colts, but was seldom known to attack a full-grown horse. In later years they found another and more deadly enemy in the Indians, who preferred horse-flesh to all other meat for eating, and after the secularization of the missions formed bands of horse thieves who became a frightful scourge in the valley of the San Joaquín.

The animals, never being stabled, sometimes listened to the call of the wild, wandering away to live and breed in a state of nature. The wild horses increased so rapidly that at last tens of thousands were running free in the San Joaquín Valley. It was a favorite but very hazardous sport with the young men, requiring the greatest nerve and best horsemanship, to hunt them with the lasso. An unexpected meeting with a band of these animals flying before the wind was a thrilling but perilous adventure. Woe to the one who lost his seat and fell under the feet of the stampeding herd! So numerous did these wild horses become that they grew to be a menace, eating up the grass and destroying the pasture needed for the more valuable cattle. Besides, they enticed the tame horses away. The government accordingly resolved to hold a general slaughter. Corrals were formed near the pueblos, and the horses, wild and tame, were driven into them, and the entrance closed. A small gate was opened to allow only one animal to pass out at a time; two or three lancers placed at this gate stabbed the wild horses as they passed out, thousands being killed in this way. In addition to this shocking method, many were killed by being driven over precipices, or into rivers.

Gentle-paced animals, called *de sobrepaso*, were reserved for the women. A Californian considered it a disgrace to ride a horse with the tail or mane clipped, and on show occasions took pains to comb out the long tails so as to show them off to the best advantage. Once a practical joker, José Antonio Yorba, clipped the tails of all the horses tied outside a certain house where there was a dance in progress. When the young fellows came out and proceeded to place their fair partners on the saddle while they mounted behind, as was the custom, they discovered the tragedy that had occurred. Great were the lamentations, for it was as though a great calamity had fallen upon them!

As might be expected of a people of such equestrian abilities, horse racing was a prime sport with them. Not even among the "colonels" of our southern states did excitement reach a higher level over a trial of speed between two or more of these noble animals than among the rancheros of California, who often wagered large sums in cattle and other stock on the results. Some very fine race horses were raised in pastoral California.

There were a number of sports played on horseback, some of which would make the modern polo seem quite tame. The *carrera del gallo* was perhaps the most popular of all, next to horse racing. "A live cock was buried with the head above ground. At a signal a horseman would start at full speed from a distance of about sixty yards, and if by a dexterous swoop he could take the bird by the head he was loudly applauded. Should he fail, he was greeted with derisive laughter, and was sometimes unhorsed with violence, or dragged in the dust at the risk of breaking his limbs or neck. Another amusement was to place on

Franz Geritz

the ground a rawhide, and riding at full speed suddenly rein in the horse the moment his forefeet struck the hide."

There were bull fights, but not so cruel as those of European Spaniards, for no horses were used and the bull was seldom killed. Then there was the *corrida de toros*, in which the chief sport consisted in baiting the bull by shaking serapes in front of him. "When the bull had become tired, and consequently less mettlesome, the gate was opened and he was driven forth at full speed. Behind him came those within the enclosure, who endeavored to seize the animal by the tail and throw him. In disputing this honor there was much jostling and coming together of horses; and it was frightful to behold such a group of men and horses sallying out of the enclosure at the risk of life and limb. There were always on these occasions men and horses more or less injured."

A very popular diversion was the bull and bear fight, for which the best that can be said is that it was not so cruel as the European bull fight, for the reason that both the participants were fighting animals, and no miserable horse was sacrificed. "We used to make bears and bulls fight," remarked Blas Peña, "for which purpose we tied together the two animals, the bull having one of his fore legs strapped and the bear one of his hind legs. Sometimes the bull came off victorious, and at other times the bear, the result depending somewhat upon the ages of the beasts. The bears were caught on Mount Diablo, with reatas made of four strips of oxhide braided together." The fight usually took place inside of a strong wooden fence, behind which, and at a short distance, was erected a high platform for the women and children, most of the men being on horseback outside the ring, with reatas ready and loaded guns, in case the bear should leap the barrier or other accident occur. The diversion was kept up for hours, or until one or the other of the animals succumbed, and it often happened that both were killed. This type of amusement was one of the least desirable of the inheritances brought by the first settlers from old Spain.

"Another diversion, also on horseback, was known as the *juego de vara* (the game of rods). The players formed in a ring, the horses facing inwards. One of the number then rode round the circle, having in his hand a stout rod of quince or other similar wood, which he gave from behind to one of the players. He who received the rod pursued the giver, directing blows at his shoulders, which the latter by the exertion of skilful horsemanship endeavored to elude, until by gaining a vacant place in the circle he was exempt from further persecution. This sport was continued for hours, and he who was not a skilled horseman received a good drubbing." Enough has been said of these games played on horseback to show, whatever may be said of the cruelty to the animal participants, that courage, physical strength, and exceeding agility were required by the players.

Next to his horse, a Californian's pride centered in the trappings with which it was caparisoned, upon which he sometimes spent several thousand dollars. A poor man might own a dozen horses, for they were the cheapest things in California, a fairly good one being obtainable for three dollars, but he was rich who possessed the complete furnishings for one. The saddle, a huge affair with a high "tree" fore and aft, was laid upon a broad apron of leather, stamped and embroidered in red, green, gold, or silver. The bridle, made of horsehair, was silver mounted; the immense wooden stirrups had long leather coverings in front, and the great cruel spurs, inlaid with silver, bore rowels with four or five points. With his horse equipped in this fashion, the inevitable lasso looped over the saddle bow, his slender, graceful figure set off by a gay blue jacket trimmed with bright red cuffs and collar, blue velvet pantaloons buttoned down the sides but left open at the knee to show the white stockings, feet in deer-skin leggings handsomely embroidered, head covered with a broad-brimmed, flat-crowned sombrero under which his thick black hair hung braided in a queue, the rider made a gallant appearance. Outfitted in this fashion, with his trusty hunting knife thrust in his legging, he was ready at a moment's notice for a little gallop of a hundred and fifty miles or so, which he often accomplished in one day by using relays of horses. If overtaken by night on the road, his saddle was his pillow, the roll of blankets strapped to it his bed, the inevitable serape his only covering, while the ever-useful lasso secured his horse as it fed on the wild oats of the valley.

It was not remarkable that the horse should have been used as the chief, almost the only, means of locomotion, considering the character of the only vehicles in the country. These carretas, or oxcarts, were very primitive affairs; the wheels were solid blocks of wood cut transversely from the butt ends of trees, and bored through the center for huge wooden axles. The deep body was arched with hoop-poles, which were covered with hides or cotton, somewhat in the manner of our "covered wagon" of overland travel fame. For long journeys a mattress and blankets were laid in the bottom for sleeping purposes, and the traveler who was not in haste could make himself very comfortable indeed. The rude contraption was innocent of springs, and the squeaking of its unoiled axles as they turned in the holes could be heard for miles. They were drawn by oxen, yoked by the horns and urged on by Indian drivers who ran alongside and poked them in the side with poles, the whole escorted by a troop of dogs. The hallooing of the drivers, the barking of the dogs, the creaking of the axles and the laughter of the children made an uproar that caused the birds and wild animals to flee before them. It is clear that not much speed could be made with one of these vehicles. Once in 1844 Francisco Rico took a whole day to go with three of these carts from the presidio of San Francisco to Yerba Buena, and the creaking of the wheels was such it could be heard a mile away—this on a "secret" revolutionary expedition! "I know of only two carriages," says Arnaz, "an old *calesa* owned by the padres of Santa Barbara, and another by José de la Guerra. They were old-fashioned, very like hand chairs with low wheels, known as *literas*. Martínez, the missionary of San Luis Obíspo, had a fine coach of leather, varnished black. He used harness with bells. In 1842-43 they began to introduce *calesas* and carts with spoked wheels from the United States." This story of Martínez and his fine carriage shows a change since the days when poor, fat, old Father Viader of Santa Clara was disciplined for indulging in the luxury of the home-made *calesa* constructed for him by the Indians.

Whether at work or at play, everything the Californian did had to have its musical accompaniment, for, like all other Latins, the love of music was in his blood. If a man who could not ride well was considered only half a man, so he who could not play upon some instrument or sing agreeably was thought to be hardly human. The men in particular had pleasing baritone or tenor voices, and did not as a rule sing in the strange high falsetto popular in Mexico. Nearly every act in their social lives was accompanied by music of some sort—baptisms, weddings, funerals, *tertulias* (evening parties), and love-making. Even the horseman galloping along the road enlivened his journey with a merry song timed to the beat of his horse's hoofs. The poor wood-cutter, working at his lonely trade in the depths of the forest, raised his morning hymn to the *Todo Poderoso* with the birds. With the large families of the Californians, it was possible to have a reunion every evening, when they sang and danced and played on the *vihuela*, a kind of guitar. Most of them were able to play by natural taste and talent, without any instruction whatever.

"Singing and dancing," says Sir George Simpson, "were as common as eating and sleeping. All are musicians, and in every house may be heard the guitar or singing." Another writer says: "All Californians could . . . play the *vihuela* or guitar. Every night they passed through the streets giving serenades and singing what occurred to them. Most men could play instruments and sing, so that musicians were easily relieved at a party. Opera music was not known, but the women could play and sing pretty songs. The usual instruments were guitars and violins, but there were some clarinets and harps, many of the women being expert players on the last-named instrument. The missions had orchestras of Indians, taught by the padres; these Indian musicians were in great demand to play for the balls given by the whites. Joaquín Carrillo, father-in-law of Vallejo, was an accomplished violinist. When a soldier he was one night playing at a ball at the house of Comandante Ruíz at San Diego. Ruíz was fond of a certain air, which he ordered Carrillo to play; and because he thought the latter too long in tuning his instrument, Ruíz ordered him put in the stocks, and sent the guests home, it being then about midnight.

"Three pianos were brought from Baltimore by Captain Smith and sold, one to José Ábrego, one to Eulogio Célis in San Pedro, and the third to M. G. Vallejo. Consul Larkin wished to borrow the instrument from Ábrego for a ball at his house in honor of Commodore Jones. Ábrego granted the request, but suggested that a piano would not be of much use, since no one knew how to play it. But to the surprise of all, the boy Pedro Estrada sat down and played on it, although he had never seen one before. It was proposed to send the boy to Mexico to be educated in music, but the advice of David Spence prevailed, who thought a carpenter more useful than a musician."

Most of the instruments used in the mission choirs were made at the missions, and were consequently rude and inferior, but it is remarkable that they could be made at all with the means at hand. Bancroft says the ancient popular songs of the Californians were introduced from Sonora.

The guitar and violin were in constant use, the players being always ready for dance and song, usually in a plaintive strain. The singing was frequently improvised, especially in honor of guests, or in sarcastic allusion to political or other events. The folk-song, comic as well as romantic, was common, and formed one of the most fascinating of the customs of the day. The Californians were very clever at improvising verses on the spur of the moment. None of the serenades or other songs of the country were in print, but passed from mouth to mouth.

After the American Conquest more was accomplished in winning the confidence and friendship of the Californians by the military bands of the United States forces than by proclamations. Upon the advice of an old trader who knew the people well, the band was put to play in the plaza at Los Angeles an hour each day at sunset. "At first the children peeped round the corners of the houses. A few lively tunes brought out the *vivas* of the elder ones, and before closing for the day quite a circle of delighted natives surrounded the musicians. The following afternoon, the people from the ranchos at a distance, hearing of the wonderful performance, began to come in." The old priest, sitting by the church door, remarked: "That music will do more service in the conquest of California than a thousand bayonets." Winning a people by music was a new and pleasing method.

In a new country, where wild game abounded, it was natural that hunting should be one of the chief recreations of the people. With only the lasso for a weapon as a rule, they showed a dashing courage in facing wild herds, in bearding the formidable grizzly, the hard-fighting elk with his great antlers, and in catching and taming the wild horse, that has seldom been equalled. In fact, small game did not seem to interest them, and we hear little of bird shooting, while few among them were disciples of Isaak Walton. Bear they hunted for sport alone, for they never took kindly to the meat of that animal, eating it only in emergencies.

Bear hunting was the favorite among these sports, in which, although it was highly exciting and dangerous, the odds were generally against the bear. He was a brave antagonist, and always faced the enemy, but the entangling lasso in the skilful hands of his opponent and the quickness and intelligence of the equine assistant made an unfair handicap. The grizzly was the gamest and most ferocious animal in California, yet despite his fierce disposition he was inclined to attend to his own business, and rarely attacked a man unless surprised or molested. The severest test of the horse was his behavior in a bear fight, a feat which was often undertaken by a ranchero single-handed, without other aid than his mount, his inseparable reata, and the knife carried in his *bota*, or legging. Don José Ramón Carrillo was a great bear hunter; it was his custom to dismount and go forward to meet the enemy alone. Holding a bull-hide shield in front of him with his left hand he approached the snarling bear, which immediately showed fight. The combat began; Carrillo, as the bear charged upon him and attempted to seize him, held up the shield to repel the assault, while with the knife in his other hand he made wary thrusts at the animal. Before long it lay dead before him. Walter

Colton describes a more unequal contest in which he was invited to participate:

"We wheeled into a mountain gorge, which opened into a long, irregular vista of savage wildness. A gallop of two or three miles brought us to a spot where the rocky barriers retreated on either hand, shaping out like a bowl, in the centre of which stood a cluster of oaks. On the lower limb of one, which threw its giant arm boldly from the rough trunk, a dark object was descried, half lost in the leaves. 'A bear! A bear!' shouted our leader, and dashed up to the tree, which was instantly surrounded by the whole troop. 'Give us pistols!' exclaimed the señoritas, as bravely in for the sport as the rest. Click, clack, and a storm of balls went through the tree-top. Down came old bruin into the midst, full of wrath and revenge. The horses instinctively wheeled into a circle, and as bruin sprang for a death grapple, the lasso of our vaquero, thrown with unerring aim, brought him up all standing. He now turned upon the horse of his new assailant, but that sagacious animal evaded each plunge, and seemed to play in transport about his antagonist. The pistols were out again, and a fresh volley fell thick as hail around the bear. In the smoke and confusion no one could tell where his next spring might be; but the horse of the vaquero knew its duty and kept the lasso taut. Bruin was wounded, but resolute and undaunted; the fire rolled from his red eyes like a flash of lightning out of a forked cloud. Foiled in his plunges at the horse, he seized the lasso in his paws, and in a moment more would have been at his side, but the horse sprang aside and tripped him, rolling him over and over till he lost his desperate hold on the lasso. The pistols were reloaded, and señoritas and caballeros all dashed up for another shower of fire and lead. As the smoke cleared, bruin was found with the lasso slack, a sure evidence that the horse which managed it knew his antagonist was dead."

For those who liked a spice of danger in the sports, elk hunting was not to be despised, for these animals were large, strong, and bold fighters. Yet, strong as they were, one of them could be dragged alive into a settlement by the reatas of two rancheros. At one time elk abounded to such an extent in the central and northern part of the province that they were hunted for their hides and tallow. On this subject William Heath Davis has an interesting paragraph:

"I often saw on Mare Island in the years from '40 to '43 as many as 2,000 or 3,000 elk. It was their habit to cross and re-cross by swimming between the island and the mainland, and I remember on one occasion sailing on the schooner *Isabel* through a band of not less than 1,000 which were crossing from the island to the main. It was a grand and exciting scene. The rancheros captured them with the lasso, which was more dangerous and exciting than killing cattle. The best horses and vaqueros were required on account of the strength, agility, fleetness, and fierceness of the elk; and on account of their wide-spreading horns great skill was required in throwing the lasso."

The chase for the wild horse, too, furnished plenty of excitement. There was no sport, however, that brought the strength, courage, and skill of both horse and rider into such full play as an encounter with a wild bull. Lieutenant Joseph Warren Revere, of the United States Navy, at one time in command of the military district of Sonoma, has a spirited description of one of these encounters:

"I have seen the fiercest and wildest mountain bull attacked and overcome by a single skilful vaquero, who led him off like a puppy led by a string. On such occasions the horse exhibits wonderful sagacity of nature, a sense of his own importance as the trusty ally of his master, and a degree of excitement and pleasure at least equal to that of his rider. The intelligence of the animal then most nearly approaches human reason, and his large expanded nostril, his reeking coat, his cautious approaches to the foe, around whom he lightly careers, like a boxer in the arena, the stiffness of his muscles when he plants and braces himself for the sudden and violent jerks of his antagonist, far more powerful than himself and, above all, the careful watchfulness of his piercing and regardful eye, form a picture of equine sagacity and attitude which would delight a Horace Vernet. And when the bellowing and raging bull, at length overcome in the struggle between strength and skill, falls heavily to earth, cowed and conquered at the feet of the victor, it is surprising to see the apparent scorn with which the noble beast looks on at the catastrophe, and how, guiltless of the meaner passion of revenge, he seeks only to recruit his exhausted strength for the next conflict."

There were lighter amusements to while away the long summer days on the ranchos. The *merienda*, or picnic, was a form of entertainment much in vogue among the Californians. These affairs were attended by whole families, and sometimes entire neighborhoods or villages, and were occasions for much jollity and innocent mirth. Those who were too old, too young, or too feeble to ride horseback had to content themselves with the carretas, but the more vigorous always preferred their prancing steeds. Each horseman carried a fair one on the saddle before him, his feet thrust forward in the stirrups, the reins held in his left hand, the lady's waist protectingly encircled with his right arm, and away they galloped over hill and dale, waking the wild echoes of the woods with their happy laughter and songs. Into the carretas tumbled the children and such of the women who perforce preferred that slow mode of locomotion, and in them also were stowed a generous supply of roast turkeys, chickens, *tamales*, *enchiladas*, *dulces*, and beef and mutton to be barbecued. Arrived at the chosen spot, generally some delightful flower-strewn dell, by the side of a clear, rippling stream, the party halted, the bountiful meal was spread on the grass, and all fell to with the hearty appetites of an outdoor people. Afterwards there would be horse-racing, guitar playing, singing, and always some love-making. Happy, unspoiled children of nature! They had no need of the artificialities of society to get out of life all the joy that it held for them.

Incredible as it may seem to the housewives of our era, "wash day" was looked forward to as a sort of fiesta by the children and others. The soiled linen was generally allowed to accumulate for several weeks, and then half the village went to the nearest springs to make a picnic of "blue Monday." Guadalupe Vallejo recalls pleasant memories of such an expedition to Agua Caliente:

"The night before, the Indians soaped the clumsy carreta's wheels. Lunch was placed in the baskets. The gentle oxèn were yoked to the pole. We climbed in under an old Mexican flag used as an awning, and the white-haired Indian teamster, who had driven the carreta since his boyhood, plodded beside with his long *garrocha*, or ox-goad. The great piles of linen were fastened on the backs of horses, led by other servants, while the girls and women who were to do the washing trooped along by the side of the carreta. Altogether it made an imposing cavalcade, though our progress was slow and it was generally sunrise before we had fairly reached the spring . . . Sometimes we heard the howl of coyotes, and the noise of other wild animals in the dim dawn, and then none of the children were allowed to leave the carreta. The women rubbed home-made soap in the clothes, dipped them in the spring and rubbed them on smooth rocks until they were white as snow, then spread them out to dry on the tops of low bushes . . . To me, at least, one of the dearest of my childish memories is the family expedition from the great thick-walled adobe under the olive and fig trees of the mission to the Agua Caliente in the early dawn, and the late return at twilight when the younger children were all asleep in the slow carreta, and the Indians were singing hymns as they drove the linen-laden horses down the dusky ravines." Idyllic days, alas, forever gone!

The Californians were a great people to make visits to friends and relatives, the whole family going and sometimes staying a week or a month. Often fifty visitors would arrive at once, and then the tortilla makers would get no rest night or day. Of a bullock butchered one morning not enough was left for breakfast the next morning.

There was no country where celebrations and feast days occurred more frequently than in California. Religious festivals were made occasions for jollity and merry-making rather than the pulling of long faces and Puritan seriousness. Colton writes of the feast of Guadalupe at Monterey in this wise:

"The old church bell has been ringing out all the morning in honor of Guadalupe, patron saint of California. Her festivities commenced last evening in illuminated windows, bonfires, the flight of rockets, and the loud mirth of children."

Christmas was the great festival of the whole year, and *La Noche Buena* (the good night) was celebrated with much pomp. After the midnight mass a sacred drama called *Los Pastores* (the shepherds), representing the Bible story, was performed by a party of young persons dressed in appropriate costumes. The whole performance was enlivened by the notes of the guitar, and was interspersed with songs and comic incidents that seemed better adapted to the stage than to the church. The party often continued the performance for some days, going from house to house, greatly to the delight of the small boys of the place.

"The *Pastorela*, composed by Padre Florencio of the Soledad Mission, a copy of which is to be found among the Vallejo documents, was often performed. It was a great favorite, and was generally given on Christmas Eve. Pío Pico used to play the part of Bato, the chief shepherd, and the Vallejos frequently took part. But the best player, the one who got most applause, was Jacinto Rodríguez, who used to go to the seashore to practice his part, uttering fearful shouts, and making all kinds of crazy gestures, to the great amusement of the boys who hid near by and watched him."

The people, whites and Indians, were much given to gambling, especially over the results of games and contests. Even the children wagered the buttons on their clothes in their little games, sometimes being left without enough to hold the clothing on. An Indian would wager away the shirt on his back, and even sometimes his wife and children. "The Spanish-Californians," says the French traveller, Duflot de Mofras, "are passionately fond of horse-racing, and the extravagant bets which they make upon them contribute not a little to their ruin. We have seen rancheros risk on the swiftness of their horses a hundred or two hundred head of cattle." Yet they gambled for excitement rather than avarice, and accepted losses with the same imperturbability as gains.

The Indians had their own games. One of the favorites was the *tekersie*, which was to send rolling a ring three thumbs in diameter, and to throw upon it two sticks, each four feet long, so as to stop its course. If one or both passed through the ring or it fell upon one or both of the sticks, it counted so many points. When one couple had taken its turn throwing the sticks, others followed, until it had gone the rounds of the party. Another, which was played by both men and women, was to divide into two bands, each with a curved stick seeking to push a wooden ball to a mark, while the other endeavored to thrust it back. It was deemed amusing at a festival to place clothing on top of a mast smeared with tallow and sprinkled with dust and ashes, and let the Indians climb for it. This was the same thing as the "greased pole" of American country sports.

"Every Saturday at the missions the Indian neophytes had a ball. Some missions had a separate place for this; at others the dance went on in the field. In 1824 Duhaut-Cilly saw twelve mission Indians, dressed in long shirts, with feathers on their heads, dance in wonderful accord, striking the ground with sticks, gesticulating with arms and legs, making signs of love, hate, terror. The body was kept curved, the knees somewhat bent. The scene was lighted up by torches. The orchestra formed a half circle of women, surrounded by a row or two of onlookers. The harmony was plaintive and wild, moving the nerves rather than the soul. While the actors rested, a horn was blown to drive away evil spirits. The padres winked at these scattered pagan superstitions."

One of the few amusements of the padre at San José was to throw rolled-up pancakes into the gaping mouths of the boys, which would be caught by the teeth and swallowed like lightning, amid laughter and jokes; again, something like our pie-eating contests. The game of billiards was introduced at Monterey in 1828. No bets were allowed, and the price of the game was one *real*. Betting on the results of the games generally formed a large part of their interest, so it seems that billiards could not have been very popular.

The arrival of a grandee in the province was always made an occasion for elaborate festivities, in which the entire population within reach joined with heartfelt enthusiasm. When Governor Pablo Vicente de Sola, the last of the Spanish governors, arrived in 1815, he was received with illuminations and general rejoicings at Monterey. A grand feast was prepared, at which the tables were loaded with the delicacies of the province—wild game, olives from San Diego, oranges from San Gabriel, wines from San Francisco, "oven-fruits" made of San Antonio flour. The table decorations consisted of flowers from the garden of Don Antonio García, whose daughters waited on the governor. After the repast soldiers gave an exhibition of horsemanship. Then came a bear and bull fight, of which Juan B. Alvarado, who witnessed the affair as a boy, has left a detailed description:

"By the large gate of the presidio entered four riders on spirited horses covered with embroidered trappings; these horsemen dragged by a lasso two large and very black bears; two others did the same with two furious bulls which were to fight. The people shouted on all sides, making bets as to which would be the conqueror in this battle of giants, some betting on the bear and some on the bull. The native musicians played on their instruments—violins, flutes, and drums. The bears and the bulls, which were not accustomed to this kind of noise, bellowed in a terrifying way; and if to the bellowing of the animals is added the noise made by the spectators, it will easily be understood that the scene presented a startling confusion. On one side men stood ready with loaded guns in case of accident. The new governor, to whom such spectacles were altogether strange, remarked, 'I am afraid. I have heard that these bears are very fierce, and that they eat Christians.' The bear and the bull were fastened together by one foot with a stout chain of sufficient length to allow them considerable freedom of action; then the reatas which held each leg of the bear were thrown off, and the beasts confronted each other. The bull lowered his head and looked threatening, and the bear rose upon his haunches, as if awaiting the onset. But for ten minutes neither advanced. The spectators began to grow impatient. The vaqueros prodded the bull, and with a roar of pain he rushed upon his adversary. The bear, with a quickness and agility astonishing in a body apparently so unwieldy, avoiding the horns, threw himself with a grasp upon the bull's neck, and both rolled over and over in desperate struggle upon the ground. The noise was terrific and the dust rose in clouds, while the onlookers shouted and yelled as they saw the fight was deadly and witnessed the flow of blood. Presently the bull, fatigued with exertion and hot with thirst, protruded his tongue, and the bear made an attempt by a change of position to seize it. But the attempt cost him his life. The bull was wary and on his guard, and with a sudden plunge transfixed his enemy and with a tremendous effort threw him in the air. As the bear fell with a ghastly wound, the bull, infuriated with his own injuries, pursued his advantage, and with a second and deadly plunge closed the battle."

The climax to the function was a grand ball at night which lasted until dawn of the next day. Again we quote Alvarado:

"The dresses were for the times elegant; those of the men were close-fitting short jackets of dove color, short breeches fastened at the knee with silver buckles, and white stockings; those of the women white *enaguas*, or skirts, of transparent muslin covered with gilt spangles which sparkled in the lamplight; short jackets of colored silk buttoned closely to the neck; hair elaborately done up in waves and curls partly confined in silken nets; necklaces of pearls from the gulf, which were plentiful in those days, and long ear pendants of the same; slippers of white satin with wooden heels which clacked as they danced. The same Indians who had assisted in the mass of the morning and the bull and bear fight of the afternoon furnished the music for the dances; and they did it well, being much more accustomed even for their church music to lively and inspiriting operatic airs and dancing tunes than to slow and lugubrious elegies and dirges. The programme consisted of *contradanzas*, minuets, Aragonese *jotas*, and various other dances usual among the Spanish population. It was the custom to accompany the dancing with the singing of appropriate verses, making the whole business of the dance a real accomplishment requiring some study."

The costumes worn in California in the time of Sola were fifty years behind those in other parts of the world, and the new governor paid the ladies the rather dubious compliment of telling them how much it pleased him to see them using the styles of the olden days in his country.

It was now the turn of the padres to welcome the new governor, which they did by escorting him in a long procession of friars and Indians over the *via crucis* (way of the cross), as the road between the presidio and Mission San Carlos was called. Following this procession came church ceremonies and a grand finale by the Indians, in which, dressed in all the bravery of feathers, beads, and war paint, they gave their native dances and a sham battle. At the conclusion of the whole affair the governor remarked that he had never been so highly entertained before in his life. The fiesta, which was probably extended to this royalist governor as an expression of the loyalty of the Californians to the king of Spain, furnished food for talk to the people for a long time.

Of the amusements, that preferred above all others by the Californians was the dance. Dancing was a passion with them from infancy to old age. The man of seventy was just as agile in tripping the light fantastic toe as the youth of eighteen, and grandmothers and grandchildren were seen dancing together. Their houses were constructed with reference to this amusement, and each had a large *sala* for the purpose. If a few people got together at any hour of the day, the first thought was to send for a violin, or perhaps one of the daughters of the house consented to perform on her harp for the occasion. So devoted were the people to this amusement that even the Sabbath was not held too sacred for it, and after dutiful attendance at morning mass, the afternoon was given over to dancing. Walter Colton says, "A Californian would hardly pause in a dance for an earthquake, and would renew it before the vibrations ceased." It seems that even the presence of a prisoner of state was celebrated by a tertulia, as William Heath Davis relates in connection with the story of his arrest and imprisonment in 1840 by Governor Alvarado:

"I was kept imprisoned for twenty-four hours at the house of the sub-prefect, Don Francisco Guerrero, at Mission Dolores; during my incarceration I was very kindly treated by the sub-prefect and his amiable wife, Doña Josefa. In the evening I was entertained by this lady with a beautiful little dancing party at her house, at which were present six or eight lovely young ladies and about as many young Californian gentlemen. We had a delightful time. On that occasion Doña Josefa, who was a graceful young woman, with full, brilliant black eyes, wore her hair unconfined, flowing at full length, rich and luxuriant, reaching nearly to her feet; as she moved in the figures of the dance, she presented a fascinating picture of youth and beauty that I could not but admire. The dancing continued until a late hour, and the affair was so very enjoyable that I hardly realized that I was a prisoner of state. The next day the sub-prefect ordered me released."

In early times balls broke up at ten or eleven o'clock at night. Those were the days of "early candle-light" affairs. But along about 1817 and later the keeping of such early hours began to be disregarded, and finally the balls lasted the night through. In 1840, on the occasion of the marriage of one of his sons, Amador remembers that there was a dance at the house of Sálvio Pacheco, at San José, which lasted all night and until nine o'clock in the morning, continuing again at eight in the evening of this second day, and kept up all night. In 1843, at the marriage of another son, dancing continued for three days and nights, with unlimited consumption of wine and food of all kinds.

To ride all day to attend a baile was a mere bagatelle. Duflot de Mofras, the Frenchman who visited the coast in 1841, accompanied a party of thirty from Sonoma to a Russian farm. They started in the morning, arrived at their destination in the evening, danced all night, all the next day, and all the following night, and on the third day started at sunrise on their homeward journey. The reader will perhaps remember the description of an affair of the sort at San Diego which lasted for eight days, part of the time on shipboard and part on shore, with only short rests taken out for eating and sleeping. One writer says that it seemed as though the young people were either riding on horseback or dancing all the time.

Doña Refugio de Bandini speaks enthusiastically of the time when she was a girl: "How often did we spend half the night at a tertulia till two o'clock in the morning, in the most agreeable and distinguished society. Our house would be full of company—thirty or forty persons at the table; it would have to be set twice. A single fiesta might cost $1,000, but in those days the receipts at my husband's store were $18,000 a month. The prettiest women were to be found at San Diego." Estevan de la Torre says that the balls given at a celebration of nuptials lasted regularly three days. The people ate, drank, and danced night and day; while some rested or slept, others continued the festivities. Coronel says that for a large ball an arbor of boughs, lined inside with cotton cloth to keep out the wind, was erected in front of the house; the ground being first well watered and beaten level. One side was left open, in front of which the men gathered on horseback, while seats were arranged around the three enclosed sides for the women. The musicians, consisting of a violinist, a guitarist, and two or three singers, stationed themselves in a corner, where they were out of the way.

"The master of ceremonies," continues Coronel, "was called *el tecolero;* from the first he was present managing everything connected with the ball. To start the festivities he led out each lady, one at a time, dancing a few steps before her as he held out his hand. The lady then arose, went to the center of the sala, lifted her wide skirts on each side with her hands, and danced a turn or two to the time of the music, then retired and another took her place. In this way every lady was called out, and there were no wall-flowers. While the women were going through the performance, the men on horseback kept up a constant skylarking, coming and going, disputing places, each endeavoring to force his horse to the front. When ladies and gentlemen were to dance a piece together, the horsemen who wished to take part dismounted, removed their spurs and hung them on the saddle-bow; then, sombrero in hand, they entered the salon and each took out his selected partner. After the piece was ended, the ladies retired to their seats and the men remounted, so that it might almost be said that they did their dancing on horseback." In the wilder dances as practiced by the less refined class, sometimes one or more men would enter the arbor on their horses, which they caused to prance about, while they sprinkled aguardiente from bottles which they carried, on the ground in front of the lady, crying out, "Do your best, my darling; you know that I am yours, and will guard you!" These demonstrations sometimes resulted in a fight outside. Of course such rowdy affairs never took place in the houses of the better class, where all was dignity and ceremony. The following is a literal translation of a printed invitation to a ball:

"José Figueroa, José Antonio Carrillo, Pío Pico, Joaquín Ortega, and the licentiate Rafael Gómez, request your attendance at eight o'clock this evening, at a ball that will be given at the house of the first named, to congratulate the directors of colonization and their estimable fellow travelers, to celebrate the election of deputies for the territory and to felicitate the country upon its enjoyment of union and peace. Monterey, November 1, 1834. Citizen Mariano Bonilla." From this it will be seen that dancing had its place even in affairs political.

In the early days folk dances, with set figures, were the rule, but later the waltz, polka, mazurka, and other European "round dances" were introduced, much to the indignation of the clergy, who in 1821 prohibited the waltz under penalty of *excomunion mayor*. Nevertheless, Juan Bandini, who was a famous dancer himself, introduced it in California in 1830, and it was danced that same year at a ball given by the governor to the *diputación* at Monterey. The Hijar colonists also brought in these modern dances when they came in 1835.

The *jota* was perhaps the favorite among the folk dances. It resembled an English country dance, or an American Virginia Reel — the men and women standing in long lines facing each other. It was accompanied by the singing of verses and a refrain, of which the following are examples:

VERSE

Palomita, vete al campo,
Y dile á los tiradores
Que no te tiren, porqu'eres
La dueña de mis amores.

Literally translated, this reads:

Little dove, go to the field,
And tell the hunters
Not to shoot thee, for thou art
The mistress of my loves.

Then followed the refrain, accompanied by a chain of hands in the dance:

El cuervo en el aire
Vuela vigilante;
Vuela para atras
Vuela pá delante.
Si la piedra es dura,
Tu eres un diamante,
Porque no ha podido
Mi amor ablandarte.
Si te hago un cariño
Me haces un desprecio,
Y luego me dices
Que yo soy el necio;
Como si quererte
Fuera necedad.
Pero anda, ingratota,
Que algun dia entre sueno
Tú te acordarás
Que yo fui tu dueño.

Literal translation:

The crow in the air
Flies watchfully.
It flies backwards,
It flies forwards.
If stone is hard,
Thou art a diamond,
For it has not been possible
For my love to soften thee.
If I offer thee a caress
Thou dost flout me,
And then tell me
I am a fool,
As though to love thee
Were folly.
But never mind, ungrateful one,
Some day, in thy dreams,
Thou wilt remember
That I was thy master.

So many of these dances were accompanied by singing or recital of verses, often improvised, that it seems the beaux and belles of the day must have done some arduous thinking as well as the practice of the steps of the figures. Dances of this sort, in which there was singing of verses by the participants, were the *zorrita* (little fox), the *camotes* (sweet potatoes), the *borrego* (lamb), *el caballo* (the horse), and the *burro* (donkey). The *burro* was almost the counterpart of the American "Old Dan Tucker." The dancers, men and women, formed a circle; then one extra man took his place in the center as burro. When the music commenced those forming the circle began to dance around the central figure. Two or three verses were sung, and at a certain word each man embraced a woman, and the person who was left alone became the donkey.

El caballo was danced by a man and woman, who, when the music began, balanced to each other. At certain designated points in the singing of the *verso*, the woman seized her skirts before and behind as if to mount a horse, the man got astride of his handkerchief, and to the sound of music they made movements as if on horseback. These descriptions would indicate that some of the modern "jazz" dances, such as the "fox trot" and "horses, horses, horses," are not so modern after all.

The *canastita de flores* (the little basket of flowers) was performed by making a ring of all the dancers, who circled round, singing. Just as the last word in the song was pronounced, each man rushed forward to embrace the girl he loved. Generally some lady was left out in the cold, and became the *dueña de las burlas* (the dame of the joke). This was repeated several times, so that the dueña was changed. This dance was a companion to the *burro*, except that in this case a lady was the victim.

In all these dances there was a great variety in the words of the verses and the refrains. In the *fandango*, which was danced by one man and one woman, to the accompaniment of castanets, the music would now and then suddenly stop and the singer would cry out *bomba!* At this signal one or other of the partners was required to recite a verse, often improvised, such as the following, sung by the man:

Entre las flores de lirio
No te pude conocer,
Que no parecias muger,
Sino Ángel del cielo empíreo.

Among the lily flowers
I could not distinguish thee,
For thou wert not like a woman,
But an angel of the empyrean skies.

The dance called the *bamba*, executed by women only, required such dexterity that only certain ones undertook it. The steps were extremely intricate, and the dancer carried on her head a tumbler of water. On the floor was placed a handkerchief with two of the corners tied together. This handkerchief the woman took up with her feet and concealed about her person while dancing, sometimes doing so with two or three handkerchiefs, which she would again place on the floor. All this she did without spilling a single drop of the water in the tumbler. The feat concluded, the *tecolero* took from her the glass, and, amid uproarious applause, she returned to her seat.

When a woman was a particularly graceful dancer, the men expressed their appreciation by placing their hats on her head, one on top of the other; when her head could balance no more, she would take the hats in her hands, dancing all the time. When she returned to her seat the hats had to be redeemed by the owners with coin, each one paying what he pleased, from *dos reales* to five dollars. There were many more folk dances of this sort, participated in more often by the humbler class. The *contra-*

danza, stepped to waltz time in slow and measured cadence, something like a minuet, with much interweaving and waving of arms, was very popular among the higher class. When well done, by two long lines of men and women, it was exceedingly graceful.

Carnival week preceding Lent was marked by the *cascarone* balls, a feature of social life as characteristic of the California of that day as the Mardi Gras was of Europe. For weeks previous to the season the housewives would begin to save their egg-shells. A hole was carefully broken in one end of the egg, the contents removed, and the dried shell afterwards filled with *oropel* (gold-leaf finely cut), colored paper, cologne water, or, as a special extravagance, with gold-dust. The hole in the egg was then sealed with wax or paper pasted on. The compliment was to break the eggs lightly over the heads of favored ones, and as the ladies generally wore their hair floating unconfined, the spangles glittering among their raven tresses as they swept through the dance had a very pretty effect. The *cascarone* season was observed with particular brilliance at Monterey and Los Angeles, the former being the capital and the latter the largest town in the department. Monterey has not yet forgotten how to give a *cascarone* ball.

It is a charming picture that one gets in a backward look at those times, with the happy people singing and dancing the care-free hours away. Who can say that theirs was not the better choice, as compared with the material progress coupled with the carking anxieties of our day? One who knew it all at first-hand, William Heath Davis, gives us a pleasing picture of the social affairs of the time:

"I have often been a guest at such gatherings, which were the sweetest part of my life, and I thought these native Californians of Spanish extraction were, as a rule, as sincere people as ever lived under the canopy of Heaven. I look back almost two generations ago to those merry days with pride and joy, at the kindness which I received and the manliness and simplicity of the welcome of the fathers of families and the womanly deportment of their wives and daughters and their innocent amusements. The native Californians were about the most contented people that I ever saw, as also were the early foreigners who settled among them and intermarried with them, adopted their habits and customs, and became, as it were, a part of themselves."

Chapter XIII

CHAPTER XIII

When the Pen Was Mightier Than the Sword

IT HAS BEEN too much the custom with historians to cast ridicule upon the "bloodless revolutions" of the Californians, the little wars in which more ink was spilled than blood. As a matter of fact, nothing sheds greater credit upon them than this very circumstance. They were not a bloodthirsty people, and killing anybody was the last thing that they wished to do, least of all their own fathers, brothers, and intimate friends. Intermarriage and friendship had bound the community together in the closest of bonds, and political disagreements, though they might cause great rancor, seldom brought the Californians to the point of wishing to take each other's lives. As Bancroft says, "They were simple-minded, and not at all sanguinary; shedding blood was abhorrent to their nature. They were different from many of their countrymen of the other provinces of Mexico in this respect." Referring to this same point, Sepúlveda has to say:

"Settled in a remote part of the centre of government, isolated from and almost unaided by the rest of the Mexican states, and with very rare chances of communication with other parts of the world, they in time formed a society whose habits, customs, and manners differed in many essential particulars from the other people of Mexico. The character of the new settlers assumed, I think, a milder form, more independence, and less of the restless spirit which their brothers in old Mexico possessed. To this the virtuous and intelligent missionaries doubtless contributed greatly."

Yet, notwithstanding the mild character of the inhabitants, the history of California under Mexican rule is one of a succession of rebellions against constituted authority. From the point of view of the American residents, who were then here in considerable numbers, these political upsets were mere nuisances, because they interfered with business; but considered in the light of the interests of the Californians, every one of them was justified. The Americans cared little for the "rights of man" so long as business went on as usual, but with the Californians liberty was the predominant passion.

There was a constantly growing resentment in the distant colony toward the central government for its indifference and neglect, and a feeling of contempt and dislike among the colonists for the Mexican governors who were sent to domineer over them. It was felt that the colony was old enough to throw off its swaddling clothes and assume its own government. In fact, the revolutions were a series of demonstrations for "home rule," which finally achieved success. From the very beginning a bitter feeling had arisen between the Californians and the Mexican government, owing to the policy of the latter in attempting to turn the province into a penal colony for Mexican convicts. The ill-feeling was further increased when the government resolved to fill all the official positions with Mexicans, to the exclusion of Californians. This feeling soon grew to one of hostility toward the people of Mexico, or as they were called, *los de la otra banda* (those of the other side). "The best of the Mexicans among us," says Alvarado, "were insulting and offensive, and were far more cordially hated than any foreigners." Personal encounters and quarrels between men of Mexican birth and native-born Californians became increasingly frequent. Alvarado himself once inflicted chastisement with his own hands upon a Mexican schoolmate named Romero, for making insulting remarks on the dress of the administration of which he was a member.

Such being the state of affairs, it was not difficult to find cause of complaint against each of the Mexican governors sent to rule the province, and one after another they were sent flying out of the country. J. M. Guinn, an impartial commentator, says on this subject:

"There were many revolutions in California during the Mexican period, but in nearly every case they were protests against petty tyrannies of Mexican-born governors. California, during the time it was a Mexican province, suffered from bad governors very much as the American colonies did before our Revolutionary War. Descendants of revolutionary sires would resent as an insult the imputation that their forefathers were the promoters of anarchy. California rebellions were more in the nature of political protests than real revolutions. They were usually bloodless affairs. In the half-dozen or more revolutions occurring in the twenty years preceding the American Conquest, resulting in four battles, there were only three men killed and six or seven wounded."

The spirit of independence mounted higher and higher; the people no longer called themselves *Mexicanos*, but *Californios*. First, Victoria, half Indian by blood, honest in purpose but dictatorial in methods, was driven out on the ground of his disregard for the constitution and his tyrannical acts. One thing that especially horrified the kind-hearted Californians was the imposition of the death sentence upon criminals for robberies of small sums. Pastoral

California never had a hangman or public executioner; the few executions that were carried out were done by the regular troops.

Figueroa, despite his Mexican origin and his Indian blood, managed by the force and charm of his personal character and the wisdom of his public acts to win and retain the respect and affection of the people until his death. After that they began to grow restive again, and when Mariano Chico arrived, preceded by an unpromising reputation and accompanied by a lady, the beautiful Doña Cruz, to whom he was not united by the bonds of matrimony, the Californians professed themselves to be outrageously insulted, and in three months Chico was unceremoniously sent up the gang-plank of a return ship at Monterey. But the devil is never so black as he is painted, and Chico was by no means without his good qualities. He made a hobby of studying the medicinal plants native to California, and prepared a number of remedies from them which he said would cure every ill the human race was subject to. This harmless fad only awakened the ridicule of the people, who, with the Spanish fondness for nicknames, dubbed him *el gobernador de las recetas* (the governor of the recipes). Victoria was called *el gobernador negro* (the black governor), in reference to his Indian blood and dark complexion. It will be seen by this that Californians did not stand in much awe of their rulers.

Chico's successor, Gutiérrez, was a good-natured, easygoing man, not a Mexican but a Spaniard by birth, but it was enough that he was a foreigner, and it was not hard to find a charge against him; so he lasted only two months, when he was sent on the right about face back to Mexico.

Micheltorena, a perfectly well-meaning and charming gentleman, won the affections of the people in spite of themselves, but he suffered from a fatal handicap in the shape of the convict army with which his short-sighted government had saddled him. Once more revolution broke out, more against his ragamuffin soldiers than himself, and he also was compelled to walk the gang-plank at Monterey, the courteous gentleman to the last, bowing to the people and expressing thanks to those who had not taken sides against him. The disrespect for Micheltorena was shown in the comic songs written about him and his army of *cholos* (rascals) and openly sung all over the state.

Even after the people had won their way and established home rule under the first native-born governor, Juan Bautista Alvarado, dissensions did not cease, for the country was still in the throes of the settling down process which naturally followed the separation from Spain. Clashes arose from the jealousy which began at an early date between north and south, ending in such rivalry between Los Angeles and Monterey, as to which should be the site of the capital, that civil war broke out in 1837 to settle it. The civil governor, Alvarado, and the military commander, M. G. Vallejo, could not agree upon the management of the political and financial affairs of the country.

Altogether, the whole Mexican period looms in history as one of constant unrest, of kaleidoscopic changes in politics, marked by many clashes at arms and personal quarrels. But, as has been said, little bloodshed resulted from these encounters, and on the few occasions when this occurred the grief of the people was intense. *Pronunciamientos* and *manifiestos* were the weapons usually employed by the leaders to win their purposes. In this sort of fighting none was more adept than the brilliant young Juan Bautista Alvarado, silver-tongued orator and political "spellbinder" of his day. William Heath Davis says the power of eloquence possessed by Alvarado was such that he could make people believe black was white, and win them to a cause even though they believed it to be wrong. In the movement to expel Gutiérrez, Davis says, "Alvarado maneuvered with such tact that he succeeded in his efforts without sacrificing any lives." In 1838 when there was a threatened uprising against him at Los Angeles, led by the Carrillos, Governor Alvarado marched to meet the revolters at Las Flores, where a "battle," waged for the most part by tongue and pen, took place. Alvarado now tried the force of his persuasive eloquence upon Carlos Carrillo, and induced him to disband his troops, thus ending all further opposition. When the Mexican government finally confirmed his appointment as constitutional governor of California, notwithstanding that he had been the leader of the revolution against it, it was probably because, so Davis thinks, "he represented the matter in a letter of marked ability to the President." This was only one more occasion in which the California leader proved that the pen is indeed mightier than the sword.

In the rebellion led by Solis, in 1829, which was in reality a "strike" of the soldiers for their pay, ink, not blood, was shed, and the only carcass seen on the field after the smoke cleared away was that of a horse that was unlucky enough to have a ball lodged in its neck. The expulsion of Chico was so adroitly managed by those who wished to get rid of him that their purpose was accomplished without coming into open conflict with the national government, and they were thus enabled to "try their wings in easy flights." In the revolt against Micheltorena the only casualties were the loss of one horse and a mule, and the chief suffering was that endured by the women and children of Los Angeles, who climbed a hill from which the firing could be distinctly heard, and, with crosses in their hands, knelt and prayed for the safety of their brave defenders, while they shed abundant tears and filled the night with their lamentations.

Franz Geritz '27

Happy the people who can reckon their battle losses in ink rather than in blood! One exception to these bloodless revolutions occurred, that against Victoria in 1831, the story of which we shall call:

Like Knights of Old

Victoria, who despised the Californians and was confident of his ability to whip them almost single-handed, when he heard of the revolt at Los Angeles, marched against them with a force of only about thirty men. In this force was numbered one who stands out from the rest, partly because of his own striking personality, and partly because of his fate in being one of the few to die on the battlefield in peaceful California. This was the young captain Romualdo Pacheco. To make his story clear we must now turn backward a step in our narrative. In 1827 Governor Echeandía, who will be remembered by the reader as the "villain" of the Fitch-Carrillo romance, decided to tear himself from the attractions, sentimental or otherwise, of San Diego long enough to go to Monterey and hold a meeting of the diputación. The San Diegans despatched him on his journey with a hearty send-off. In his train were two young men who had come with him from Baja California, Agustín Zamorano and Romualdo Pacheco. Being at the susceptible age, the two lost no time in laying their hearts at the feet of two of San Diego's fairest daughters, the Señoritas Argüello and Carrillo. As both the young men wished to accompany their chief to Monterey, and neither was willing to leave his lady-love behind him, arrangements were made to celebrate the weddings before the departure. The festivities were most elaborate, and, Alvarado tells us:

"The entire population of San Diego turned out, and afterwards, when the gubernatorial party set out with a military escort for Monterey, the people accompanied it a long distance on its journey. A number of the principal citizens continued with the party all the way. It is said that the march altogether, graced as it was by the presence of the young brides and their relatives and friends, was the merriest and most enjoyable that had ever taken place in California." Alas, that so bright a beginning should have so sad an ending!

In the revolution against Victoria, in 1831, young Pacheco elected to remain loyal to his government, and so joined the governor's forces. When the two parties met at Cahuenga Pass, Victoria, perhaps to show his contempt for his opponents, advanced alone and called upon Captain Portilla, his former officer, to come over to his side, with his soldiers. They refused, upon which Victoria ordered his men to fire a volley, but, as the shots went over the heads of the enemy, they were probably aimed to frighten rather than harm them. At this moment Pacheco, perhaps through a misunderstanding of the order, rode forward alone on his beautiful black horse into the space between the two parties. On the other side was a dare-devil named José María Ávila, a man of herculean size, and said to be the best horseman in Los Ángeles. Ávila, who had armed himself with a lance made of a long stake with a bayonet point strapped to it, believed that Pacheco was challenging to single combat, and rode forward to meet him, with leveled lance. While the others looked on in stupefaction, the two rushed at each other, like knights of old. Pacheco swerved to avoid the lance thrust; Ávila was carried past by the impetus of his horse, but, turning in his saddle, he drew a pistol and shot Pacheco through the heart. The struggle then became general, and in the combat that followed, Ávila in turn was unhorsed and killed, some say by Victoria himself.

This was the first blood shed between men of Spanish ancestry in California, and it was with the deepest mourning that the citizens who had taken no part in the contest carried the bodies of the two young men to the pueblo of Los Angeles, where they were followed to the grave by all the inhabitants, irrespective of political convictions. By the death of young Pacheco the territory lost a brave officer and true gentleman. Estevan de la Torre thus describes him: "Pacheco was a tall, slender, well-built man, extremely good-looking, and with a fine carriage and very gentlemanly manners. In character and conduct he was strictly moral. Never did a caballero come from Mexico so perfect in all respects."

This perfect young knight left a widow to mourn him, and an infant son but a month old, the Romualdo Pacheco who grew up to serve a term as governor of California after the American Conquest.

It was not simply in the form of pronunciamientos and manifiestos that the Californians made use of the pen in preference to the sword. A curious custom brought from old Spain, which took root and flourished exceedingly in the new soil of California, was that of settling disputes in verse rather than by duels with pistols and coffee for two. Notwithstanding the low state of education in the province, there was a general taste for poetry. As Bancroft says:

"There were not lacking verse-makers among them, though in poetry no attempt was made to achieve the upper regions of Parnassus, their half-fledged muse being apparently content to flutter 'round the mountain's base. Like their language, the Spanish are a poetic, rhythmic people; yet stern, majestic, and with a melancholy tone. In their softer moods they are touchingly sweet and tender, but when roused their tongue is terrible. All through these pastoral days there was material for a hundred pastoral poems, only there was not present any discovered Theocritus or Virgil to write them."

The country was full of "poetasters," as Vallejo calls them, and the pages of his own memoirs are sprinkled with quotations from their effusions. These writers spared no one, from governor or congressional candidates to rivals in love. Party rancor, which might otherwise have resulted in the spilling of blood, dissipated itself in the hurling of verses, sometimes little better than doggerel, by the partisans, at each other's heads. The eve of a political campaign generally found walls and doors covered with the *decimas* (stanzas of ten lines) of one side or the other, calling very pointed attention to the demerits and faults of the opposing side. The lampooned candidate, far from sending in a challenge to mortal combat to the authors of the scurrilous stanzas, retired to his chamber and set himself diligently to work to compose an even more withering reply in the same form, which he then scattered broadcast through the town. Bancroft thinks this was an unmanly way to carry on a contest, but opinions may differ as to whether it is more manly to perforate the body of one's opponent with a pistol ball or to make holes in his reputation with poetic darts. In the latter case, the contestants at least lived to fight another day.

Let it not be thought that these shafts of ridicule caused no pain, for many a victim would greatly have preferred to meet his enemy face to face with sword in hand than endure the laughter of his associates when the true aim found a tender spot. As an instance, in the political upheaval of 1836 which led to the expulsion of Governor Gutiérrez, among the exiles was numbered one Judge Castillo Negrete, who, before setting sail for Mexico, fired a parting shot at his victorious opponents, Alvarado and Vallejo, in the form of a tirade in verse. That the shot hit the mark was proved by the mental squirmings of the two gentlemen attacked, and their strenuous efforts at refutation of the charges contained in the so-called poem.

Every change in politics, which occurred with bewildering rapidity during the Mexican period, was celebrated in verse, more or less worthy of the name. That the output of the poetasters should have been so poor, as considered from a literary point of view, is explained by Vallejo by the general lack of educational advantages. In this connection he remarks, "In California there were many poetical geniuses, but they lacked the opportunity to cultivate the spirit of the muses."

Nor was it simply in the field of politics that poetry was employed as a vehicle of expression. The lover found it his best means to soften the obdurate heart of the lady fair whom he might be courting, and while he lightly touched his guitar under her barred window he raised his voice in the tender strains of a love song. This custom of the serenade continued long after American occupation. Even when Robert Louis Stevenson visited Monterey in 1880 it was still in vogue, and he writes of it:

"Night after night serenaders would be going about the street, sometimes in a company and with several voices and instruments together, sometimes severally, each guitar before a different window. It was a strange thing to lie awake in nineteenth century America and hear the guitar accompany, and one of these old, heart-breaking Spanish love songs mount into the night air."

These ballads were not in print, but passed from mouth to mouth in the manner of folk-songs. Some of them have recently been rescued from oblivion and put in printed form, with the musical score. As we have already seen, even the dances were punctuated and illustrated with the recital of impromptu verses, requiring a ready wit on the part of the dancer. Another quaint survival from the old country was that of wandering reciters of poetry, who went from house to house, somewhat in the fashion of the minstrels of the ancient times, and, striking an attitude, declaimed some poem, comic, heroic, or sentimental. These uninvited elocutionists no doubt expected at least a dinner in return for their efforts at entertainment. Let us now hear the story of:

The Judge and His Deadly Poems

Among all the Californians there was none who made a more effective use of the weapon of versification than a certain Judge Joaquín Buelna, a resident of the town of Santa Cruz, although it must be admitted that the opinion of his contemporaries concerning the literary value of his effusions differed markedly from his own. There were two occasions in particular when his plan worked to perfection. The first was in connection with the only attack ever made upon California from the sea, unless we count the premature raising of the flag at Monterey by Commodore Jones an attack.

In 1818 Monterey was sacked and burned by the Buenos Aires insurgents against Spain. This attack was really an attempt to coerce the Californians into joining the revolt, for up to that time they had remained loyal to the mother country. Its leader was the insurgent Captain Bouchard, one of the company of the famous "pirate of the Gulf of Mexico," Lafitte, hero of Byron's poem *The Corsair*. Hyppolyte de Bouchard is described as a strong, determined man of fiery temper, who exercised an iron rule over his men, something like his notorious master, "scarce seen to smile, and seldom heard to sigh, whose name appals the fiercest of his crew."

California, situated far from the center of hostilities, got little news of the progress of the revolution, especially as all trading ships had been stopped from coming by the insurgents. Had it not been, in fact, for their sufferings for lack of the commodities for which they had depended upon these ships, they would not have been affected in any particular by the great movement for liberty going on in the south. They had almost come to believe that they were safe from attack, but at the end of the summer of 1818 they suffered a rude awakening, when two privateers, or pirates, as they regarded them, appeared off Point Pinos. Governor Sola did all he could, with the totally inadequate means in his power, to resist the invaders, but he was so completely overmatched that he was finally compelled to retreat with his small force to the Rancho del Rey, on the present site of the town of Salinas.

Meanwhile, wild excitement prevailed among the noncombatants of Monterey, who saw themselves in imagination victims of the dreaded pirates. Dark stories of the buccaneers of early days and the bloody outrages committed by them upon the helpless people of the lower coast came to mind. The governor gave orders in the dead of night for the immediate flight of the women and children, and so great was the panic, that instead of devoting the little time at their disposal to packing the carretas with food and clothing, the people gave way to grief, and the poor women and children departed in a destitute condition. M. G. Vallejo writes feelingly of this occasion, in which he took part as a child:

"How well I remember that night! My good and venerated mother (may she rest in Paradise) placed herself in a carreta which had for a bottom two ox-hides, with two more for a top. There, after supping on some strips of beef half roasted without any salt, she surrounded herself with her family. Half a dozen blankets, which she had received from Father Florencio at the mission of Soledad, formed all our bed-clothing. Some were sitting, some stretched out on the hides, crying with the cold, while others shivered, and my poor mother cared for them all with an inimitable patience."

This was about as near to real war as California has ever

arrived. The people were divided between the missions of San Antonio and San Juan Bautista until conditions should permit their return to their homes.

In the meantime, the invaders were busy sacking and burning the presidio and town of Monterey. Few buildings escaped, and even the orchards and gardens were destroyed. After trying in vain to persuade the Californians to make common cause with them against Spain, the insurgent ships set sail on November 27, and Governor Sola went to work at once to rebuild the burned houses of Monterey. He worked to such purpose that in a few months all the inhabitants returned, and the town was in better condition than before the attack.

But what has our poetical friend, Judge Buelna, the reader may well ask, to do with these war's alarms? To make this clear a few words about the mission at Santa Cruz and the neighboring town of Branciforte are necessary. The church at Santa Cruz was especially well furnished with valuable ornaments; many of them were of gold and silver, and would therefore have made a rich prize for marauders. As for the town of Branciforte, we have already seen that it represented one of the early colonizing mistakes of the Spaniards in California, chiefly on account of the character of the colonists selected for the purpose. These people made constant trouble. When the Bouchard insurgents burned Monterey the fire was plainly seen across the bay at Santa Cruz, and the people, believing that the rich and flourishing mission there would be the next to be attacked, prepared to sack it themselves, with the idea that their depredations would be concealed in the spoliation committed by the enemy. The *juez comisionado*, Don Joaquín Buelna, naturally objected to this and called out troops to prevent it. The people were already beating on the church doors with hammers, and had baskets ready to fill with the golden ornaments. Those from Branciforte sacked the padre's house and the warehouses, excusing themselves by saying, "Since it must be lost, it is better that Christians should take it than the heathen invader." They even accused the judge of being in with the insurgents, and threatened to attack his house. Paying no attention to these threats, that gentleman calmly sat down and wrote some verses, of which he sent a copy to each of the rioters:

Que lenguas, que matadores
Los que viven sin gobierno;
Que es menester otro infierno
Para los murmuradores!

How loud-mouthed, how murderous,
Are those who live without restraint!
Another hell is needed
For such malcontents!

"Ignorant persons believed that the art of poesy was first cousin to that of necromancy, and believed themselves to be excommunicated by these verses," says Vallejo, "so, collecting the stolen articles, they went in a procession to return them to the priest. After administering a severe reprimand, all the while with an amused smile on his face, the good-hearted padre forgave them, and all returned to their homes to celebrate the reconciliation."

Thus was it proved again that the pen is indeed mightier than the sword, at least when it is dipped in bad poetry, as this same Judge Buelna had occasion to verify once more in a wholly different matter. It appears that the charms of Doña Guadalupe, his wife, attracted the attention of a number of young gallants, who attempted to pay court to her "in the very beard" of her husband. This annoyed him exceedingly, but far from challenging the would-be lovers to a succession of duels, as one might reasonably expect of a fiery Spaniard, the canny judge fired his verses, loaded with denunciations of their treacherous and dishonorable conduct, at them, and soon had the satisfaction of seeing them slip away, one by one! Whether this action on the part of the gallants was the result of an awakening of conscience, or because they could not endure the badness of the poetry, history does not say, but M. G. Vallejo remarks: "His *decimas* were *pesimas* (very heavy), and had no literary merit whatever, but to Judge Buelna they brought political and domestic tranquillity."

The Californians were all great politicians, but chief among them was Don Juan Bautista Alvarado, the silver-tongued orator and political "spell-binder" of whom we have already heard many times. Alvarado, through his natural talents and superior education, was a leader in the politics of the province and a member of the diputación by the time he was twenty-seven years old. As an *hijo del pais*, endowed with great personal magnetism and the gift of eloquence, he was extremely popular with all classes. Besides all this, his knowledge of the English language and frequent association with foreign residents guaranteed him their support. He took part in many movements against the central government of which these foreign residents did not always approve, some of them regarding him as a trouble maker, but, as Bancroft says, he was generally right in the stand that he took. He himself refused to be classified as a "revolutionist," but wished rather to be called "patriot." Speaking on this point in his *Historia de California*, he says:

"Never in my life have I been a revolutionary, but always have I served my country with the best will, and in various capacities. If on two occasions I was compelled to grasp the lance and carry the sword with the object of freeing Alta California of the presence of incompetent governors and their bad companions, that conduct was certainly dictated by the purest patriotism, and cannot be classified as that of a revolutionary, who sacrifices everything—country, honor, friends, and family—for the sake of his thirst for power."

Alvarado's constant political activities naturally involved him in many controversies, especially in the frequent clashes between Californians and those of Mexican birth, which became more and more rancorous as time went on. To quote Bancroft, "This mutual abuse continued until even the most respectable families of the place were not spared. The hostility became so intensified that it showed itself at public and private gatherings, and even at church. It must be said that the conduct pursued by both sides was equally reprehensible. At last the Californians abandoned these vile practices, and resorted to the more manly course of open rebellion against their ruler, who too often richly deserved it." As an illustration of the methods used in these political quarrels we will here quote a story told by Alvarado himself, under the title of:

A Frightened Cook

"This happened in the year in which I contracted marriage with Doña Martina Castro. I had my house well furnished. Among the number of my servants there was a French cook by the name of Raoul. That foreigner understood his business perfectly, and was so proud of his knowledge of the culinary art that he became angry if he was not given the title of *Señor profesor*. I appreciated fully the magnitude and value of Raoul's services, so I showed him much consideration and, always, when my official business permitted it, sat down promptly at the table, for Raoul became very angry if at the call of the bell any guest was absent. Having noticed that my señora and I both treated him kindly and paid him promptly, he became fond of us, and assured us that if through some unexpected misfortune we should some day lose our patrimony, he would continue to serve us without any remuneration. While I did not put too much faith in those promises, yet I was glad to see my young wife assured of the services of the most erudite professor of cookery that had up to that time come to exercise his noble art at the port of Monterey. Imagine, then, my readers, what was my astonishment on a beautiful morning in the month of February, when Raoul presented himself in the reception sala, called to a young girl who served as maid to my wife, and told her that he desired to speak to me very urgently. The moment I received the message from the Señor Profesor of the kitchen, I went to meet him. I was somewhat alarmed on seeing him paler and more out of countenance than usual; but, pretending not to notice the disorder of his dress and the paleness of his face, I asked him, 'What's the matter?' 'Señor,' he replied, 'I cannot remain with you a minute longer! This house is under a curse, and all the people who live in it are going to die very soon.' I could not help being surprised at such language in the mouth of a man who had always conducted himself in my presence in a worthy and modest manner; but, as I suspected he had lost his reason, I took no offense at his behavior, and kindly asked him upon what reasons he based the belief that he had just expressed. 'I base it, Señor,' he replied, 'on what I have just seen; go out of the door and see whether I have reason for wishing to leave your house promptly!' More to please him than for any other reason, I went into the street. Raoul went along with me, and as soon as he was outside the door he raised his right arm and pointed in the direction of the flag-staff, saying, 'Look, Señor, look at what is on the point of the staff!' I gazed at the place indicated, and to my great surprise I saw hanging from the halyard of the flag an enormous skull. I was astonished at the boldness of my enemies, who had not scrupled to profane the sanctuary of the dead with the object of giving me to understand that they hated me. Without losing a moment, I ran to the staff, seized the cord from which the skull hung, and little by little pulled it down until at last the skull touched my hands. I untied it reverentially, took it to my study and placed it on the table, where I was in the the habit of writing. When the skull was deposited in a safe place I called Raoul and directed him to prepare breakfast; but he roundly refused, and notwithstanding that I offered to raise his salary, he did not wish to remain in my house. Seeing that he was determined to leave my domicile, I paid him what I owed him and permitted him to go in search of another patron. The frightened Frenchman did not even stop for that, but, terrified at the thought of the skull, lost no time in taking passage on board of a ship which was ready to sail for the roadstead of Santa Barbara.

"Desiring to know the authors of the joke which had deprived me of the Professor Raoul, I called the *regidores* of the town and ordered them to ascertain who had taken the skull from the cemetery of the presidio church, and flung it to the breeze in place of the flag, but the guilty persons could not be found, in spite of the best efforts. I gave up the investigation, and in deference to the religious ideas of the women of Monterey, after keeping the skull on my desk about a week, ordered it taken with all ceremony and funeral pomp to the church and put in the place designated for it. I ascribed the insult to some person of Mexican birth, for I refused to believe that one of the sons of California would be guilty of such sacrilege as to desecrate the sanctity of the house of God and extract from it the skull of a Christian."

In view of the wiles practiced even in our own day to capture a good cook, one is almost led to wonder whether there was more than politics in this little tale. In any case if the trick was played by any resident of Santa Barbara, it failed in its purpose, for "Professor" Raoul moved to Los Angeles, where he "played safe" by entering the service of one of his own countrymen, Louis Vignes, at that time owner of the most extensive vineyard in California. Vignes, who had neither wife nor children, received Raoul with open arms, and kept him to the end of his days in 1843, when he "breathed his last sigh and his immortal soul passed to a land where it is to be supposed there are no skulls; although it is said that from time to time Saint Peter permits the entrance into his kingdom of certain numskulls. Can this be true?" The somewhat irreverent ending is Alvarado's own. He then goes on to give, rather sadly, his opinion of the rewards to be expected from a political career:

"I, who had the misfortune to become a public man before reaching legal age, can assert that politics, in republican countries, is the most ungrateful career that a man can follow, and that which brings the most unhappiness. Would that in all my life I had never figured in politics! It is true that a high-sounding title sounds melodious in the ears of a vain man, but the recollections which it awakens are not very pleasing when to the father of a family who finds himself in reduced circumstances people say, 'Your Excellency, Señor Governor, I come to collect the rent of the house which is now overdue from you for eight days!' Since my experience, acquired at the cost of immense sacrifices and disillusions of every kind, gives me a certain right to give advice to young men, I come forward to tell youth to abstain from politics and devote itself to learning some useful trade; the former brings only troubles, while the latter is an infallible means to reach the height of prosperity; this is a positive fact."

So writes one of the most distinguished and attractive of all the Californians, of whom Bancroft gives the following encomium, partly based on personal acquaintance:

"Don Juan Bautista Alvarado was a man of medium stature, stout build, fair complexion and light hair. He had a genial temperament, courteous manners, rare powers of winning friends; and had more brains, energy, and executive ability than any three of his contemporaries combined. In most of his many controversies he was right, as well as successful. Though compelled to support himself by political intrigues, he never used his position to enrich himself, and in his latter days he had a hard time to pay his rent. He was patriotic and full of good intentions for his country."

Chapter XIV

CHAPTER XIV

Social Customs

IF I WERE to be asked what was the chief characteristic, the most striking social custom, of the Californians, my reply would be, their hospitality, the warm and uncalculating welcome which they offered to the guest in the house. Every foreign visitor, from the earliest days when they had but meager fare to offer, down to the lavish times of the cattle barons, gives the same testimony—that the Californians were the most generous hosts in the whole world. This characteristic they shared to a degree with all the inhabitants of the great west. The pioneer in his lonely cabin in the heart of the western prairies of the United States extended as hearty a greeting to the infrequent wanderer who came his way as the immigrant from Spain who had set up his hearthstone in the flowery vales and sunny hillsides of far California. Isolation and loneliness had much to do with the unusual development of this pleasing quality; the settler in a new land can best appreciate the feelings of a stranger in a strange country. It was the cordiality and sincerity of this welcome, as well as the natural charm of the place, that induced many a foreigner to cast in his lot forever with the Californians. One such, who came without any intention of remaining, writes in these words of the reasons for his decision:

"Receiving so much kindness from the native Californians, I arrived at the conclusion that there was no place in the world where I could enjoy more true happiness and true friendship than among them. There were no courts, no juries, no lawyers, nor any need of them. The people were honest and hospitable, and their word was as good as their bond; indeed, bonds and notes of hand were entirely unknown among the natives."

Their liberality was such that a person could travel from San Diego to Sonoma without a coin in his pocket, and never want for a roof to cover him, a bed to sleep on, food to eat, and even tobacco to smoke. So says Bancroft, and this statement may be carried even further, for many hosts were in the habit of leaving a small pile of money in the spare room, to save the guest the embarrassment of asking for a loan if he found himself short of funds; and horses were always supplied to those whose own had become jaded. California would indeed have been a paradise for loafers, but fortunately not many of that tribe had yet reached there. Nor let it be thought that this generosity was confined to the rich. Serrano says that while traveling he once came to the house of some poor people who had but one bed; this they wished to give him and themselves sleep on hides spread on the ground. The guest resisted, but they considered themselves slighted, and he was forced to yield. The same hospitality was extended to strangers as to acquaintances; and if any one attempted to pay for services rendered, the poorest Californian refused it, saying, "Señor, we are not in the habit of selling food." Housewives held that articles of food should not be sold to neighbors, and gave of their abundance to those who lacked anything.

"On arriving at a rancho," says Arnaz, "the traveler was received with joy, and the best things were prepared for

Franz Geritz '27

him, with horses and servants on leaving. Even their beds were given up. When the missions flourished a man could travel from one end of California to the other, obtaining horses, servants, food, etc., without cost to him, and this hospitality was kept up, or nearly so, by rancheros after the decline of the missions."

When a guest arrived at a ranch house, he was welcomed with the phrase *la casa es suya* (the house is yours), which, though theoretical rather than positive, added to the good feeling. The key to the gate was perhaps given to him, the house was his own, and all its inmates were his servants. On retiring to rest the family united in pronouncing a benediction and calling on all the saints to watch over him. Only one reservation was made—the young females of the house were somewhat jealously guarded, and it often happened that the guest did not even see them. Amador says: "When I was a young man every one retired for the night at eight or nine o'clock, immediately after supper. Each young person of either sex slept in an apartment under lock and key. The parents always arose very early in the morning in order to open the doors, the father those of the boys' rooms, the mother those of the girls'."

"Any stranger traveling through the country," says Robinson, "could stop at any one of the missions as long as he pleased—for months, if he chose; his plate would always be laid at table, and every possible attention paid to him. When ready to leave, all he had to do was to tell the padres, and his horses would be ready, with a guide, and provisions for the road, which were generally a chicken or two, a boiled tongue, a loaf of bread, boiled eggs, a bottle of wine, and a bottle of brandy, and the traveler was at no expense whatever."

Hospitality at the ranchos was only limited by the means of the host. As a consequence there were no hotels in California, for every door was open to the guest, whether friend or stranger. When a foreign ship came into port, the Californians loaded it with prodigal supplies of cattle, vegetables, milk, poultry, hay, and grain, for which they would accept not one peso in recompense. Lavish feasts were set forth at presidios and missions for the officers and crews of the vessels; and all this hospitality was embellished by the fine manners and courtesy of the Castilian. Whether Protestant or Catholic, and no matter what their nationality, the men of these vessels were always loath to leave this land of warm hearts and uncalculating friendship.

When the chain of missions was complete, citizens, government officials, missionaries, and strangers, could travel comfortably from one end to the other of the five hundred miles between San Diego and San Francisco and enjoy the hospitality of some mission every night, without being under the necessity, as was formerly the case, of carrying heavy loads of provisions and sleeping by the roadside. Horses were plentiful, and it was always possible to procure fresh mounts without expense. The average distance from one mission to the next was about thirty miles, that distance being exceeded in only a few cases. The famous *Camino Real* (king's highway), which linked the mission establishments together, was hardly more than a bridle path, but the unshod horses were hardy and swift, accustomed to rough traveling. As communication became easier, visitors at the missions were more frequent, and the reports of the corporals of the mission guards show that nearly every day some traveler arrived or departed. The loneliness of the missionaries must have been greatly relieved by this travel from the outside world. Harrison G. Rogers, companion of Jedediah Smith in the first entrance into California by Americans overland, and himself a staunch Calvinist, pays this warm tribute to the fat and jovial Padre Sánchez, of Mission San Gabriel, where the whole party was hospitably entertained:

"Old Father Sanchus has been the greatest friend that I ever met with in all my travels; he is worthy of being called a Christian, as he possesses charity in the highest degree, and a friend to the poor and distressed. I ever shall hold him as a man of God, taking us in when in distress, feeding and clothing us, and may God prosper him and all such men."

The writings of the advance guard of Americans, those who constitute what I have called the "peaceful invasion," are full of warm encomiums of the generous spirit of the Californians. J. B. Dye, pioneer of 1832, writes, "After I became acquainted with the language and the people of California, I could travel from Sonoma to San Diego without a horse of my own or spending a cent of money. Never was there a more hospitable, generous, and kindly people on the face of the earth than the native-born Californian." Walter Colton, Protestant chaplain in the service of the United States navy, speaks of them in terms of even warmer praise, as follows:

"Their hospitality knows no bounds. Were the De'il himself to call for a night's lodging the Californian would hardly find it in his heart to bolt the door. He would think they could manage against his horns, hoofs, and tail in some way. They are always glad to see you, come when you may; take a pleasure in entertaining you while you remain, and only regret that your business calls you away. If you are sick there is nothing which sympathy and care can devise or perform which is not done for you. No sister ever hung over the throbbing brain or fluttering pulse of a brother with more tenderness or fidelity. This is as true of the lady whose hand has only fingered her embroidery or swept her guitar as of the cottage girl wringing from her laundry the foam of mountain stream; and all this from the heart! If I must be cast in sickness or destitution on the care of the stranger, let it be in California; but let it be before American avarice has hardened the heart and made a god of gold."

All agree that never was there a more generous or more truly charitable people than the Spanish Californians. Unsatisfied hunger was unheard of, for any man had but to make his need known to have it immediately relieved. Don José Martínez, though but one of many, serves as a good example of this liberality. He was a large-hearted man, and the people of the surrounding country were constantly in receipt of favors at his hands. If any one called at his house wanting a horse it was never refused. If one wanted a bullock and had not the means to pay for it, the patrón would send out a vaquero to lasso one and bring it in, so that the man could take it home, to pay for it when convenient, or not at all if not convenient. "If true generosity and genuine philanthropy entitle a man to a place in the kingdom of heaven," says William Heath Davis, "I am sure that Don José Martínez is received there as one of the chief guests." And now let us hear what one of their own descendants, Dr. Platón Vallejo, has to say on this subject:

"Hospitality was the freest thing in the world in the old pastoral days. There were no week-end limitations, no tape measurements of dates. Your guests arrived, and at once your house and appurtenances became theirs. How long they stayed was purely a matter of their pleasure—not yours. Nor was this rule ever violated. In the daytime the men mounted horses, inspected herds, climbed ridges, where the air was brisk, and perhaps had a brush with a grizzly bear, which declined to let them peaceably pass. The women stayed at home, sewed, gossiped, ate more or less 'dulces' or sweets, and had a quiet, congenial, good time.

"The evenings were given over to pure merriment. Every hacienda had its stringed band of several pieces, harp, guitar, and violin—once in awhile a flute. And every night, rain or shine—except at times of death or sorrow—there was a baile. In this everyone had his part. The elder people stepped the stately contradanza. The budding generations enjoyed the waltz and the beautiful Spanish folk dances to the accompaniment of the castañetas, and even the little ones had their own figures to romp through. In short, the occasion was one for all around pleasure—of the natural, unconscious style, without restraint or starchiness, where not a few, but everyone, enjoyed themselves. I am an old man now, but I was young once, and remember that time very well indeed. And nothing in my early or later recollections makes a prettier picture than some of the evening scenes I have witnessed between four patriarchal adobe walls.

"Nor was the hospitality by any means confined to their own race. The same sincere welcome was extended to the visitors from other lands, from the United States, from England, from France. Many of these were so captivated with the life that they settled here, intermarried with us, became part and parcel of California, and were our constant friends."

In a land where food and lodging were to be had for the asking, and where there were few luxuries to tempt the envious, it goes without saying that thieves were few, and crime of any kind not rampant; that is to say, in the period before the arrival of foreigners in large numbers. Let us quote here from J. M. Guinn, whose opinion is based upon study of the original documents:

"How was the municipality or corporation of Los Angeles governed under Spanish and Mexican rule? Not by mob rule, as some writers intimate. Comparatively few capital crimes were committed in California under Spanish domination or Mexican rule. The era of crime in California began with the discovery of gold. There were no Joaquín Murietas or Tiburcio Vasquezes before the days of '49. While there were disturbances in the territory and several governors were deposed and sent back to Mexico, municipal governments were well administered. I doubt whether the municipality of Los Angeles has ever been governed better or more economically under American rule than it was during the last twenty-five years that the 'Most Illustrious Ayuntamiento' controlled its civic affairs."

The Californians got along with less law, and lived under less judicial restraint than people of most communities of similar size in the world. About the most important of the officers of justice, not even excepting the governor, was the alcalde, whose official position was much like that of our mayor, though with larger powers. "An alcalde," says Walter Colton, "under the Mexican law has a large scope in which to exercise his sense of moral justice. Better to err a furlong with mercy than a fathom with cruelty." His powers were almost unlimited. He judged all kinds of cases, settled all manner of disputes. There was not a judge, so thought Colton, on any bench in England or the United States whose power was so nearly absolute as that of the alcalde of Monterey. It involved every breach of the peace, every case of crime, every business obligation, every disputed land title within the space of 100 miles. There were no lawyers in the old pueblo to worry the judge, and no juries to subvert justice and common sense by foolish verdicts. Sometimes the alcalde was judge, jury, and executioner all in one, but contestants were permitted to ask for trial by *hombres buenos* (good men) which differed from our trial by jury only in the number of jurors, they having three or five, as ordered by the magistrate. The plaintiff and the defendant simply appeared before the alcalde and stated their case on either side, produced their witnesses, if they had any, and the alcalde decided the case without delay. "I believe," writes William Heath Davis, "that more substantial justice was done in this way than in the courts of the present day, with all their elaborate machinery and prolonged course of proceedings."

The alcalde decided all cases of minor importance, punishable by fine or imprisonment, while cases of greater magnitude, like those of murder and other high crimes, were brought before the governor at Monterey, and his decision in the matter was final. It was said that the alcaldes as a class were men of good, strong, common sense, and as a rule were honest in their administration of justice and sought to give every man his due. The insignia of the office was a gold or silver headed cane, from the top of which dangled black tassels. This cane was carried, either by the magistrate himself or a representative, on all official occasions, particularly when an arrest was to be made, and great deference was paid to it and its bearer by the people at large, who looked up to the alcalde as a person of undisputed authority. That he needed the wisdom of Solomon to decide the great variety of affairs brought before him is amply proved by some of the cases quoted by Walter Colton, who was appointed alcalde of Monterey in 1846:

"A poor fellow came to me today and complained that his wife had run away with another man, and wanted that I should advise him what to do. I asked him if he desired her to come back; he said he did, for he had five children who required her care. I told him he must then keep quiet; for the harder he chased a deer the faster it would run; that if he kept still she would soon circle back to him. He hardly seemed to understand the philosophy of inaction: I told him there was hardly an animal in the world that might not be won by doing nothing; that the hare ran from us simply because we had chased it; that a woman ran for the same reason, though generally with a different motive; the one ran to escape, the other to be overtaken. He consented to try the do-nothing plan, and in the meantime I shall try to catch the villain who has covered a humble family with disaster . . . A Californian who had been absent some two years in Mexico, where he had led a gay, irregular life, finding or fancying on his return grounds for suspecting the irregularity of his wife, applied to me for a decree of divorce. I told him it was necessary on so grave a subject that he should come into court with clean hands; that if he would swear on the cross that he had been faithful himself during his long absence, I would then see what could be done with his wife. He wanted to know if that was United States law; I told him it was the law by which I was governed—the law of the Bible, and a good law, too—'Let him that is without sin cast the first stone.' 'Then I cannot cast any stone at all, sir,' was the candid reply. 'Then go and live with your wife; she is as good as you are, and you cannot require her to be any better.' He took my advice, is now living with his wife, and difficulties seem to have ceased. Nothing disarms a man like conscious guilt of the offense for which he would arraign another."

After reading these decisions of a "Daniel come to judgment" one is not surprised that the people of Monterey should have respected this man, alien to them in both race and religion, who dealt out even-handed justice to them in the troubles of their simple lives. He also did them the great service of building a good schoolhouse—Colton Hall—which still stands in Monterey in good condition, for which he paid out of the slender proceeds from the sale of town lots, the labor of convicts, taxes on liquor shops, and fines on gambling. "There were no taxes on lands and improvements; the cost of governing was paid by men's pleasures and vices. Under Mexican rule municipal funds were obtained by revenues on wine and brandy; from licenses of saloons and other business houses; from tariff on imports; from permits for dances, from fines and fees for bull-rings and cock-pits and on gamblers. Not even a private dance could be given in the pueblo without the alcalde's license, in return for which the purse of that functionary was enriched by a fee of $3.00."

The whole foundation of jurisprudence in early California was the administration of the law "in accordance with the principles of natural right and justice," and with honest magistrates the system operated well. With the other kind, the consequences were the same as in our own times and country—utterly destructive to all equity. "Thus we see," says Bancroft, "that in matters of morality, private or political, it was among the pastoral Californians much as it is with us today; vice in the high circles was winked at, while the poor were severely punished. As a rule it was some miserable Indian or soldier, or person in the lowest grade of society who suffered such punishments as twenty-five lashes daily given for nine days. This is in accord with what is observed in our own day—that the rich and influential of all times and nations may commit all the crimes of the decalogue with impunity. And, though justice was then plain and crude, it differed not so much after all from justice now, which neither in America nor Europe, nor yet in Asia, is often found wholly unadulterated."

Notwithstanding defects, there was comparatively little crime in pastoral California. The South American, Don José Arnaz, says: "I can assert that from 1840 to 1843 perfect security for the person prevailed in California towns and highways, except from savages in remote localities. I heard of but one murder and robbery." Governor Victoria, who boasted that he would make it possible for any man to leave his purse in the public plaza at Monterey and be able to find it in the place where he left it on his return, came near to making his boast good; but the people looked upon him as a bloodthirsty monster. When he sentenced two Indians to be shot for robbing the warehouse at Mission San Carlos of a small amount of property, the missionary came and threw himself at the governor's feet to beg for their lives, but he was inflexible, and the Indians were shot. Another Indian boy was tried, convicted, and shot for having stolen some buttons from the military stores, valued at about $2.50. The people were shocked by the severity of these sentences, by which many of them were moved to tears, and it was largely because of them that the uprising against Victoria and his expulsion from the country took place. Estevan de la Torre writes, "The executions produced great discontent in a country where sentence of death had rarely been practiced." Moreover, they were unconstitutional, acts of despotism, yet Victoria was favored by many of the American residents because crime was materially reduced under his rule, and business prospered.

Thomas O. Larkin tells some amusing stories of the course of justice in those days. As some of the jails were very uncomfortable, even filthy, the prisoners were often kept outside; and as they often got no food but a hunk of raw meat once a day, they were allowed to go home to get better; and it is to be said for them that they always returned to the prison door when ordered. Once a complaint was made to the alcalde by a person who had been robbed that the thief was every day out of prison and every day passed the victim's house. The alcalde apologized and promised that thereafter the prisoner should take his daily morning and afternoon *paséo* on the other side of town. Sometimes the alcalde put some of the Indian prisoners to work on his own farm. When they became tired of the fare they ran away on his worship's horses, always choosing fat ones, for they were very fond of horsemeat. The alcaldes picked up drunken Indian cooks and stewards in the afternoons of feast days and discharged them next morning in time to cook their masters' breakfasts. Monterey prisoners were often banished to San Diego; those of San Diego to Monterey—which was fair—and when they committed a second crime, they were banished back to the original place.

In pastoral days in California it was customary to take boys to see executions and public punishments, to serve as a warning. Rafael Pinto relates that he was present at the execution of two robbers at Monterey. The minister of Mission San Carlos addressed the parents on the necessity of watching their children. Pinto's brother-in-law, with whom he lived, then held the boy tight with one hand, and with the other gave him a severe flogging. Pinto pleaded that he had done nothing to deserve punishment, but it did not avail him. The brother-in-law answered that it was true that he had done no wrong, and that he was a good boy; but that the flogging was inflicted so that he should remember that day throughout his life—and, as Pinto said, "*No se me ha olvidado, por cierto*" (and I have never forgotten it, for certain).

From justice to fashion is rather a long leap, but a book of this sort is necessarily discursive, and with the Californians the question of personal adornment occupied a place as high as, or perhaps even higher than, that of the law. Dame fashion was not as changeable a body with them as in our day, and when Governor Sola came to take possession of his office in 1815 he thought he was addressing a genuine compliment to the ladies at his inaugural ball when he congratulated them on being fifty years behind the times in their dress. When the Frenchman, Duhaut-Cilly, came in 1827, he could not restrain a secret smile at what he regarded as the ridiculous attempts of the señoritas to imitate the latest Paris fashions, though he was by no means insensible to their natural charms—"the freshness and gayety scarcely repressed by the presence of strangers." This backwardness in taking up new styles was owing chiefly to the isolation of California from the rest of the world. Even Mexico and South America received more frequent reports of what was going on in the fashionable circles of Europe than this most remote province, with the consequence that at least in the earliest years Californians developed a style of dress distinctive in many respects to themselves. After the entrance of foreigners in appreciable numbers, especially of the Hijar colonists in 1834, fashions unfortunately lost much of their individuality and standardization began to get in its deadly work. Bancroft gives a description, culled from many sources, which may be regarded as in general the distinctive dress of the Californian:

"A broad-brimmed hat of dark color, gilt or figured band round the crown, lined under the rim with silk; short silk or figured calico jacket; open necked shirt; rich waistcoat, if any; pantaloons open at sides below the knee, usually of velveteen or broadcloth, and trimmed with gold lace, or short breeches and white stockings; deer-skin shoes, dark brown and much ornamented; a red sash round the waist, and the whole covered with a poncho or serape. The last-named garment was always a mark of the rank or wealth of the owner, and was made of black or dark blue broadcloth, with velvet trimmings, for the rich, down to the coarse but showy blanket poncho of various colors used by the poorer classes. The women wore gowns of silks, crepe, calico, etc., according to means, made with short sleeves and loose waist worn without a corset; shoes of kid or satin, sashes or belts of bright colors; and almost always necklace and earrings."

Husbands of that day were free of worry about "Easter bonnets," for the women wore no head coverings but the rebozo, a scarf or shawl wrapped around the head and shoulders. It was only on horseback that they wore hats, generally wide-brimmed for the purpose of saving their fine complexions, of which they were justifiably proud. For the paséo on foot the parasol was very much favored, and in fact was nearly as characteristic of Spanish women in general as the fan. Their abundant hair was generally worn loose or in long braids hanging down the back, though married women preferred to wind it in a coil on top of the head, fastened with a high comb, of tortoise shell or horn, according to wealth. The American captain, Henry Fitch, was said to have brought on one of his voyages from Peru four tortoise-shell combs, which sold at $600 each, one of them to José de la Guerra y Noriega for his wife, one to Mariano Estrada, one to Joaquín Maitorena, afterwards elected deputy to the Mexican Congress, and the fourth to General Vallejo. In considering the prices paid for such things it must be recollected that the traders charged exorbitant prices for their commodities, and that Californians were practically at their mercy.

In their dress the Californians were like the birds, in that the males wore the gayest plumage. Señor Arnaz thus describes the attire of a rich ranchero of the '40's:

"Shoes of deerskin embroidered with gold and silver thread; breeches of cloth, velvet, or satin reaching to the knee, bordered with gold braid and silver buttons, and open on both sides to show full under-drawers of white linen; vest of velvet, silk, or cloth, and over it a short jacket of blue, black, or green cloth embroidered in gold or silver thread." Add to this outfit a gay sash of red satin bound around the wearer's slender waist and a wide sombrero with a cord of silver or gold encircling the crown, worn jauntily tipped on one side, and we have a figure beside which the females seem comparatively plain. Yet they had their adornments, for the richer among them, though they dressed very quietly for the church and street, had silk and satin dresses, with gold necklaces and earrings set with genuine and beautiful pearls from Baja California fisheries, which they wore at the dances. Bancroft speaks of their wearing "imitation" pearls. This was not true of the wealthier class. Don Bernardo Yorba, of Santa Ana, had stored away 150 dress patterns of silk and satin of the finest sort, and whenever a son or daughter married, a trunk full of dresses worth $80 to $100 each was given to the bride. The dress worn by the middle class of females in the '30's is described by Robinson as a chemise with short embroidered sleeves, richly trimmed with lace, generally hand-made, a muslin petticoat flounced with scarlet and secured at the waist by a silk sash of the same color, shoes of velvet or blue satin, a cotton rebozo or scarf, a pearl necklace and earrings, with the hair falling in broad plaits down the back. Some substituted for the rebozo a rich and costly shawl, the graceful management of which added much to its effect.

But it was always the caballero who cut the most dashing figure, and among them all there could have been none more striking than that of Don Tomás Yorba. Upon his head he wore a black silk handkerchief, the four corners of which hung down his neck behind. An embroidered shirt, a cravat of white jaconet tastefully tied, a blue damask vest, short breeches of crimson velvet, a bright green cloth jacket, with large silver buttons, the invariable sash, and shoes of embroidered deerskin, comprised his dress. With his tall figure arrayed in this costume and his sword hanging by his side, he was every inch the Spanish caballero. On feast days it is said that his entire display, including the broad sombrero held on with a throat strap, silver-mounted saddle, bridle, and spurs, often exceeded a value of a thousand dollars.

Notwithstanding that the styles changed so little during the first years that a man could wear his grandfather's hat or coat without causing remark, yet some variations are noted by writers in the different epochs. In 1780, says Amador, men, soldiers and civilians alike wore knee-breeches of cloth or velveteen, fastened in a band at the knee with a silver buckle, with stockings of wool or silk. Gómez states that up to 1834, when the Hijar colony came from Mexico, the dress worn by the men was a big green silk handkerchief tied around the head, the knot in front; another kerchief round the neck; a wide blue vest worn partly open to show a sash of crimson silk—often two or three belts—a blue jacket adorned with big metal buttons; short wide breeches fastened at the knees; leggings tied on with colored silk bands; wide brimmed hat tied on with a strap; the braided hair falling over the shoulders. Blas Peña adds that the queue, tied with a rosette of ribbon, was worn until 1840, when it was abandoned for short hair. "On arriving from Mexico in 1834," says Hijar, "I was surprised to see the men with hair as long as that of the women, worn in a braid over the back or gathered in the crown of the hat."

Our poetical friend, Judge Buelna, did not fail to seize the opportunity to air some of his satirical verses, in bad rhyme and worse grammar, addressed to the first native rancheros who adopted the new style introduced in 1834, of wearing frock coats, with long pantaloons, and suspenders to take the place of sashes. He did well to bemoan the passing of the old fashions, for the new were not nearly so graceful nor so picturesque.

"A custom which called my attention in 1840, in Santa Barbara," says Arnaz, "was the *camorra* of the women—a black silk band laid around the forehead and tied in a knot at the nape of the neck. This gave the women of Santa Barbara a different appearance from others in Southern California." This band sometimes had a star or other ornament fastened to it in front, as noted by Dana. It was regarded as ill-bred to expose the ears, so the hair was allowed to cover them; nothing is more certain than that fashion repeats itself, as witness the "bobbed" hair worn over the ears in this year of 1928.

In 1847 there was general excitement over talk of introducing bonnets, apropos of which the *Californian* had in its April issue the following paragraph: "For a month past the question has been agitated among the women, shall they, or shall they not, adopt the use of bonnets? From present indications the ayes have it. But who will supply them?"

Many Californians wore silver spurs, and silver plated work on their saddles and reins; and on arriving at the house of a friend, they would give the servant a dollar to take off their spurs. General Vallejo says that after the discovery of gold he used to fling the boy who held his horse an ounce, equivalent to sixteen dollars. But it was not long after that until he had fewer ounces to fling about.

As to their food, there is little doubt that the plain but nourishing diet upon which they lived, with an almost complete absence of pastries and condiments, had much to do with their excellent health and digestion. There was large consumption of beef, fresh and jerked, but the people never took kindly to pork, mutton, deer, or bear meat. They would not even use pork lard in their cooking, saying that it was only fit to make soap of. Duhaut-Cilly, in 1827, said that Californians did not consider venison fit to eat. Sweets were used sparingly, perhaps because sugar was all imported and was no doubt expensive.

There were many cooks expert in the preparation of their own sort of dishes. Señor Arnaz even asserts that they could have compared with those serving at the celebrated *bodas de Camacho* (nuptials of Camacho) described by Cervantes in his *Don Quixote*. These cooks were particularly expert in the making of soups and stews, in which they could hardly have been excelled by any in the world. Tortillas, cakes of flour or cornmeal beaten to the thinness of a wafer between the hands and baked before the fire, formed their only bread. *Frijoles* (dried beans) fried in fat appeared at every meal, and red peppers entered into the composition of nearly every dish.

Wine was sometimes taken with meals, but more often water was the only drink, for the early Californians inherited the abstemiousness of their Spanish ancestors, and were moderate in eating and drinking. It was only after they had deteriorated through the influence of a bad class of foreigners that intemperance was observed among them. The European breakfast of a simple cup of coffee or chocolate, with a tortilla or dish of pinole, was usually taken very early in the morning, for, as I have said before, the Californians, though not fond of hard work, were not slothful, and even the rich often left their beds before daybreak. The principal meal was taken at noon, and usually consisted of an excellent soup, cunningly flavored and thickened with rice, vermicelli, or dumplings; then followed the *puchero* (stew) of meat and vegetables cooked together, highly flavored with red or green peppers, onions or garlic, and sometimes tomatoes. The California women had many appetizing ways of cooking vegetables which added a greater variety to their *cuisine* than might have been expected. They also knew ways of cooking fish and all sea foods that might very well be added to our modern menus. They concocted wonderful *conservas* (preserves) of fruit, but as a rule gave little time to the preparation of desserts. It was a habit among the commoner people to use a rolled-up tortilla as a spoon to dip up frijoles or stew, eating a mouthful of the spoon along with the rest.

Some of their most famous dishes, such as tamales and enchiladas, though sadly deteriorated from their former savory estate, have remained with us and are in great demand among present-day Californians. Most of their dishes required much time in the preparation; for instance, it took all of two days to prepare a good pot of tamales; hence I fear that even though it were possible to rescue a collection of their delectable recipes from oblivion and print them in a book, they would not meet with the approval of modern cooks.

There are many odds and ends in the way of customs peculiar to the Californians that do not seem to range themselves in any particular category. For instance, there was their tendency to gossip, which they had in common with all small communities, and which is by no means unknown in our own day. In much the same way as our New England farmers, who are said to settle the affairs of the nation while they sit on a box in the corner grocery and whittle a stick, so the men of California gathered in groups on the street with their serapes wrapped about them and talked over the business of Fulano (such and such a one). And in every pueblo there was a coterie of old ladies, themselves past the days of youthful folly, who constituted themselves a board of censors of the conduct of the townspeople, after the manner of the old in all times and places. The overhanging balconies with which most of the houses were equipped gave them a fine point of vantage from which they could observe the comings and goings of the younger persons, whom they did not scruple to admonish at every opportunity. In fact, it was considered the bounden duty of every elderly woman to scold the young girls, and old men were privileged to apply physical correction to boys or young men, even though not of their own family, when they believed it to be needed.

Salutations were matters of great politeness and ceremony. Whoever met a military chief or padre was expected to remove his hat while still a hundred *varas* away. Friends, such as Bandini and Pico, addressed each other as *estimado* or *amado compadre*. Father Junípero taught the Indians of San Carlos to salute every one with *Amar á Dios* (love God), a fashion which spread all over the country and was used even by the pagan Indians. If a son wrote a letter to his father he began it with, "*Mi muy estimado padre* (my very esteemed father)." Compare this with the "Dear Dad" of our own day!

A small peculiarity was the calling of the month of May *María*. Another was the blessing of houses. Alfred Robinson tells of being present when Bandini's house at San Diego was blessed, in 1829. All the leading people of the place were present at the ceremony, which took place about noon. The padre went through the different apartments, sprinkling holy water on the walls and uttering prayers in Latin. The company then sat down to an excellent dinner, after which came the invariable music and dancing, followed in the evening by a general ball.

There was a custom among the women of saving their soiled clothing for weeks for a general grand wash-up. On such occasions, after their own clothes were done, they would ask their neighbors for theirs, which they washed without any recompense. "My clothes were thus often washed without charge," says Hijar. These great washings usually were done at some place where there were natural springs. Near Monterey, in a delightful little glen, there were a number of these springs, or waterholes, where the women did the town washing by kneeling on the ground and dipping the clothing directly in the pools. This place was called *Los Aguajitos* (the water-holes) by the early Californians, and Washerwomen's Cañon by the Americans. Frequently days were passed at these places, all the family eating and sleeping in the camp under arbors of tree branches until the work was done, when they returned home and celebrated with feasting, dancing, and singing. So little did they need, to be happy, in those days!

They were strict observers of the habits of good society. In 1833 Governor Figueroa sent to the president of the ayuntamiento the pamphlet which Joaquín Gómez de la Cortina published about the rights and duties of society. The personal cards of most of the Mexican governors of California bore the arms of their ancestors, and a family motto, either religious or warlike, or still oftener referring to some act of gallantry. Governor Figueroa's card bore the words *Honor y Lealtad* (honor and loyalty). "One governor did not like to see the Spanish people decline in social dignity, and in 1799 he wrote to the viceroy, referring to rather indecorous means resorted to by the poor subalterns to subsist; such as letting their wives and daughters wash their own clothes, and make bread and sew for others, and at the same time fail to procure shoes and stockings for the children." Considering that these soldiers more than half the time could not get their pay from the government, the governor's criticism seems not to come with a good grace.

An interesting custom was the use of the *rúbrica* in making signatures to documents and letters. J. M. Guinn writes entertainingly of this custom:

"*Rúbricas* were intricate flourishes of loops, circles, and zigzag lines following each name, that in Spanish documents take the place of our English seal. Every man had one of his own, as distinct from his neighbor's as the brand on his cattle, and fully as necessary, for his signature was not legal without the *rúbrica*. These *rúbricas* are wonders of the penman's art, and the mystery is how the writer could construct two alike, unless he kept a copy before him. Only among the people of illimitable patience in a land of *poco tiempo* would men go through life repeating such autographical montrosities."

The higher the social standing of the writer, the more intricate as a rule was his rúbrica, so that they may be regarded as marks of class distinction. I have seen examples that cover half a page of foolscap, and took their authors half a day to construct each time they were written. What a picture it gives of those old leisurely days! Foreigners who settle in the country in the ante-gold period—such as John Bidwell, Abel Stearns, John A. Sutter, and others—hasten to adopt this with other customs of the country, and it was not long before each had devised his own particular rúbrica. One may almost judge of a man's character by his rúbrica; that of Abel Stearns consisted of one long, curving sweep of the pen, indicating the busy man of rather brusque manners, which he really was, while that of Sutter, the polished, suave gentleman of the old European school, is more elaborate.

One of the interesting customs which the Californians shared with our Anglo-Saxon ancestors on the other side of the continent was that of selecting Christian names for their children from the Scriptures. Thus María, Encarnación, Concepción, Refugio, Dolores, Jesús, José, etc., formed the same religious note in California as Jeremiah, Abraham, Isaac, Praise-God, etc., in New England.

Many of the first foreign settlers seem to have formed a marked opinion of the superiority of the females over the males of the Spanish Californian race, in industry, moral character, and sound common sense. Although some of this prejudice may be the natural affinity of opposite sexes, yet there seems to have been some foundation for this belief. Certainly the women were much more industrious, and while those who could afford it employed Indians to perform all menial labor, others worked very hard, in the fields as well as in the house. They cut wood, cultivated the gardens, carried water from the springs, prepared the food for the family, all in the most laborious manner, without common conveniences. Sewing was a most painstaking occupation, for it was all done by hand, and there was much fine embroidery and lace work used, even on the garments of the men. The best work was put on the beds and bedding, which even the poorest women made the objects of greatest display. Pressing and ironing were done with the hand until the piece became perfectly smooth.

One of the unusual duties of the women was daily to comb and braid the long hair of their male relatives, that is, as long as queues remained in fashion. No doubt they were not sorry when this fashion went into disuse. Some of the women took charge of the sowing and harvesting of the crops. Fermina Espinosa, owner of the Santa Rita Rancho, worked like a man, doing all the ranch work, including breaking colts, lassoing cattle, etc., while her husband did nothing but eat, sleep, smoke, and "increase an already numerous family." But she at least had the satisfaction of enjoying the respect of all who knew her. "Señor V. Ávila of Sal-si-puedes Rancho had four daughters, fair and blue-eyed, who worked like men, roamed the mountains in male attire, guarding stock and felling timber. They also made blankets and cheese, and drove the old wooden-wheeled oxcart here and there as duty demanded. One girl married, the rest remained single to care for the old father."

Coronel says that although the women were but poorly educated, their morals were good and they were industrious and neat. They were both charitable and hospitable, and would care for a sick stranger as tenderly as for one of their own. Torres says, "California mothers were tender, and as wives were affectionate. The few unfaithful wives were Mexicans."

The women were without exception excellent swimmers, perhaps surpassing the women of all other countries in this art. In summer they all resorted to the rivers or seashore to enjoy this recreation. They were also expert horse-women.

Hayes writes in his *Emigrant Notes*, "California women are an interesting race in many respects—a kind-hearted, amiable, industrious set. I like them better than the men, although these too have their virtues, as well as their faults." Alfred Robinson says, "In few places of the world, in proportion to inhabitants, can be found more chastity, industrious habits, and correct deportment than among the women." "The women of California," says Amador, "were always noteworthy for their excellent conduct as daughters, sisters, wives, and mothers. They were virtuous and industrious, and devoted to their family duties." William Heath Davis, who married one of the *hijas del país* himself, writes: "During my long and intimate acquaintance with Californians, I have found the women as a class much brighter, quicker in their perceptions, and generally smarter than the men. Their husbands oftentimes looked to them for advice and direction in their general business affairs." Charles Howard Shinn remarks that, "The grace, modesty, and beauty of the women of the time were the admiration of every visitor."

I am glad to have this opportunity to offer a tribute to these very fine women, who have not always received the appreciation from historians that their merits deserve. I myself have enjoyed the friendship of many of their descendants who retained the sterling qualities for which their mothers and grandmothers were noted. In the matter of industry they remind one of our pioneer women of the middle west, who knitted while traveling on horseback, in order not to waste a moment of time; so their California sisters always kept a piece of lace work or embroidery within easy reach, in order to catch it up in odd minutes. As their own writers are fond of saying, "May their souls rest in Paradise!"

As for the men, though they lacked some of the more solid virtues of the women, they had many attractions.

They were kind-hearted, liberal, ready to open both heart and purse to those poorer than themselves. They were neither money-makers nor money-lovers, and for this have been unduly criticized by some writers who place too high a value upon the material side of life. Handsome, graceful, athletic, light-hearted, generous, of decent morals until corrupted by outsiders—let us remember the Californian kindly for these attractive qualities, and forget that he was improvident, careless of the morrow, and that ambition had never sung her siren song in his ears. And let us forever regret that through his very best qualities, his unsuspicious frankness and trust of strangers, he was grossly sinned against by the people of the United States.

What a contrast there is between the characters of the first settlers on the opposite coasts of our country! Almost as though climate had something to do with it, we see landing on the "stern and rock-bound" shore of the stormy Atlantic the solemn-visaged Puritans, men seeking "to merit heaven by making earth a hell"; while to the "delightsome" land of California, as some of the earliest discoverers term it, came these wanderers from old Castile, seeking to make of this world a paradise, singing and dancing their happy lives away on the edge of the Peaceful Sea!

Appendix

APPENDIX

INDIANS

Approximate estimate of the comparative number of Indians in various California groups in 1770 and 1910; compiled by Doctor A. L. Kroeber in *Handbook of the Indians of California* in the Bureau of American Ethnology, Bulletin 78.

Groups	1770	1910	Groups	1770	1910
Yurok	2,500	700	Gabrielino, Fernandeño, San Nicoleño	5,000	(x)
Karok	1,500	800	Luiseño	4,000	500
Wiyot	1,000	100	Juaneño	1,000	(x)
Tolowa	1,000	150	Cupeño	500	150
Hupa	1,000	500	Cahuilla	2,500	800
Chilula, Whilkut	1,000	(x)[1]	Diegueño, Kamia, Mohave (total)	3,000	1,050
Mattole	500	(x)	Halchidhoma (emigrated since 1800)	1,000	....
Nongatl, Sinkyone, Lassik	2,000	100	Yuma (total)	2,500	750
Wailaki	1,000	200	Chimariko, New River, Konomihu, Okwanuchu	1,000	(x)
Kato	500	(x)	Achomawi, Atsugewi	3,000	1,100
Yuki	2,000	100	Modoc in California	500	(x)
Huchnom	500	(x)	Yana	1,500	(x)
Coast Yuki	500	(x)	Wintun	12,000	1,000
Wappo	1,000	(x)	Maidu	9,000	1,100
Pomo	8,000	1,200	Miwok (plains and Sierra)	9,000	700
Lake Miwok	500	(x)	Yokuts	18,000	600
Coast Miwok	1,500	(x)	Costanoan	7,000	(x)
Shasta	2,000	100	Esselen	500	(x)
Northern Paiute in Calif.	500	300	Salinan	3,000	(x)
Eastern and Western Mono	4,000	1,500	Chumash	10,000	(x)
Tübatulabal	1,000	150	Washo in California	500	300
Koso, Chemehuevi, Kawaiisu	1,500	500			
Serrano, Vanyume, Kitanemuk, Alliklik	3,500	150			
Total of groups after deducting non-California Yumas, non-natives resident in California, and others of doubtful affiliation				133,000	16,350

[1] *The "x" indicates that the numbers in the groups so marked had become so reduced by 1910 that it was not considered worth while to estimate them separately, so such groups were all added up together.*

THE SPANISH GOVERNORS OF CALIFORNIA

Gaspar de Portolá, governor of the Californias, Alta and Baja, 1768 to 1770. First ruler of the province of Alta California, rather as military commander than as civil governor, to..............July 9, 1770

Felipe de Barri, governor of the Californias, residing at Loreto.......... 1770-1775

Felipe de Neve, governor of the Californias, residing at Loreto from March 4, 1775; at Monterey from.......... ....February 3, 1777, to September 10, 1782

Pedro Fages..........September, 1782, to April, 1791

José Antonio Roméu..........April 16, 1791, to April 9, 1792

José Joaquín de Arrillaga, governor *ad interim* from.......... ....April, 1792 to October, 1794

Diego de Borica, governor from..........October, 1794, to January 6, 1800

José Joaquín de Arrillaga, governor *ad interim* from..........1800 to 1804
Constitutional governor from..........1804 to 1814

José Argüello, acting governor from..........1814 to 1815

Pablo Vicente Sola, governor from.......... ....August 15, 1815, to November 22, 1822

THE MEXICAN GOVERNORS OF CALIFORNIA

Pablo Vicente Sola, hold-over from the Spanish administration to.... ....November, 1822

Luís Argüello, governor *ad interim* from.......... ....November 22, 1822, to November, 1825

José María de Echeandía, governor from.......... ....November 22, 1825, to January, 1831

Manuel Victoria, governor from....January, 1831, to December 9, 1831

José María Echeandía, governor from.......... ....December, 1831, to January, 1833

(Pío Pico has been inaccurately regarded by some writers as governor during this period.)

José Figueroa, governor from....January, 1833, to September 29, 1835

José Castro, acting governor from....September, 1835, to January, 1836

Nicolás Gutiérrez, acting governor from January, 1836, to May 3, 1836
Mariano Chico, governor from..............May 3, 1836, to July 31, 1836
Nicolás Gutiérrez, acting governor from..
....September 6, 1836, to November 4, 1836
Juan Bautista Alvarado, revolutionary governor from....................
....December, 1836, to July, 1837
Constitutional governor from........July, 1837, to December 31, 1842
Manuel Micheltorena, governor from..
....December 31, 1842, to February 22, 1845
Pío Pico, governor from....................February 22, 1845, to July, 1846

THE TWENTY-ONE MISSIONS
The dates of their foundings and their founders

1. San Diego de Alcalá. July 16, 1769. Junípero Serra.
2. San Carlos Borroméo. June 3, 1770. Junípero Serra.
3. San Antonio de Padua. July 14, 1771. Junípero Serra.
4. San Gabriel Arcángel. September 8, 1771. Junípero Serra.
5. San Luís Obispo de Tolosa. September 1, 1772. Junípero Serra.
6. San Francisco de Asis. October 9, 1776. Francisco Palóu.[1]
7. San Juan Capistrano. November 1, 1776. Fermín Francisco de Lasuén.
8. Santa Clara. January 12, 1777. Tomás de la Peña.
9. San Buenaventura. March 31, 1782. Junípero Serra.
10. Santa Barbara. December 4, 1786. Fermín Francisco de Lasuén.
11. Purísima Concepción. December 8, 1787. Fermín Francisco de Lasuén.
12. Santa Cruz. September 25, 1791. Fermín Francisco de Lasuén.[2]
13. Nuestra Señora de la Soledad. October 9, 1791. F. F. de Lasuén.
14. San José de Guadalupe. June 11, 1797. Fermín Francisco de Lasuén.
15. San Juan Bautista. June 24, 1797. Fermín Francisco de Lasuén.
16. San Miguel Arcángel. July 25, 1797. Fermín Francisco de Lasuén.
17. San Fernando Rey de España. September 8, 1797. F. F. de Lasuén.
18. San Luís Rey de Francia. June 13, 1798. Fermín Francisco de Lasuén.
19. Santa Inés. September 17, 1804. Estevan Tapis.
20. San Rafael Arcángel. December 14, 1817. Vicente Francisco Sarría.
21. San Francisco Solano. July 4, 1823. José Altimira.

[1] *Engelhardt gives the date of San Francisco de Asis as October 8.*
[2] *Engelhardt gives August 28 as date of founding of Santa Cruz.*

PRESIDENTS OF THE FRANCISCAN MISSIONS OF CALIFORNIA

With their terms of service

Fray Junípero Serra	1769–1784
Fray Francisco Palóu	1784–1785
Fray Fermín Francisco Lasuén	1785–1803
Fray Estevan Tapis	1803–1812
Fray José Señan	1812–1815
Fray Mariano Payeras	1815–1819
Fray José Señan	1819–1823
Fray Vicente Francisco Sarría	1823–1825
Fray Narciso Durán	1825–1827
Fray José Bernardo Sánchez	1827–1831
Fray Narciso Durán	1831–1838
Fray José Joaquín Jimeno	1838–1844
Fray Narciso Durán	1844–1846

PRESIDIOS AND MUNICIPALITIES

Dates of founding

Presidios and military towns

Presidio of San Diego	July 16, 1769
Presidio of Monterey	June 3, 1770
Presidio of San Francisco	Sept. 17, 1776
Presidio of Santa Barbara	April 21, 1782

Civic Municipalities

San José	November 29, 1777
Los Angeles	September 4, 1781
Branciforte (now extinct)	1797

Mission Pueblos

San Luís Obispo	September 1, 1772
San Juan Capistrano	November 1, 1776
San Juan Bautista	June 24, 1797
Sonoma	July 4, 1823

SOME GREAT NAMES IN THE HISTORY OF HISPANIC CALIFORNIA

Alvarado, Juan Bautista; first constitutional native-born governor, served from 1836 to 1842.

Anza, Juan Bautista de; leader of the first party of settlers from Sonora to San Francisco, first white people to cross the Sierra into California, 1775-1776.

Ayala, Juan Manuel de; captain of the ship *San Carlos*; first to pass through the Golden Gate, August 5, 1775.

Bucareli, Antonio María; Viceroy of Mexico, whose powerful support aided in the settlement of California in 1769.

Cabrillo, Juan Rodríguez; discoverer of Alta California, 1542.

Crespi, Fray Juan; diarist and chaplain of the Portolá expedition of 1769; missionary and explorer.

Gálvez, José de; Visitor General of Mexico, organizer and administrator of the expedition of 1769, which was carried to a successful conclusion largely through his able management.

Lasuén, Fray Fermín Francisco de; third president of the Franciscan missions of California, serving from 1785 to 1803; founder of nine of the missions; regarded by some writers as the equal of Serra in ability.

Moraga, Gabriel; noted Indian fighter, serving in 46 campaigns in California; explorer of the great Central Valley; son of José Joaquín Moraga, member of the Anza expedition and first comandante of San Francisco.

Ortega, José Francisco; an officer in Portolá's command; the first to actually lay eyes on San Francisco Bay. He was highly regarded by Father Serra, who at one time asked the Mexican government to appoint him as governor of Alta California, but without success.

Palóu, Fray Francisco; Serra's chief assistant in the missions of California; second president of the missions, from 1784 to 1785; founder of the mission of San Francisco de Asis (Mission Dolores). As the author of the first book ever written in the province, *Las Noticias de la Nueva California*, and later of *La Vida de Junípero Serra*, he is regarded as the father of California literature.

Pérez, Captain Juan; commander of the ship *San Antonio*, which arrived in the nick of time to save the expedition at San Diego from abandonment in 1770; Pérez was the first to explore practically the whole northwest coast, for which Cook and other English commanders received the credit.

Portolá, Gaspar de; commander of the first expedition to settle Alta California, in 1769; first governor of California; discoverer of San Francisco Bay.

Serra, Fray Junípero; founder of the Franciscan Missions of California; first president of the missions, 1769-84; usually considered California's greatest; chosen for the nation's Hall of Fame at Washington in 1928.

Vallejo, Mariano Guadalupe; most distinguished of the native-born Spanish Californians; the richest and most influential man in the province during the Mexican régime.

Vizcaíno, Sebastián; commander of the sea expedition in 1602 which explored the California coast as far as Cape Mendocino; first to enter and land in Monterey Bay, December 16, 1602. The conditions of his voyage up this unknown coast make it one of the most heroic exploits ever performed by ocean navigators.

Note. The above list naturally includes but a small number of the men who won fame during the Spanish-Mexican period. A complete list would make a book in itself

SURNAMES USED IN THIS BOOK

Pronunciation[1]

Ábrego (Ahb'-ray-go)
Aguirre (Ah-geer'-ray)
Alvarado (Ahl-vah-rah'-do)
Amador (Ahm-ah-dore')
Amesti (Ah-mes'-tee)
Anza (Ahn'-sah)
Arce (Ahr'-say)
Argüello (Ahr-goo-ay'-o)
Arrillaga (Ahr-ee-yah'-gah)
Arroyo (Ahr-roy'-o)
Ávila (Ah'-vee-lah)
Bandini (Bahn-dee'-nee)
Benítez (Ben-ee'-tess)
Bernal (Bare-nahl')
Bodega (Bo-day'-gah)
Bonifacio (Bo-nee-fah'-see-o)
Borica (Bo-ree'-kah)
Boscana (Bose-kah'-nah)
Buelna (Boo-el'-nah)
Carrillo (Cahr-ree'-yo)
Castañares (Cahs-tahn-yahr'-ess)
Castro (Kahs'-tro)
Catalá (Caht-ah-lah')
Célis (Say'-lees)
Chico (Chee'-ko)
Coronel (Ko-ro-nel')
Costansó (Kose-tahn-so')
Covarrúbias(Ko-vahr-roo'-bee-ahs)
Cuesta (Koo-es'-tah)
Domínguez (Do-meen'-gess)
Durán (Doo-rahn')
Echeandía (Ay-chay-ahn-dee'-ah)
Esténega (Ess-ten'-ay-gah)
Estrada (Ess-trah'-dah)
Estudillo (Ess-too-dee'-yo)
Fages (Fah'-hess)
Figueroa (Fee-gay-ro'-ah)
Gamboa (Gahm-bo'-ah)
Guerrero (Gayr-ray'-ro)
Gómez (Go'-mess)
Guerra y Noriega
(Gayr'-rah ee No-ree-ay'-gah)
Hernandez (Ayr-nan'-dess)
Higuera (E-gayr'-rah)
Hijar (E-har')
Lasuén (Lah-soo-en')
López (Lo'-pess)
Lugo (Loo'-go)
Malarín (Mahl-ah-reen')
Menéndez (May-nayn'-dess)
Machado (Mah-cha'-do)
Martínez (Mahr-teen'-ess)
Micheltorena
(Mee-chel-to-ray'-nah)
Morelos (Mo-rayl'-ose)
Negrete (Nay-gray'-tay)
Nieto (Nee-ay'-to)
Noé (No-ay')
Ortega (Ore-tay'-gah)
Pacheco (Pah-chay'-ko)
Pedrorena (Payd-ro-ray'-nah)
Peralta (Pay-rahl'-tah)
Pico (Pee'-ko)
Pinto (Peen'-to)
Portolá (Pore-to-lah')
Prudón (Proo-done')
Quintana (Keen-tah'-nah)
Quixano (Kee-hah'-no)

[1] *Where there is a variation of rule between Castilian and Spanish-American usage as in the soft c or double ll, the author has preferred the American.*

Requeña (Ray-kayn'-yah)
Rezánof (Ray-zan'-off) (Russian)
Ripalda (Ree-pahl'-dah)
Rivera (Ree-vayr'-rah)
Romero (Ro-may'-ro)
Ruiz (Roo-ees')
Sal (Sahl)
Sánchez (Sahn'-chess)
Sepúlveda (Say-pool'-vay-dah)
Serra (Sayr'-rah)
Serrano (Sayr-rah'-no)
Soberanes (So-bayr-ahn'-ness)
Sola, or Solá. (So'-lah or Solah')[1]
Solano (So-lah'-no)
Soler (So-layr')
Soto (So'-to)
Suñol (Soon-yole')
Tapia (Tah'-pee-ah)
Torres (Tore'-ress)
Uria (Oo-ree'-ah)
Vallejo (Vah-yay'-ho)
Vargas (Vahr'-gahs)
Verdugo (Vare-doo'-go)
Viader (Vee-ah-dare')
Valle, del (Vah'-yay)
Yorba (E-ore'-bah)
Zamorano (Sahm-o-rah'-no)
Zúñigas (Soon'-yee-gahs)

[1] *Sola is now commonly accented on the first syllable, but all Spanish encyclopedias accent it on the second—Solá.*

NAMES OF PERSONS AND PLACES MOST COMMONLY MISPRONOUNCED

California—should be Cahl-ee-for'-nee-ah, not Cal-ah-for'-nee-ah.
Cabrillo—should be Cah-bree'-yo, not Cabrillo, as in English.[1]
Camino Real—should be Kahm-ee'-no Ray-ahl', not Camino Reel.
Farallon—should be Fahr-ah-yone', not Farallon as in English.[2]
Los Altos—should be Loce Ahl'-tos, not Loss Altus.
Los Angeles—should be Loce Ahng'-hel-ess, not Loss An'-geles with soft g.
Los Gatos should be Loce Gah'-tose, not Loss Ga'-tus.
Rodéo—should be Ro-day'-o, not Ro'-deo.
Norte, del—should be Del Nor'-tay, not Del Nort.
Suñol—should be Soon-yole', not Soonole.
Vallejo—should be Vah-yay'-ho, not Vallayo.[3]

[1] *American usage. Castilian would be Cah-breel'-yo.*
[2] *American usage. Castilian would be Fahr-ahl-yone.'*
[3] *American usage. Castilian would be Vahl-yay'-ho.*
This list might be drawn out ad infinitum.

APPENDIX

CHRONOLOGICAL SUMMARY OF IMPORTANT EVENTS IN THE SPANISH PERIOD OF CALIFORNIA HISTORY

Discovery of Alta California by Juan Rodríguez Cabrillo .... September 28, 1542
Landing of Francis Drake in California .... June, 1579
First landing in the Bay of Monterey, by Sebastián Vizcaíno .... December 16, 1602
Settlement of San Diego by Junípero Serra and Gaspar de Portolá .... July 16, 1769
Founding of San Carlos Mission at Monterey .... June 3, 1770
Settlement of San Francisco by Juan Bautista de Anza .... March, 1775
Founding of San José .... November 29, 1777
Founding of Los Angeles .... September 4, 1781
Death of Fray Junípero Serra .... August 28, 1784
Discovery of the Columbia River by Captain Bruno de Heceta .... July 17, 1775
Visit of first foreigner, J. F. Galaup de la Pérouse, September 15, 1786
Founding of Fort Ross by the Russians .... September 10, 1812
California becomes a province in the Republic of Mexico .... November 19, 1823
Outbreak of the Solis rebellion .... November 12, 1829
First movement for the secularization of the missions, January 6, 1831
Arrival of John Augustus Sutter 1839
The revolt against Governor Manuel Victoria 1831
Decree by Figueroa for secularization of the missions, August 9, 1834
Coming of the Hijar colony from Mexico 1834
Revolution led by Juan Bautista Alvarado 1836
Alvarado superseded by Manuel Micheltorena .... August, 1842
Revolution and expulsion of Micheltorena .... March, 1845
The Cahuenga capitulation of California to the United States .... January 13, 1847
Signing of the Treaty of Guadalupe Hidalgo in Mexico formally transferring the province of Alta California to the United States .... February 2, 1848

PRINCIPAL SPANISH PLACE NAMES OF CALIFORNIA

Pronunciation[1]

Alameda (Ahl-ah-may′-dah)
Álamo (Ahl′-ah-mo)
Alcatraz (Ahl-ka-tras′)
Aliso (Ahl-ee′-so)
Almaden (Ahl-mah-den′)
Altos, Los (Loce Ahl′-tose)
Alvarado (Ahl-vah-rah′-do)
Alviso (Ahl-vee′-so)
Amador (Ahm-ah-dore′)
Amargosa (Ahm-ahr-go′-sah)
Angeles, Los (Loce Ahng′-hel-ess)
Año Nuevo (Ahn′-yo Noo-ay′-vo)
Arenas, Punta (Ah-ray′-nahs, Poon′-ta)
Asunción (Ah-soon-see-one′)
Benicia (Bay-nee′-see-ah)
Bodega (Bo-day′-gah)
Bolinas (Bo-lee′-nahs)
Buena Vista (Boo-ay′-nah Vees′-tah)
Cabrillo (Cah-bree′-yo)
Calaveras (Cah-lah-vay′-rahs)
Capistrano (Cahp-ees-trah′-no)
Carmelo (Kar-may′-lo)
Carpintería (Kar-peen-tay-ree′-ah)
Carquínez (Kar-keen′-ess)
Catalina (Caht-ah-leen′-ah)
Cazadero (Cahs-ah-day′-ro)
Chico (Chee′-ko)
Colorado (Co-lo-rah′-do)
Concepción (Cone-sep-see-one′)
Contra Costa (Cone′-trah Cose′-tah)
Coronado (Co-ro-nah′-do)
Corte Madera (Cor′-tay Mah-day′-rah)
Cruz, Santa (Sahn′-tah Croos)
Monte, del (Del Mon′-tay)
Norte, del (Del Nor′-tay)
Diablo (Dee-ahb′-lo)
Dolores (Do-lo′-res)
Dorado, El (El Do-ra′-do)
Estanislao (Ess-tahn-ees-lah′-o)
Farallones (Fahr-ah-yone′-ess)
Fresno (Fres′-no)
Gatos, Los (Loce Gah′-tose)
Gaviota (Gah-vee-o′-tah)
Jolla, La (Lah Hoy′-ah)
Jolon (Ho-lone′)
Lagunitas (Lah-goo-nee′-tahs)
Laureles (La-oo-rel′-ess)
Lobos (Lo′-bose)
Madera (Mah-day′-rah)
Madroño, not madrone (Mah-drone′-yo)
Mariposa (Mah-ree-po′-sah)
Matilija (Mah-tee-lee′-hah)
Mendocino (Mayn-do-see′-no)
Merced (Mayr-sed′)
Mesa (May′-sah)
Milpitas (Meel-peet′-ahs)
Mokelumne, Indian (Mo-kel′-um-nay)
Monterey (Mone-tay-ray′)
Nevada (Nay-vah′-dah)
Pájaro (Pah′-hah-ro)
Palo Alto (Pah-lo Ahl′-to)
Paraíso (Pah-rah-ee′-so)
Paso de Robles (Pah-so day Ro′-blays)
Plumas (Ploo′-mahs)

[1] *The meanings and romance of the names in the above list, with many others, Indian and Spanish may be found in* Spanish and Indian Place Names of California; *Sánchez.*

Presidio (Pray-see′-dee-o)
Rio Grande (Ree′-o Grahn′-day)
Sacramento (Sahc-rah-mayn′-to)
Salinas (Sah-lee′-nahs)
San Andreas (Sahn Ahn-dray′-ahs)
San Benito (Sahn Bay-nee′-to)
San Bernardino (Sahn Bare-nahr-dee′-no)
San Buenaventura (Sahn Booayn-ah-vayn-too′-rah)
San Carlos (Sahn Cahr′-lose)
San Diego (Sahn Dee-ay′-go)
San Francisco (Sahn Frahn-sees′-co)
San Gabriel (Sahn Gahb-ree-el′)
San Geronimo (Sahn Hay-ro′-nee-mo)
San Ignacio (Sahn Eeg-nah′-see-o)
San Isidro (Sahn Ee-see′-dro)
San Jacinto (Sahn Hah-seen′-to)
San Joaquín (Sahn Ho-ah-keen′)
San Juan Bautista (Sahn Hoo-ahn′ Bah-oo-tees′-tah)
San Juan Capistrano (Sahn Hoo-ahn Cahp-ees-trah′-no)
San Julian (Sahn Hoo-lee-ahn′)
San Leandro (Sahn Lay-ahn′-dro)
San Lorenzo (Sahn Lo-rayn′-so)
San Luís Obispo (Sahn Loo-ees′ O-bees′-po)
San Luís Rey (Sahn Loo-ees′ Ray)
San Mateo (Sahn Mah-tay′-o)
San Miguel (Sahn Mee-gel′)
San Nicolás (Sahn Nee-co-lahs′)
San Pedro (Sahn Pay′-dro)
San Quentin (Sahn Kayn-teen′)
San Rafael (Sahn Rah-fah-el′)
San Ramón (Sahn Rah-mone′)
Santa Ana (Sahn′-tah Ahn′-ah)
Santa Barbara (Sahn′-tah Bahr′-bahr-ah)
Santa Cruz (Sahn′-tah Croos)
Santa Fe (Sahn′-tah Fay′)
Santa Gertrudis (Sahn′-tah Hare-troo′-dees)
Santa Inez (Sahn′-tah Ee-nays′)
Santa Lucia (Sahn′-tah Loo-see-ah)
Santa María (Sahn′-tah Mah-ree′-ah)
Santa Teresa (Sahn′-tah Tay-rays′-sah)
Sausalito (Sah-oo-sah-lee′-to)
Sierra (See-er′-rah)
Soledad (So-lay-dad′)
Suñol (Soon-yole′)
Sur (Soor)
Tamalpais (Tah-mahl-pah′-ees)
Tuólumne, Indian (Too-ol′-um-nay)
Vallejo (Vah-yay′-ho)

Bibliography

BIBLIOGRAPHY

Alvarado, Juan Bautista, *Historia de California.* (MS.) Bancroft Collection, University of California.

Amador, José María, *Memorias sobre la historia de California.* (MS.) Bancroft Collection, University of California.

Anza, Juan Bautista de, *Diario.* (MS.) Bancroft Collection.

Arce, Francisco, *Memorias Históricas.* (MS.) Bancroft Collection.

Archives of the Missions, in the Bancroft Collection.

Arnaz, José, *Recuerdos.* (MS.) Bancroft Collection.

Ávila, Juan, *Notas Californianas.* (MS.) Bancroft Collection.

Bancroft, Hubert Howe, *History of California; California Pastoral.*

Bandini, Juan, *Historia de California.* (MS.) Bancroft Collection.

Bidwell, John, *California in '41-48.* (MS.) Bancroft Collection.

Blackmar, Frank Wilson, *Spanish Institutions of the Southwest.* Johns Hopkins Press, Baltimore, 1891.

Boscana, Gerónimo, *Chinigchinich.* (Appendix to the first edition of Robinson's *Life in California.*) Bancroft Collection.

Briones, Brigida, *A glimpse of domestic life in 1827.* Century Magazine.

California Publications in Archæology and Ethnology, edited by Alfred Louis Kroeber. (University of California Press.)

Clark Galen, *Indians of the Yosemite Valley and Vicinity.* (H. S. Crocker Company, San Francisco, California.)

Colton, Walter, *Three Years in California.* (A. S. Barnes and Company, New York; H. W. Derby and Company, Cincinnati, 1860.)

Coronel, Antonio Francisco, *Cosas de California.* (MS.) (Dictated for H. H. Bancroft.) Bancroft Collection.

Dale, Harrison Clifford, Ed., *The Ashley-Smith Expeditions*, with original diaries. (The Arthur N. Clark Company, Cleveland, 1918.)

Dana, Richard, *Two Years before the Mast.* (Houghton, Mifflin and Company, Boston, 1869.)

Davis, William Heath, *Sixty Years in California.* (A. J. Leary, San Francisco, 1889.)

Duhaut-Cilly, Auguste Bernard, *Voyage autour du monde.* (A. Bertrand, Paris, 1834-35.)

Dwinelle, John Whipple, *The Colonial History of San Francisco.* (Towne and Bacon, San Francisco, 1863.)

Dye, Job Francis, *Recollections of California.* (MS.) Bancroft Collection.

Engelhardt, Charles Anthony, in religion Zephyrin, *The Missions and Missionaries of California.* (The J. H. Barry Company, San Francisco, 1908.)

Fitch, María Antonia Natalia, a Elijia Carrillo, *Narración de la viuda Fitch.* (MS.) Bancroft Collection.

Guerra y Noriega, José de la, *Documentos para la Historia de California.* (MS.) Bancroft Collection.

Guinn, James M., Articles on the *Early days of Los Angeles* in the annual publications of the Historical Society of Southern California.

Hijar, Carlos N., *California in '34.* (MS.) Bancroft Collection.

Janssens, Victor Eugene Auguste, *Vida y Aventuras.* (MS.) Bancroft Collection.

Kotzebue, Otto von, *Voyage of Discovery in the South Sea.* (Sir Richard Phillips and Company, London, 1821.)

Kroeber, Alfred Louis, California Publications in Archæology and Ethnology. (University of California.)

Langsdorff, George Heinrich von, *Voyages and Travels in various parts of the world.* (H. Colburn, London, 1821.)

La Pérouse, Jean Francois de Galaup, *Voyage round the World.* Translation. (J. Johnson, London, 1798.)

Larkin, Thomas Oliver. *Private and Official Correspondence.* (MS.) Bancroft Collection.

Lugo, José del Carmen, *Vida de un ranchero.* (MS.) Bancroft Collection.

Lyman, George D., *The Scalpel Under Three Flags in California.* Publications of the California Historical Society, San Francisco, 1925.

Mofras, Eugene Duflot de, *Explorations du territoire de L' Oregon et Californias.* (A. Bertrand, 1844.)

Newmark, Harris, *Sixty Years in Southern California.* (Knickerbocker Press, New York, 1926.)

Ord, James, *Memoirs,* edited by Henry W. Shoemaker, Altoona, Pa. (Altoona Times-Tribune, 1920.)

Ord, Maria de las Angustias de la Guerra, *Ocurrencias.* (MS.) Bancroft Collection.

Ortega, José Francisco, Several important records of early events: *Comunicaciones del comandante, etc.; Correspondencia; Fragmento de 1769; Informe de 30 Nov., 1775; Memorial, etc.* (MS.) Bancroft Collection.

Osio, Antonio María, *Historia de California.* (MS.) Bancroft Collection.

Pattie, James Ohio, Personal Narrative, edited by Timothy Flint. (E. H. Flint, Cincinnati, 1833.)

Pico, José de Jesus, *Acontecimientos*. (MS.) Bancroft Collection.

Powers, Stephen, *Tribes of California*. (Washington Government Printing Office, 1877.)

Revere, Joseph Warren, *A Tour of Duty in California*. (C. S. Francis and Company, New York, 1849.)

Rezánof, Nikolai Petrovitch, Reports to the Russian Government. (MS.) Translations in the Bancroft Collection.

Robinson, Alfred, *Life in California*. (Wiley and Putnam, New York, 1846; W. Doxey, San Francisco, 1891; T. O. Russell, San Francisco, 1925.)

Rogers, Harrison G., *Journal of the Jedediah Smith Expedition to California in 1826*. (In the *Ashley Smith Expeditions*, edited by Harrison Clifford Dale.)

Sánchez, Nellie Van de Grift, *California and Californians, Hispanic Period*. (B. F. Lewis Company, Chicago, Ill., 1926.) *Spanish and Indian Place Names of California; Their Meaning and Their Romance*. (A. M. Robertson, San Francisco, California.)

Sepúlveda, Ignacio, *Historical Memoranda*. (MS.) Bancroft Collection.

Serrano, Florencio, *Apuntes de California*. (MS.) Bancroft Collection.

Shinn, Charles Howard, *Ranch and Mission Days in Alta California*, written by Mr. Shinn from notes obtained from Guadalupe Vallejo. (In the Century Magazine, Vol. XIX.)

Spence, David, Historical Notes. (MS.) Bancroft Collection.

Tikhmeneff, P., *Historical Review of the Russian-American Company*. (MS.) Translation in the Bancroft Collection.

Torre, Estevan de la, *Reminiscencias*. (MS.) Bancroft Collection.

Torres, Manuel, *Peripécias de la vida Californiana*. (MS.) Bancroft Collection.

Vallejo, Guadalupe, Notes on California rancho and mission life furnished to Charles Howard Shinn. (Century Magazine, Vol. XIX.)

Vallejo, Mariano Guadalupe, *Historia de California*, 5 Vols. (MS.) Bancroft Collection.

Vancouver, George, *A Voyage of Discovery to the North Pacific and Round the World*. (G. G. and J. Robinson, London, 1798.)

Index

INDEX

A

B

B

C

D

E

F

G

H

I

J

K

L

M

N

O

P

Q

R

R

S

S

S

T

U

V

V

W

Y

Z

THE CHICANO HERITAGE

An Arno Press Collection

Adams, Emma H. **To and Fro in Southern California.** 1887

Anderson, Henry P. **The Bracero Program in California.** 1961

Aviña, Rose Hollenbaugh. **Spanish and Mexican Land Grants in California.** 1976

Barker, Ruth Laughlin. **Caballeros.** 1932

Bell, Horace. **On the Old West Coast.** 1930

Biberman, Herbert. **Salt of the Earth.** 1965

Casteñeda, Carlos E., trans. **The Mexican Side of the Texas Revolution (1836).** 1928

Casteñeda, Carlos E. **Our Catholic Heritage in Texas, 1519-1936.** Seven volumes. 1936-1958

Colton, Walter. **Three Years in California.** 1850

Cooke, Philip St. George. **The Conquest of New Mexico and California.** 1878

Cue Canovas, Agustin. **Los Estados Unidos Y El Mexico Olvidado.** 1970

Curtin, L. S. M. **Healing Herbs of the Upper Rio Grande.** 1947

Fergusson, Harvey. **The Blood of the Conquerors.** 1921

Fernandez, Jose. **Cuarenta Años de Legislador:** Biografia del Senador Casimiro Barela. 1911

Francis, Jessie Davies. **An Economic and Social History of Mexican California** (1822-1846). Volume I: Chiefly Economic. Two vols. in one. 1976

Getty, Harry T. **Interethnic Relationships in the Community of Tucson.** 1976

Guzman, Ralph C. **The Political Socialization of the Mexican American People.** 1976

Harding, George L. **Don Agustin V. Zamorano.** 1934

Hayes, Benjamin. **Pioneer Notes from the Diaries of Judge Benjamin Hayes, 1849-1875.** 1929

Herrick, Robert. **Waste.** 1924

Jamieson, Stuart. **Labor Unionism in American Agriculture.** 1945

Landolt, Robert Garland. **The Mexican-American Workers of San Antonio, Texas.** 1976

Lane, Jr., John Hart. **Voluntary Associations Among Mexican Americans in San Antonio, Texas.** 1976

Livermore, Abiel Abbot. **The War with Mexico Reviewed.** 1850

Loyola, Mary. **The American Occupation of New Mexico, 1821-1852.** 1939

Macklin, Barbara June. **Structural Stability and Culture Change in a Mexican-American Community.** 1976

McWilliams, Carey. **Ill Fares the Land:** Migrants and Migratory Labor in the United States. 1942

Murray, Winifred. **A Socio-Cultural Study of 118 Mexican Families Living in a Low-Rent Public Housing Project in San Antonio, Texas.** 1954

Niggli, Josephina. **Mexican Folk Plays.** 1938

Parigi, Sam Frank. **A Case Study of Latin American Unionization in Austin, Texas.** 1976

Poldervaart, Arie W. **Black-Robed Justice.** 1948

Rayburn, John C. and Virginia Kemp Rayburn, eds. **Century of Conflict, 1821-1913.** Incidents in the Lives of William Neale and William A. Neale, Early Settlers in South Texas. 1966

Read, Benjamin. **Illustrated History of New Mexico.** 1912

Rodriguez, Jr., Eugene. **Henry B. Gonzalez.** 1976

Sanchez, Nellie Van de Grift. **Spanish and Indian Place Names of California.** 1930

Sanchez, Nellie Van de Grift. **Spanish Arcadia.** 1929

Shulman, Irving. **The Square Trap.** 1953

Tireman, L. S. **Teaching Spanish-Speaking Children.** 1948

Tireman, L. S. and Mary Watson. **A Community School in a Spanish-Speaking Village.** 1948

Twitchell, Ralph Emerson. **The History of the Military Occupation of the Territory of New Mexico.** 1909

Twitchell, Ralph Emerson. **The Spanish Archives of New Mexico.** Two vols. 1914

U. S. House of Representatives. **California and New Mexico:** Message from the President of the United States, January 21, 1850. 1850

Valdes y Tapia, Daniel. **Hispanos and American Politics.** 1976

West, Stanley A. **The Mexican Aztec Society.** 1976

Woods, Frances Jerome. **Mexican Ethnic Leadership in San Antonio, Texas.** 1949

Aspects of the Mexican American Experience. 1976

Mexicans in California After the U. S. Conquest. 1976

Hispanic Folklore Studies of Arthur L. Campa. 1976

Hispano Culture of New Mexico. 1976

Mexican California. 1976

The Mexican Experience in Arizona. 1976

The Mexican Experience in Texas. 1976

Mexican Migration to the United States. 1976

The United States Conquest of California. 1976

Northern Mexico On the Eve of the United States Invasion: Rare Imprints Concerning California, Arizona, New Mexico, and Texas, 1821-1846. Edited by David J. Weber. 1976